50ish

A Journey Around the World to
50 Countries in 50 Weeks,
Interviewing Women in Their 50s

Donna Marie Lynch

Enjoy the journey
Donna Lynch

ISBN-13: 978-1453658154
ISBN-10: 1453658157

Published by DML Publishing

This book is a true story. I have changed a few names by request. All statistics and historical information were given to me by tour guides or found on Wikipedia or The World Factbook, but I don't guarantee their accuracy. Some stories are folklore and Web site facts could be outdated. If you do not wish to be bound by the above, you may return this book to the publisher for a full refund.

Look for pictures on
www.50ishthebook.com

This book is dedicated to my Mother.
I miss her every day.
She was my rock, my best friend,
and my inspiration.

Acknowledgments

I have to thank so many people who helped make this one of the best years of my life.

I thank all my incredible friends who found time to join me. Kathy McAree, who keeps me up on food and wine and helped with my first interview. Joanne Hunston, who not only joined me for five weeks in Europe, but held a fund-raiser, found me several places to stay and people to interview, and was my Canadian interviewee. Linda Brennan, who looked after booking and showed up for a Baltic cruise with two weeks' notice. Laura Dowell, whose laughter and friendship and "cup-half-full" attitude got us through many hot flashes, squat toilets, and the extreme heat of Southeast Asia. My sister Lynda McKinney and niece Colette Lynch, who joined me in the Caribbean for a fun-filled cruise and helped me run around trying to find interviewees in countries we only visited for one day. Finally, Ann Scott, who emailed me one day and showed up two days later in my final country to celebrate the completion of my journey.

I also have to thank all the generous people who gave me a place to lay my weary head, fed me, and showed me around their countries, especially my cousin Gail Lynch in London, who allowed me to use her home as a flophouse while I wound my way around Europe.

The journey would not have been complete without the 50ish women around the world, many who had only known me a few minutes, who agreed to be interviewed. I thank them for sharing their life stories with me. The world is full of incredible, inspirational women.

Table of Contents

The world is a book and those who do not travel read only page one.

- St. Augustine

Introduction

"We didn't want to ruin your birthday," confessed my sister and mother the morning of my fiftieth birthday celebration. They had visited Mom's doctor and learned of her diagnosis of lung cancer three days earlier, which was my actual birthday. But on this day, as the truth spilled out, my stomach turned and the tears fell. I knew Mom had not been feeling great and had gone through some tests, but I didn't expect to hear the word cancer.

My dear, sweet mother had blossomed so much in the six years since my father's passing. After years of caring for my dad and suffering his constant verbal abuse, she had come into her own and was really enjoying life. This was the woman who never spoke a harsh or critical word and who could come up with a one-liner to make us laugh so hard we couldn't stop. She was the person I most looked up to in the world.

Despite this devastating news, Mom, in true Mom fashion, insisted my birthday party go on. Even though she started out a little weak, she ended up partying until two a.m. Although she looked frail to those who hadn't seen her for some time, she held court on the deck with all our friends, relatives, and neighbours. Under the starry July night sky we partied on. Games were played, cake was devoured, and jokes flew. Laughter really is the best medicine.

The doctor didn't deliver a prognosis as far as days, months, or years left to live, and Mom wasn't given, nor did she want to have any major intervention. She accepted that it might soon be her time to go, and as she did with everything in her life, she just lived life. No dramatics, no pity party, she just carried on. I think she knew she didn't have long and stoically neglected to tell us how much pain she really was in.

Even though we believed she would be around at least another year, my siblings—Lynda, Glen, and Ian—and I, along with Mom, made plans for her funeral. Mom even picked her favourite songs, including "Amazing Grace", which reminds us all of our brother Denis, who drowned at twenty-one, in 1973. While we pulled together as a family we felt fortunate that there was no need for awkward conversations or reconciliations, as we each had a great relationship with Mom. There was no doubt about our love for her, or hers for us. Her favourite line was "I love you all one-quarter," and this love was unconditional.

In the weeks following my fiftieth birthday, I tried to come to grips with losing this amazing woman and wondered what I would do when she was gone. I wondered where I would live, as I had moved back into the family home with Mom shortly after my father died. I was also trying to wrap my head around turning fifty: what had I done in my first half-century, and what was I going to do with the next? My mind was struggling with these questions, my stomach was in constant turmoil, and sleep was elusive.

One night while unable to sleep, I got on my computer and saw that someone had sent me the Facebook map that has you put a pin in all the places you have travelled to. When I was finished pinning, the results came back with a staggering forty-three countries. I had never counted before.

The next morning I awoke with the number fifty in my head and an idea of what to do after Mom passed away. Here was my idea: to travel to fifty countries in fifty weeks and interview women in their fifties, and then write a book about my experience. I wrote my idea down, as all the self-help gurus recommend, and started telling friends about my idea that very night. I never told Mom of my plans, as I didn't want her to think I was waiting for her to die. I now regret not telling her, but she knew I would use my inheritance to travel. She knew me better than anyone.

Lynda and I had planned a Mediterranean cruise before we knew about Mom's illness, and decided we could still go before Mom got to a stage where we couldn't leave her. However, two months after her diagnosis we were about to leave and she started to have some peculiar symptoms. We told her we were going to cancel the trip, but she insisted we go. "I promise to be here when you get back," she said.

Mom had been to Naples, Italy, years ago, so when our ship docked there, we phoned her. It was only a few days before the end of our trip and she said she was feeling good. Unbeknownst to us, she really started to decline the next day. Within another day, Ian and Glen took her to hospice and spent the day with her. At one a.m. she passed away peacefully in her sleep.

The boys, as we call my brothers, had decided not to try to find us because we were due home in two days. So it wasn't until three hours before we arrived home, when we called them from Vancouver, that we learned she was gone. We were gutted, sitting on a bus, sobbing loudly. We felt so guilty for not being with her to hold her hand, say good-bye and have one last laugh.

Later, when I talked to the hospice doctor, she told me Mom was so proud of us for travelling together and would not have allowed us to cancel. She also told me Mom had said she was "ready to go and not afraid" (she was deeply religious and ready to meet her maker). The doctor felt that when we called from Naples we gave her permission to go. I've now recovered from the guilty feelings of not being there at the end and am instead focused on the image of her smiling face while she waved us off on our trip. I'm also happy my brothers were there for her and were able to have their own good-byes. My sister and I tended to take over where Mom was concerned, and they might not have had that special time with her had we been there.

Grief was, unfortunately, a familiar emotion for me. Almost seventeen years before Mom died, my precious daughter Carly died of pneumonia. She was born with a muscular disorder and we had been told she wouldn't live past two, but at ten months old, on Mother's Day, she died in my arms.

From that experience I learned that, for me, the only way to deal with grief is to keep as busy as possible. So after Mom's death, with my cruise luggage barely unpacked, I walked into my workplace, gave my boss six months' notice, and started making plans for my journey. I sent out the following e-mail to everyone I knew and asked that it be passed along to friends and family:

Hi, my name is Donna Lynch. I am a Canadian woman who just turned fifty. For a full six months before I turned fifty, I couldn't stop thinking about "turning fifty". Am I where I thought I would be at fifty? Do I "feel" fifty? Does fifty really mean I am "over the hill"?

I am not really where I thought I would be, in part because I am divorced and never really imagined I would get to this age and be single. But here I am, and I'm actually enjoying it. It would be great to be in a relationship, but being single is okay too. I am able to do what I want, when I want.

Do I "feel" fifty? Not for a minute. I am not sure what fifty is supposed to feel like, but of course when I was younger I thought fifty was OLD. I definitely don't feel old.

Does fifty mean "over the hill"? Well, it does mean that life is probably more than half over, and to me this means I should enjoy whatever comes next.

So I have decided to follow my passion. My passion is travelling, and what better way to seek some of my answers to the fifties questions than to travel around the world and ask other fiftyish women around the world about their experiences.

In my travels I have seen many monuments, churches, mountains, and museums, but I have never really come to know the people of the countries I have visited.

What I would like to do is visit fifty countries and meet with fifty women, who are close to fifty years old. I would like to spend at least a few days talking with each woman and exploring her country. I would like to ask each woman the same group of questions; not just the ones above, but several more about health, culture, heritage, and religion.

I hope to go to both developed and developing countries, on every continent. My mother recently passed away, and I have inherited the money to pay for all my expenses, but if the women in some of the countries want to do some kind of fund-raiser, either before I get there or while I am there, I will take that money to people in other countries that may benefit from some financial help.

So, I am looking for: women aged forty-seven to fifty-two, who would be willing to answer questions and maybe spend a few days showing off part of their country.

If you know people who would be willing to let me contact them to set up a meeting in their country, I would love to hear from you.

Thanks, Donna

While I waited for replies, I started working out an itinerary. I wanted to work out a route where I followed the sun, to avoid carrying around cold-weather gear. Since I was leaving in May, Europe seemed the best place to start. After looking at hundreds of brochures and Web sites, I decided Morocco, Syria, Jordan, and Turkey would have to be first, because by June they would be too hot to enjoy. Being able to look at a world map and just pick out countries I wanted to see was both overwhelming and wonderful!

Before I got any further in my plans, my friend Joanne called to ask if she could join me for five weeks. Her dates worked out perfectly for when I would be leaving Turkey, so I suggested she meet me in London. She said she could arrange accommodations and interviews in Poland, Ireland, and Scotland, and I had been given a contact in Hungary, so together we worked out an itinerary and the first leg of my trip started to take shape.

I got all the shots, took all the pre-travel drugs, applied for visas, and then booked the tours and the hotels not covered on the tours. I bought all the necessary travel items, secured my travel insurance, and ordered an extended page passport—an ordinary passport would not work for this trip!

Shortly after I purchased my ticket to London for May 1, I found out I didn't have to work for two weeks in March. So I decided to get my first two countries completed before I left for Europe. I found a good deal to Mexico, with a stopover in California on the return portion.

I also worked on the questions I would ask the women I met. I asked my friends for suggestions, and even e-mailed Oprah to see if she had any suggestions. (I didn't hear from her.) I settled on questions about marriage, education, religion, employment, children, and menopause, that word that brings a nervous laugh or outright embarrassment to everyone but a menopausal woman. I wanted to be able to ask everyone the same questions, but knew I must be mindful not to offend anybody. Many people wanted me to ask questions about sex, which was not something I could pull off. I don't even discuss my friends' sex lives, so I was not prepared to ask strangers about theirs.

Based on the responses from my initial e-mail, I sensed that my hopes to have other people host fund-raisers were not realistic. In fact, my request may have even deterred some people from getting back to me. I still carried on with my own event. It was a garage sale with a twist. It wasn't a Saturday morning event and it wasn't in a garage. Rather, it took place on a Saturday evening in my living and dining rooms. Friends brought all the junk they had around the house that they had been meaning to put in a garage sale one day, and with the help of the party atmosphere and a splash of liquor, everyone found that another person's junk would be his or her new treasure. It was a great success and we raised $2,200. I didn't know exactly where I would distribute the funds, but had no doubt I would find many worthy causes.

With bags packed and my first few months' itinerary established, I wondered how the year would unfold.

Will I make it to fifty countries in fifty weeks? How will I arrange a meeting with a woman of around fifty in each country? Will I be able to do it all within my budget? At fifty, will I physically be able to cope with the constant moving? Will I meet Mr. Right, as all my friends predict? Only time will tell.

The Questions

1. How old are you?
2. Are you single/married/divorced?
3. How long did you know your husband prior to marrying?
4. How old were you when you got married?
5. Did you live together before you married?
6. How many children do you have? Boys? Girls?
7. What is the level of your parents' education?
8. What is your level of education?
9. What is your children's level of education?
10. Did your parents stay married?
11. Are your parents still alive?
12. Do you work outside the home?
13. Do you follow a religion?
14. Is religion a big part of your life?
15. Does your spouse follow your religion?
16. Do your children follow your religion?
17. Where else have you lived?
18. Have you travelled, and would you move to another country?
19. Do you have menopausal symptoms?
20. Do you take any medications?
21. Do you feel your life is better than your parents'?
22. Do you have hobbies?
23. Can you describe yourself?
24. Are you where you thought you would be at fifty?
25. Are you happy?

Travel is fatal to prejudice, bigotry and narrow-mindedness.

Mark Twain

Chapter 1

Mexico

"Do you want to join me in my first country?" I asked my friend Kathy.

"Absolutely! I'd love to," she replied, without hesitation. And so the journey began.

I arrived in Puerto Vallarta, Mexico, on Easter weekend. Kathy had arrived the night before me, preparing everything for the perfect beginning to my journey. She had already arranged a better room (the first was too noisy); stocked the fridge with water, juice, wine, and snacks; picked up towels for the pool, set up an Internet connection on her computer, and placed a chocolate Easter bunny on my pillow. From our sun-soaked balcony overlooking the pool we sipped Mexican wine, talked about our plans for the week, and watched all the happenings around the hotel. In an effort to keep the guests from leaving the hotel, the management provided on-site water aerobics, volleyball, bingo, Spanish classes, mixology classes, and many more fun activities. We weren't sure we would actually join in, but it was fun to watch from the comfort of our balcony.

My only goal for the week was to find an interviewee, conduct the interview, and relax. I wanted a week of calm before the rush of the next forty-nine countries. Kathy, who owns a culinary tourism business, had been very busy planning her upcoming season, so her goals were to just check out the local restaurants and relax. With a city full of great restaurants and no real to-do list, it promised to be a great week for both of us.

Puerto Vallarta (PV) is located on the beautiful blue waters of the Bay of Banderas and is backed by the tropical Sierra Madre Mountains. I had been there many times, but this was Kathy's first time, so I wanted to show her the lively waterfront esplanade called the Malecon. Because it was Easter weekend there was an extra energy in the city, and the locals, who celebrate Easter in a big way, outnumbered the tourists. The Malecon positively vibrated with musicians, dancers, and sand artists. The massive sand sculptures had religious themes. The "Last Supper" was at least five times life-size and was so intricately sculpted, it was sad to think it would be destroyed within days by the wind and surf. We soaked up the atmosphere, enjoyed the entertainment, browsed the food and craft vendors, and watched all the families, including small children, party into the night.

The aroma from the food vendors was wonderful, and some of it looked great, but we gringos with our delicate bellies were wary of food that might have sat in the sun all day. Instead, we settled on the Cheeky Monkey, a restaurant that sold margaritas and beer for a dollar. Can't beat that! The owner, Troy, became our new friend and is now one of my biggest cheerleaders. He loved the idea of my journey.

Kathy was so excited about some of the fine dining in Puerto Vallarta she had made dinner reservations, before arriving in Mexico. One of these restaurants, the Hacienda San Angel, is in a villa once owned by Richard Burton. (Liz and Richard are part of PV folklore, having owned property and spent time there while shooting *The Night of the Iguana* in the 1960s.) This beautiful colonial villa sits on top of a hill with panoramic views of the city and the bay. The courtyard was decorated with antiques, huge bouquets of tropical flowers, and religious statues. The patio where we dined, beside a pool, was a perfect place to enjoy the setting sun. The ambience was so romantic we both wished for male companions rather than each other, but Kathy and I always have fun together, and her being a "foodie" makes dining out that much more interesting. She will ask what is in the sauce, whether the fish is fresh or frozen, and what wine will enhance the flavour, even if she already knows, just to see how well-informed the staff is. As for me, if the waiter flirts and the food tastes good, I am happy.

Even though the owner was American, the menu English, and the prices in U.S. dollars, our waiter and the cuisine were Mexican. Kathy, not only a food expert but also a wine connoisseur, ordered a fantastic bottle of Mexican wine. The local calamari, tortilla soup, and fresh shrimp were delicious. Kathy found the service superb and I found that our waiter did the appropriate amount of flirting, so we both left very contented.

During the week, with Kathy on her culinary search, we visited several other great restaurants, a trend I knew I would not be able to continue in every country. I did have a budget to consider.

When we weren't sampling PV with our taste buds we worked hard at relaxing. (This is not something that either of us does well.) I do not generally just sit in the sun, but we did find shaded lounge chairs where we managed to spend a few days by the pool near the beach. I preferred the pool to the ocean for swimming, but I liked being near the beach to watch the vendors, dressed all in white, peddle their wares. They aren't supposed to come past the rope onto the hotel property, but if you make eye contact, they sneak over. I like to see what new merchandise they come up with every year, as I have been coming to PV since the early 80s'. This year the newest items were colourful purses woven from recycled plastics and juice containers. I didn't want one but they were selling well, and I was pleased to see the vendors finding such a great way to recycle, clean up the beach, and make money.

Most people don't like the vendors bothering them, but I don't mind because I don't like shopping. Having the "store" come to me is great. I was tempted by lots of beautiful jewellery, but decided that this time in Mexico, no matter how cute the salesman, I wouldn't buy anything. Instead, when the vendors plunked down in the sand beside us, I would ask them questions about their families, their jobs, or whatever other topics came up. One fellow told me that he had been selling various items on that beach for twenty-five years and had raised five children, all of whom went to, or were still going to, university. He was a very proud father. Once the vendors knew our names, they often would just sit down and talk. Of course, they still tried to get us to buy something, but were also happy to visit.

Despite the heat (PV averages between twenty-four and twenty-nine degrees Celsius), we managed to go on our walk most days. The second day, on the way to the marina district, an area I am familiar with, we got lost. Kathy was not too impressed and lost all faith in my navigating abilities. She also started worrying about leaving me alone to travel the world to places I was not familiar with. I explained to her that I'm someone who doesn't mind getting lost because I know I will find my way eventually and always get to see something I might never have seen otherwise. Of course, we did find our way to the marina district, but not before winding our way past a golf course and through a beautiful subdivision of exquisite homes and gardens that I was unaware were so close to the hotel. We were hot and exhausted by the time we reached the marina, but found a restaurant on the docks to enjoy a delicious seafood lunch and margaritas, while imagining life on one of the impressive yachts tied up in front of us.

On the days we weren't relaxing (and, really, we never did get the hang of relaxing during our week), we explored more of downtown PV, both the old and the new sections, and two nearby towns: Bucerias to the north and La Jolla de Mismaloya to the south.

The local bus took only about forty minutes to get us to Bucerias, in the next state of Nayarit. This once small town has grown a lot since my early days in PV, with new condos and hotels popping up all along the waterfront. What was once a small local village is now competing with PV for the tourist dollar. We enjoyed our walk on the beach, watching the surfers and lunching on some freshly caught seafood. But we were disappointed with the village, as it was choked up with construction equipment and lacking any real vibrant centre. This town was definitely suffering from growing pains. After a precarious walk through town, trying to avoid gaping potholes, noisy construction sites, and uneven pavement, we hopped on the bus back to PV.

By day five, we had been having a lot of fun, but I had not found a woman to interview. In the early days of our stay we had asked cab drivers, restaurant staff, and vendors if they knew anyone, but either they didn't understand my broken Spanish or they didn't know anyone in the right age category. Some of my friends had been in PV a few months before I arrived, and they had asked me to deliver some photos to people they had met in La Jolla de Mismaloya. As it was getting down to the wire, I was hoping these people would know a suitable interviewee.

Kathy, who was still reeling from getting lost when "I knew where I was going", insisted we take a taxi to Mismaloya. Although the destination is a rewarding and beautiful beach, the twenty kilometre journey is a white-knuckle, breakneck-speed race along a very curvy coastal road. From past experience, I know the bus ride is particularly scary, so I was happy to cab it. As it turned out, the taxi driver thought he was Mario Andretti, so the ride was just as bad as the bus.

We did, however, arrive safe and sound, and headed straight for the beach to find the restaurant where the friends of my friends worked. The second we reached the beach we were bombarded by vendors competing for our attention. "Come on my boat." "Come snorkel with us." "Eat at my restaurant." "Best fish here." "Our beach chairs are free." "Have a look at my jewellery. It's almost free." Despite all their yelling, what actually stopped us was a quiet sign with a simple, tempting offer: massages for twenty-seven dollars an hour.

As luck would have it, the woman we booked our massages with, named Concepcion, looked to be in her fifties, so rather than take the chance that the other people would know someone, I jumped right in—or rather had Kathy jump right in, as she speaks more Spanish than I do. She told Concepcion what I was doing and asked if she would be willing to be interviewed. She agreed, and we arranged to come back later for massages and the interview.

We then found Teo's Place, the restaurant recommended by my friends, at the far end of the beach, overlooking the site where they filmed *The Night of the Iguana*. It was a restaurant built on the sand so close to the shore that the tables and chairs had to be moved back as the tide came in. The staff set us up with lounge chairs and umbrellas along with tasty Mexican food. We found it a great place to people-watch and enjoy the sun, sand, and ocean. While Kathy and I enjoyed margaritas, guacamole, and quesadillas, I started to review my questions for Concepcion. That's when I realized Kathy's Spanish might not be sufficient for the translation.

As we pondered how to sort out this translation issue, we overheard a Mexican guy speaking great English, so we struck up a conversation with him and explained my dilemma. He was more than happy to write out my questions in Spanish. I offered him beer in exchange, but he was simply happy to help. Nothing stumped him until I came up with the term *hot flash*. He needed an explanation and, after some thought, came up with the right words.

So, off we went for our massages, which were wonderful, followed by my first interview.

~

Concepcion – 53

We thought we were clever getting the questions written out, but never considered how we were going to understand the answers. Fortunately, one of Concepcion's work friends, who understands both languages slightly better than the rest of us, joins us to help out. Concepcion seems a little overwhelmed by all the attention, but also curious to find out why I would want to interview her. I try to explain as best I can and we start the questions. She laughs when we tell her about the guy on the beach writing out the questions, but realizes it will certainly help.

She tells us she is fifty-three. I had thought she was a little older, but then realize she lives in a climate of constant sun, which has aged her skin considerably. She has short hair, a round face and body, and I tower over her. She is probably less than five feet tall, but I know she is a strong woman, having just had an excellent massage from her hands.

She says she was married at twenty-one and divorced at forty-one. I think she tries to tell us why she divorced, but it doesn't come out in translation. She is happy to report she has a boyfriend, who she has been seeing for about a year. Talking about him brings a broad smile to her face. The interview becomes more of a girls' gabfest and a few other co-

workers mingle around. Kathy and I aren't sure what the gals are saying amongst themselves, but all seem to be enjoying the moment and we think they may be teasing Concepcion about the boyfriend. She doesn't seem to mind.

She tells us of her twenty-eight-year-old son and thirty-year-old daughter, and is very proud to say that, although her parents had very little education, she and her children are all high school graduates. She has had many more opportunities than her parents and feels her life has been much better than theirs. Her father has passed away but her mother is still alive at eighty-nine. All her family members have lived in this area, near Mismaloya, their entire lives, and although she has never travelled far from here, she loves her family and home and cannot imagine living anywhere else. "But," she adds, "I would love to travel more in my country."

Concepcion is a devout Catholic and attends church regularly. She sadly explains that, as important as God is to her, He isn't to her children, and it upsets her that they don't attend church with her.

I will have to rethink the order of the questions because I am going from God to menopause, but that is how they are written out. Just as we get to it, Concepcion starts having a major hot flash. She turns bright red and waves her hand in front of her face in an effort to cool down, then points to the translation our friend wrote down and laughs. The scary part for me, only a year into menopause, is that she says she has been having hot flashes for eight years! As for hormone replacement therapy (HRT) or other medications, she doesn't take any.

I really don't have to ask the last question, because I am sure I know the answer, but I ask anyway, "Are you happy?"

"Si," she answers with her beautiful wide smile. Kathy and I thank everyone who tried to help, give Concepcion a big hug and leave, pleased with ourselves for finding such a sweet lady to be the first of my interviewees.

~

So that was it, my first interview! I didn't get to all my questions, because of the language barrier and not having our beach friend write them all down, but it was a good learning opportunity for future interviews and we had lots of fun. From that point on I was determined to find my interviewee earlier and find a translator, if necessary, who could sit in on the whole interview.

On the way to the airport I was surprised by a marriage proposal. The cab driver, upon finding out I was Canadian, immediately fell in love and popped the question. He had apparently seen several documentaries of Canada and thought it looked fantastic. So, although I would like to think it was my stunning beauty and sparkling personality that seduced him, it was more likely my citizenship that attracted him. I had to decline, as there were still forty-nine countries to go. My friends were sure Mr. Right would be on this journey, but I was quite sure he was not that cab driver.

It was a great first week. I left Mexico with a subtle start to a tan and looked forward to the next forty-nine weeks and forty-nine countries.

Chapter 2

U.S.A.

"Sure, come on down, but you will have to wait until I return from Washington," Debbie had said when I called and asked her to be my American interviewee. Debbie was my niece-in-law back when I was married in the late '80s. Despite my divorce five years later, we have continued to stay friends throughout the years.

From Puerto Vallarta I flew to Mexico City, where I had a four-hour stop. I couldn't pass up an opportunity to see the city, so I hired a cab to take me on a tour. I expected crazy traffic and smog-filled air. Instead, there were clear blue skies and busy, but not chaotic, drivers. Then I realized it was a Sunday, so that may have had a lot to do with it. The city reminded me of many European cities, with a central plaza, a looming cathedral built over 250 years ago, and a maze of narrow cobblestone streets.

From there I flew to Las Vegas for a few days, because Debbie wasn't home from Washington yet. In Vegas I fed two of my addictions: live theatre and poker. I saw four shows and played in three poker tournaments. (I didn't win any money.) Finally I flew into Los Angeles, where Debbie picked me up and took me to her home in Corona, about seventy-five miles south of the city.

Debbie works for Wyland, the popular marine life artist and conservationist who paints the Whaling Walls. At the time of my visit, he had ninety-six whale murals around the world and was preparing to finish three more before doing his one hundredth wall for the Beijing Olympics. The week before I arrived he was invited to the White House for the annual Easter Egg Roll. Each year nineteen thousand kids arrive on the White House Lawn for this fun and playful event. Debbie and some of Wyland's staff joined him to help paint a mural with all the children. They even had a brief meeting with President Bush.

As I have visited Debbie many times in the past and have seen most of the tourist attractions Southern California has to offer, this trip was mainly just to hang out and catch up. We spent a few evenings with a group of Debbie and Mike's friends, who welcomed me like I was one of the gang. They meet weekly at the restaurant where their son Joe works. Since this was the election year, I questioned them on who they thought the next president would be. The consensus was that McCain would win. They all liked him, but not his war policies. They were already tired of the months of politicking and were not looking forward to the eight months that were still to come. I was looking forward to hearing election news in my future months of travelling.

On another night we met up with a group of Debbie's girl friends from high school, all still friends after thirty-three years. Being with women in their fifties generally means a discussion about menopause will ensue, and this group was no exception. Hot flashes, mood swings, and irritability were common occurrences amongst the group, but the solutions varied. One woman jumped up to show her estrogen patch, another couldn't say enough about a balancing cream called Kokoro, and yet another was on hormone replacement therapy. We had lots of laughs comparing stories of our funny and forgetful menopausal moments.

On one of Debbie's work days, her son Joe and I drove to Sea World in San Diego. My first trip there had been with this family when Joe was about five, so being driven down the freeway by this handsome, six-foot-five twenty-year-old was certainly an odd feeling. We had a fun day exploring Sea World, and for me the highlight was the dolphins, which we were able to touch and feed.

Debbie and I also spent a day in Los Angeles. We started in the downtown area with an Art Deco tour. I was glad to be with a group, as this was not an area of the city I would have wanted to explore on my own. Doing a walking tour gave us a whole new perspective on the city.

Art Deco came from an Exposition of Arts and Decoration in 1925 in Paris. The movement was then brought to the U.S., and for the next five to ten years, several buildings were designed with this new style. The facades, lobbies, and elevators were the main focus for this exciting new movement. The facades had lavish ornamentation; zigzags, spirals, sculptures, coloured terra-cotta, and usually a tower at the top. The lobbies were designed with many different kinds of marble, Lalique glass, and beautiful artwork. The inside of the elevators looked like confessionals, with very intricate wood designs. Apparently, L.A. has one of the largest collections of Art Deco architecture anywhere in the world.

Most big cities in the States are relatively safe and tourists flock to them, but I have always found it odd that Los Angeles is not one of them. There is so much potential there and some of the buildings are amazing, but we saw many street people and shady-looking characters, and it appeared that the city planners had made no effort to clean up the city or promote tourism.

An area that has definitely made its mark with the tourists is, of course, Beverly Hills, and we did an obligatory drive through it and then strolled down Rodeo Drive. I was looking for movie stars while Debbie was looking for fancy cars. She was luckier than I was, as we saw many Rolls Royces, Lamborghinis, and Maseratis, but did not spot one celebrity. We also did some window-shopping and dreaming, but that was all we could afford.

~

Debbie – 51

Debbie is fifty-one. I think of her as a "typical American": married with one son and one daughter; both she and her husband work (they commute over an hour to get to their jobs); they own a beautiful home with a swimming pool and have a huge motor home for weekend getaways; she loves car races and football; she follows politics at both the local and national level; the Fourth of July is her favourite holiday and she is extremely patriotic. It doesn't get more American than that!

I really don't have to ask her most of the questions because I know the answers already. She was married for a short time to her first husband (married too young), and has been married to her second husband, Mike, for over twenty-three years. Her children are Allison, twenty-three, a budding journalist, and Joe, twenty, a future restaurateur. I was sad not to get a visit with Allison, who was away at the time. She is currently a counsellor at NASA Space Camp in Alabama, but hasn't given up her dream to be a journalist one day.

As patriotic as Debbie is, she also says she would move to Canada or Mexico if she had the chance.

She completed two years of university and is now Director of Operations for Wyland, but had many jobs leading up to this and worked at more than one job at a time in the past. She took several years off when her children were younger and was always involved in their activities. She was a Girl Scout leader for years, and helped with every sports team her children were on. She is now and has always been an extremely active woman. She likes to spend her free time hiking, kayaking, walking, and doing needlework. Yosemite has always been one of her favourite places.

We had talked about menopause many times during my visit and I know she is thankful for HRT, which has helped her with many menopausal symptoms, including major mood swings. It seems no medications, however, help with the scatterbrain aspect of menopause, and we had many laughs when one of us would misplace something or forget where we were in a conversation. She says she loves her job, is very proud of her children, and yes, she is happy at this stage of her life.

~

I said a fond farewell to Debbie and left, knowing I might have had my hardest interview in Mexico, with the language barrier, and then my easiest, with a dear friend that I know so well. I took a deep breath and wondered how the next forty-eight countries would unfold.

Chapter 3
Canada

"Why would you want to interview me? There are many more interesting people than me," Joanne said, when I asked her to be my Canadian interviewee. She really doesn't understand how special she is. However, she did agree to be interviewed, and within days of my call she had started organizing a fund-raiser, contacted people in several countries, and asked if she could join me for five weeks of the trip.

Joanne and I have been friends since we were nineteen, and we travelled together in Europe for five months when we were twenty-two. She moved north to Dawson City, Yukon, in the early '80s. There, she met her husband, Fletcher, who managed Diamond Tooth Gerties, the only legal gambling hall in Canada with liquor and entertainment at that time. Eventually I ended up there as well, and spent five summers living with them and working as a blackjack, roulette, and poker dealer.

When they moved to Halifax, Nova Scotia, in 1995, I drove across Canada with Joanne and their children, Alister and Whitney. When the kids were young, Joanne and Fletcher honoured me by asking me to be the official guardian of their children should anything happen to them. Needless to say, this is a family very close to my heart. Even though they live on the other side of Canada, we have stayed very close, with visits back and forth, and I have many great memories of holidays spent together. They now live in Sydney, Nova Scotia, on Cape Breton Island.

After completing my first two countries I spent a few weeks at home. I had time to finish up some final details for the coming months and say my good-byes to everyone.

I arrived in Sydney at the beginning of May. As much as I love the west coast of Canada where I grew up, I have always envied the east coast for the heritage and culture that still exists there. The Maritime Provinces have their own music, dance, traditions, and even a different accent. Most of the people I met in Sydney were born in the area. On the west coast, and especially in my city of Victoria, it is hard to find locally born residents like myself.

While there is a large Scottish heritage in Nova Scotia, there are also Irish and French descendants, with some towns that are French-speaking only. In the phone book there are more surnames starting with Mc and Mac than any other name. Celtic music, bagpipers, and highland dance performances can be found throughout the province.

My week in Sydney was busy, as is always the case when Joanne and I are together. We golfed, hiked, visited with her many friends, held a fund-raiser, attended Whitney's university graduation, and explored the Cabot Trail. I even got to play poker at the Sydney Casino with Alister, which was a peculiar experience for me, as he wasn't even born when I was a poker dealer working for his dad—and he played much better than I did!

The Cabot Trail, around the northern tip of Cape Breton Island, is a 298-kilometre loop of spectacular coastline, with lush green mountain passes and small fishing villages. Lobster and crab traps are everywhere. Joanne and I spent a day exploring and hiking our way around the trail. We saw a coyote and a fox, but didn't find the gigantic moose we saw the last time we hiked there. It is truly a picturesque part of the world, with stunning cliffs, winding forested trails, dramatic ocean scenes, and spectacular hiking. Although we only did short hikes, there are much longer trails, and camping sites are available. We would have loved to do some kayaking and whale watching, but there just wasn't enough time. It really is an outdoor adventurer's dream location.

When I left Victoria at the beginning of May, the spring flowers were in full bloom, but in Nova Scotia there was still ice floating in the river. The golf course had just opened the weekend I arrived, and although it wasn't in the best condition, Alister and I enjoyed a golf game. (He was better at that too!) Whitney and I also spent a day catching up and visiting a game reserve where we got an up-close look at bears, moose, and other local wild animals. It has been such a joy watching these two great kids growing into such wonderful young adults.

As I mentioned earlier, the minute I told Joanne of my plans for this trip she started working on a fund-raiser. She had recently been introduced to a woman named Annett Wolf, and Annett agreed to come and speak to a group of women she didn't know, for a cause she knew nothing about. Now that's a good woman! Joanne arranged to use the beautiful and spacious home of a friend for the event. She organized donations and contributions for a silent auction and a raffle, and invited over thirty women to hear Annett speak. It all came together quite seamlessly on a sunny Sunday during my visit.

Annett Wolf is an entertaining Danish woman in her seventies, with a life story that kept us spellbound for over an hour. No one moved, spoke, or took a bathroom break in that time. For a group of women, that was an amazing feat.

Annett is an award-winning producer, director, writer, and interviewer. She started her talk with stories of growing up during WWII with a Jewish mother and detailed how they lived through that experience, and continued on to the next forty years, telling us about how she had interviewed and done film profiles of many actors, including Fred Astaire, Nick Nolte, Michael Caine, Burt Reynolds, Gene Hackman, John Travolta, Charlton Heston, and Elvis Presley. She followed Elvis through his last two concerts and produced a film called *Elvis in Concert*, which was screened after he died. She also worked with the California gangs, the Bloods and the Crips, and brought them together in an unbelievable project that produced a musical. Her time now is spent dedicated to saving the

Arctic wolves. It was a fantastic day, and we raised almost $1,200 that I could add to my fund for people in need at future destinations.

~

Joanne – 51

Joanne describes herself as a "doer" and that is an understatement. She is involved in every possible activity she can be. She says she has slowed down, and by explanation says, "I don't curl anymore, I just instruct the junior curling program and coach a boys' curling team." Her own children aren't even in the sport anymore, but she still coaches. At school, where she is a teacher's aide, she helps coach sports teams, which is not part of her job; it is strictly a volunteer position. She is the ultimate participant, coach, volunteer, and organizer. She does it all. If I think I don't know how to relax, she takes that to a whole other level. Her only problem is that she tries to fit it all into one day and gets frustrates when that doesn't work out.

Joanne and Fletcher have been married for twenty-three years. Their son Alister is twenty and their daughter Whitney is twenty-three. Both Joanne and her husband work full-time now, but she only worked on a casual basis until her kids were in high school. Then she went back to school to get her teacher's aide certificate. This is a perfect job for her, as she is such a warm, helpful person. I know she has made a difference for several of the kids she has worked with.

Both of her parents are still alive, in their early eighties and still married after fifty-two years. When asked if she feels her life is better than her parents, she says, "No, I feel our lives have been similar."

Is she where she thought she would be at fifty-one? "Yes and no. Physically, yes; married, yes; kids in college, yes. But I thought I would be further ahead financially," she says. Joanne and Fletcher have always lived in small towns where real estate values have not increased as rapidly as other places in Canada, so if they wanted to move back to the west coast, they probably couldn't afford the house prices.

Would she move to another country if she could? "Yes," she answers, which surprises me. I didn't think she would ever leave her kids, but perhaps she has realized they will both be moving to other cities when they graduate. She doesn't know where she would move, but would give another country a try, even if only for a while.

Joanne won't admit to menopause, but does admit to the odd hot flash and definitely some moments of forgetfulness. She says that over the years she has learned to be mellower, and is thankful for her kind and tolerant husband. It comes as no surprise when she answers the final question about happiness with, "Yes, I am very happy!"

It was another great week with some of my dearest friends. I looked forward to Joanne joining me in a few weeks' time in Europe.

A journey of a thousand miles starts in front of your feet.

—Lao-tzu

Chapter 4
England

"I don't have to travel the world to find fifty women from fifty countries, I could just stand on any corner in London and find them," I told my cousin Gail the second day I was there.

I stayed with Gail, her husband Joe, and their son Harry in Northwest London. High Street (the main street) a block from their home had so many nationalities represented that I truly could have found all my women there. The area was packed with Chinese, Italian, Vietnamese, Arabian, Polish, Jamaican, Irish, Indian, and Japanese restaurants and take-out joints, as well as African and Asian hairdressers. Walking down the street I heard more people speaking foreign languages than speaking English.

I lived in London for six months, twenty-nine years ago, and had been back several times. Getting around was fairly easy for me, as I was familiar with the "tube" (subway), and I always feel welcomed back the first time I hear "mind the gap", which is an announcement repeated constantly as a train approaches the station and the doors open.

Of course, there I was, thinking I was so smart. I offered to help a woman who didn't know how to navigate the underground system and promptly put us both on the wrong tube. On some tracks the trains coming through can be going to different destinations, so you have to listen to an announcement or read the front of the train. We did neither, and once we were underway I realized my mistake and had to admit to her that I was not so smart after all. We had to get off at the next stop and wait for the next train. I laughed, but I don't think she thought it was too funny. So much for my random act of kindness.

London is a fabulous city with so much to see and do, but it is one of the most expensive cities in the world. I did, however, find lots to do for free. As I was wandering around aimlessly the gigantic sign outside the British National Museum reading "Free Entrance" caught my eye, as it was meant to do. It really is amazing that this magnificent museum offers free admittance. It is a museum of human history and culture, and there are more than seven million pieces of antiquities and artwork from the world over.

Watching the Changing of the Guard at Buckingham Palace is also free, but as many times as I have been to London, I have yet to see it happen. I never seem to get there at the correct time. I did wander by the palace and watched the guards that were standing guard, to see if they moved. I was convinced some of them were statues, they stood so still, until they finally stepped out of their box to march from one side to the next. It looked to me like a very hard and boring job.

I rested in Hyde Park (one of many parks in the middle of the city), and then ventured over to Harrods, where I found many limos and town cars, chauffeurs at the ready, waiting outside. Inside, a "Once-a-Year Sale" was taking place. Hundreds of women were scrambling over half-price designer bags that were still at least eight hundred dollars. I didn't bother to check out the many floors of designer clothes.

I did spend money, though. I had to feed my theatre addiction and went to four plays in three days. I saw *Wicked*, *Hairspray*, *Dirty Dancing*, and *Blood Brothers*. I enjoyed all of them, but *Hairspray* was my favourite. I loved the music and dancing, and the performers were excellent.

My cousin Gail was not only my host, but also my interviewee.

~

Gail – 47

Gail is a cousin on my father's side and one of the only relatives from his side of the family that I know. I first met her when we were in our early twenties, and then again a few years ago, when my brother and I stayed with her for three days. She has been kind enough to offer her place as my home base while I wind my way around Europe and Great Britain.

It is obvious that I take after my father's side of the family, because Gail and I look alike. She has a picture of herself as a teenager, and it could be me in the picture. It is an odd feeling, meeting her at this stage of our lives and feeling such a connection. It is like we have known each other forever.

Gail is forty-seven, making her too young to have any menopausal symptoms, or so she says. I saw her looking for misplaced items several times; her symptoms are starting whether she admits it or not. She is in the publishing business and describes herself as "annoyingly competent". This helps explain why she works long hours and never leaves work undone. (There is a pattern here. My first four interviewees have all been hard workers and apparent overachievers. Is that our age group, or just a coincidence?)

Gail's friend Annabelle wrote this about her: Gail believes she's "annoyingly competent", eh? That would be correct, except I don't feel that she's one bit annoying. We met when I was eighteen and she was twenty-one and we have never, not once, had a cross word between us. She makes me laugh until I could die, with her throwaway witticisms and observations, is a great listener and adviser, is supremely tolerant of people, can analyse any situation in the blink of an eye, is flexible, totally dependable, and always puts others first. Far from being just "Mrs. Nice", though, she is also extremely creative, very political, a fiercely loyal friend, and a passionate and articulate advocate. She is, most definitely, the person you'd want with you on a desert island. She'd be knitting tents from bamboo in no time, would keep you going with amusing and interesting stories, and would be working out who'd be the most suitable and proactive person to address the message in the bottle to.

Now that's a good friend.

Gail is another one who married young, but after four years it was over. She has been with Joe for more than eighteen years, married for the last seven years. Their son Harry is fourteen.

Both Gail's parents have passed away. Her father was injured during WWII and suffered throughout the rest of his life. He was an alcoholic, like my father and all but one of the eight children in their family. Her mother stuck it out (like mine did), and they stayed married until his death in his late seventies. Her mother died a few years later.

She is not as enamoured with her home country as my first few interviewees were, and would move to New York City in a heartbeat. She is stressed out with work and a teenager, but when I ask if she is happy, she hesitates only slightly before replying, "Yes."

~

I really enjoyed getting to know Gail, Joe, and Harry. They made me feel like one of the family. From their welcoming home I left for Morocco, Jordan, and Syria. No more close friends to count on, no more familiar places, no more English being spoken. The real adventure was starting!

Chapter 5

Morocco

"How could we be so stupid?" we all asked in unison. My new tour mates, Chris and Carita, our tour guide Aziz, and I were standing in the middle of the desert without a vehicle. We were in the Anti-Atlas Mountains in Morocco on a "road between two mountains", as Aziz described it. In the last hours of driving, we had passed only a few nomads with their goats, a couple camels, miles of sagebrush and desert sand. We had just let our driver, Mohammed, drive off to look for the other jeep we were travelling with but had lost sight of. After about fifteen minutes he hadn't returned.

This was a few days into my one-week Moroccan tour. The day before, the other jeep broke down, so we assumed it had happened again. As we had seen the jeep about five minutes earlier, we guessed it couldn't be far behind us. Why we decided to get out and let the driver leave us there was beyond me; however, four of us—three experienced travellers and our tour guide—just hopped out and watched him drive away.

There was one larger shrub amongst the smattering of smaller sagebrush, so we had a little shade, and we all had water—but again, what were we thinking? In the distance, about three hundred metres away, was a group of flat-roofed adobe huts. Eventually, Aziz started off to see if we could get out of the sun and wait there, but surprised us all by turning around about halfway there.

"What happened?" I asked.

"I can't go any closer because there are only women there," he said.

"So why is that a problem?" Chris asked.

"A Muslim man cannot speak to a Muslim woman without another man from her family present," he explained, as though we should know this.

As far as he was concerned we would have to stay stranded in the shade of one shrub, rather than have him go against his customs. So we sat kicking ourselves for our foolish decision and wondering where Mohammed was.

Fortunately for us, the women must have seen Aziz and had gone to find their men. After a few minutes one of the men came to find out who these strange people, with no vehicle, in the middle of the desert, were. Aziz, who spoke English, French, Berber, and Arabic, determined they were Arabs and explained what had happened. They invited us into their home.

They were a family of six brothers, with their wives and children. They lived in the middle of the desert with no other homes for miles and miles around. They had built up the area with palm trees and a large garden. I saw no electricity and no sign of water, only their five buildings, a few cows, and a couple of very aggressive, loudly barking dogs.

One of the brothers led us to one of their outer buildings. He put out a straw mat and then an intricately woven, colourful carpet for us to sit on. Another brother brought in freshly steeped tea in a beautiful silver teapot, on an equally beautiful silver tray, covered with an elegant embroidered cloth. Aziz poured the sugary mint tea in precise Moroccan style. The higher you can hold the teapot, the longer the tea is draining, the better the style. That is not an easy feat, as the tulip-shaped glasses are not very big. He did it with great expertise.

A few minutes later, a shy woman stood outside the door, waited to be invited in, and then brought us just-off-the-coals hot bread. It was delicious pita-style bread and a welcome treat. Eventually we asked about the beautiful carpet we were sitting on and one of the brothers explained that the women were weaving the carpets in the house. "Can we see them?" we asked. They seemed pleased that we asked and led us into the main house.

The main part of the house was one large room, with very little furniture, bamboo mats, and their own handwoven carpets on the floor. Sitting on the floor in front of a loom were three women, with several children crawling all over them. The women took it all in stride and kept weaving. There was another woman cutting up onions, and she had a couple more kids crawling all over her. All the women were dressed in colourful long skirts, mismatched tops, and head scarves. I could only guess how old they were, but decided they were between fifteen and thirty, and assumed they were the wives of the brothers. There was also an older fellow—Grandpa, I assumed —sitting in the doorway. He was not interested in interacting with us.

They spoke no English or French, only Arabic, and Aziz was outside with the men, so we tried to communicate with sign language and by shouting. I know better, but somehow I always talk louder to people who don't understand me.

After some initial hesitation, the children were fascinated with us and were crawling all over us, instead of their mothers. They ranged in age from one to five.

While we waited to be rescued we took everyone's photos. They loved looking at their pictures and really got a kick out of watching themselves in videos. Considering they didn't even have electricity, this must have seemed like magic to them. The women on the loom never stopped working, but watched and laughed at their kids having so much fun.

After a while a young woman, probably about fourteen, appeared from the garden and put a cassette into an old boom box that ran on a car battery. Moroccan music filled the air, adding to this unique experience. The young women then left, but came back with baskets woven from recycled juice packs, reminding me of the purses in Mexico. We negotiated a price with the little cash I had in my pocket, as I had left my purse in the jeep. I paid about one dollar and thirty cents for a little basket and she seemed pleased with the exchange. I would have paid more if I had brought more cash, but of course this was not a planned shopping trip.

Three hours passed before Aziz and the brothers signalled Mohammed, using a mirror to reflect the sun. We were saved! Mohammed explained that he didn't find the other jeep, but when he turned around to come back, he lost the road back to our location. So he had been driving around looking for us all that time. We were lucky he didn't run out of gas.

The other jeep had not broken down, but had just taken another road, so that group ended up waiting and worrying about us and not having near as much fun. I resolved to never to let my only means of transportation drive off without me again. However, our bad decision turned out to be an incredible experience, allowing us to see how these people eked out a living in the desert, while enjoying their hospitality.

Besides that adventure, we spent a week in hotel rooms with no soap, generally no hot water, rough towels, and hard beds; stayed two nights in a Berber village, sleeping on floor mats and sharing one toilet with nine people; drove on the most frightening roads (enough to scare the bravest of souls); and more than once, while walking, I was nearly ploughed down by a motorcycle. However, I had one of the best weeks of my life and decided I'd found a new favourite country.

Morocco—or "Maroc", as the locals call it—is absolutely stunning. The landscapes vary from stark orange desert to breathtaking mountains, canyons as magnificent as the Grand Canyon and stunning valleys of lush palm groves. There are four mountain ranges in Morocco, and we drove over and through two, the High Atlas and the Anti-Atlas ranges. Erosion has left behind a sculpted and dramatic landscape in these mountains, with colours ranging from vibrant red to dark green to beautiful light sage green.

We also travelled many miles in the desert, and although some of it is just flat, unappealing sand and sagebrush, other portions where the sand dunes glisten in the sun are magnificent. Riding camels in the Sahara will go down as one of my favourite days, since it was peaceful, beautiful, and hilarious. Our camel-trekking guide took great pleasure in only leading us up the dunes so he could laugh at us as we went down, almost falling over the front of our camels. My squealing seemed to make his day.

We passed nomads and goatherds in the middle of nowhere and camels wandering free in the vast open desert. Watching people carrying more on their heads and backs than seemed humanly possible left me wondering how strong they must be. I also mused that the over-packed bikes, donkeys, carts, and vehicles are a study in balance the Moroccans seemed to have worked out.

The kasbahs (ancient fortresses of stone), often over five hundred years old, dot the hillsides everywhere. Some are just crumbling ruins, while others have been restored to their previous magnificence and still others have been turned into hotels. Trying to learn all the history would require more than a week of exploring, but it was fun meandering through the buildings and imagining the life of long ago.

One day we walked through a village built on the side of a canyon and the narrow canyon floor was chequered with garden plots. Amongst the palm and almond trees women were doing their washing in a tiny stream. Most of them covered their faces when we approached. It seemed that in the rural areas the women, as well as some of the older men, dressed traditionally, but the children and most men wore modern clothing. (In the bigger cities most men and women dressed in modern attire.)

The most fascinating thing we saw by far, however, was goats climbing trees. It was amazing to watch these clumsy-looking animals climb the limbs of the argan tree. They were in search of the argan nut. The argan tree is unique to Morocco. The nut is used to produce argan oil for cooking and traditional Moroccan medicines; the oil is also used in cosmetics which have become popular worldwide. At one time, argan nut harvesters would wait for the goats to eat the nut and take the seed from the dung, but now they pick the nuts themselves, crack the seed and roast it—a much cleaner way, I think.

The only big city I visited on my own was Marrakech. First on my agenda was to visit the famous market in the old part of town. I should have done more research because I didn't know a market is a "*souk*" and the old town is the *medina*. Those words would have helped me when I asked for directions and prevented me from getting lost for over an hour.

Marrakech is new and old and crazy. The streets are crammed with motorcycles, cars, and donkey carts all vying for the right of way. The new part could be anywhere in the modern world; the old part is an ancient walled city that I am told is over a thousand years old. Within the walls is an amazing labyrinth of four thousand very narrow streets and alleys lined with mosques, *riads* (Moroccan homes with an inner garden), and souks. You could wander for days, which I almost had to do, because once inside the walls I was lost again. The smells, the colours, and the vast selection of goods to buy could keep you distracted forever. Eventually two young boys, looking for a reward, helped me find my way to the main square of Djemaa el-Fna.

Djemaa el-Fna is where all the action is. I had barely stepped into the square when I had a snake wrapped around my neck. The snake charmers not only charm the snakes, but do a decent job on the women as well. Not only did I allow them to put the snake on me, I paid for it. I realized as I walked away how stupid that was, but it all happened so fast that I was under their spell. Then there are storytellers who launch into a story, and when they are halfway through they collect money. If they don't feel they have received enough, they wait for more before finishing their tale. I didn't fall for that one, but only because they tell their stories in Arabic.

There are also fortune-tellers, men with monkeys, acrobats, dancers, musicians, food vendors, and more touristy knickknack stalls. The funniest stall I saw had a man selling false teeth. I hate to guess where he got them from. To add to this chaos are cars, motorcycles, and horse and donkey carts driving right through the middle of the square.

At five every afternoon, the food vendors start setting up, and throughout the rest of the evening you can choose your dinner from any of one hundred or so stalls. The vendors bring the food, the cooking facilities, the clean-up crew, the benches, and the tables. There is no drinking alcohol anywhere in view of a mosque, and as most mosques have very tall minarets there are few places that serve alcohol.

The food was scrumptious everywhere we went and the rich aromas followed us throughout our stay. One of the traditional dishes is *tajine*, a stew slow-cooked in a *tajine* clay pot. The stew—comprised of meats (lamb, beef, or chicken), veggies, dates, prunes, and nuts—is placed in the bottom of the pot and a cone-shaped lid is placed on top. The stew cooks for hours and is served with couscous or rice. Locally grown nuts, dates, and olives are used in abundance in Moroccan cuisine, and spices are masterfully combined for mouth-watering results. Some specialties, such as sheep's head, were a bit adventurous for my tastes. I passed that one up.

I had another marriage proposal as well. As it is rather unusual to see a woman travelling alone, Moroccan men were astounded when they found out I was alone and not married, and I became the object of their affection very quickly. One very nice young shop owner thought I should leave my group and stay in Morocco to marry him. I'm sure I broke his heart when I declined, but he was much too young.

While we were travelling throughout the country, Aziz explained a few things about the Berber culture, as he and our drivers were Berbers. He told us that of the thirty-two million Moroccans, over 50 percent are Berbers. One of the more interesting stories was about the way marriages are arranged in some of the very traditional villages. They line up the young men on one side of a room and bring in young women from another village to line the other side. The men then throw a small pebble at the woman they like and if she picks it up they will marry. Aziz said that arranged marriages are still very common.

Aziz did not go that route, however, and married a woman he met at his sister's wedding. He appeared to be "the modern man" with his clients, but in fact was a very traditional Muslim. When I met him, his wife was expecting a baby in a few months. One week after the baby was born they would have the circumcision and naming ceremony. At that time he would have to kill a sheep. I laughed when I found out that this tradition will carry on even though Aziz lives in an apartment in the city. He told me he planned to bring the live sheep into his apartment, keep it on his balcony until the celebration day and then sacrifice it, on the balcony. When we drove back into Marrakech I kept looking at all the balconies to see if there were any sheep, but I didn't spot any.

Aziz also told us about their King Mohammed VI, who has been king since 1999. He succeeded his father Hassan, who, he explained, was not a nice guy. The current king is trying very hard to modernize Morocco, and although women have had the right to vote for a while, it was as recent as 2004 that he passed several laws improving women's rights regarding marriage, custody, and divorce. At the time of my visit the king was also really trying to push tourism, with a current campaign to have ten million visitors in 2010. His picture hung in most homes we visited, right beside the picture of Mecca.

It appeared to me that the country was advancing in many ways, but traditions are still held in high regard, especially in the rural areas. I met two girls who had been to college, but were engaged and planned to quit work immediately after the marriage to stay home and, in their words, devote their lives to their husbands first and their children second. I don't necessarily think this is a bad thing, but it sounded as if they felt they had no choice in the matter.

In the middle of the week we spent a few days in a tiny Berber village nestled in a valley surrounded by mountains. The drive to the village was breathtaking in more ways than one. The views were amazing, but it was one of the most frightening roads I have ever been on. The narrow, windy road circled the side of a mountain and there were no barriers on the cliff side. We were very fortunate not to meet any vehicles going in the opposite direction. I really don't know what we would have done. There was no space to back up or pull over, it was too narrow. Once we were about two miles from the village, the drivers dropped us off so we could walk and enjoy the views and countryside at an easier and safer pace, but we always kept the jeeps in sight, not making the same mistake twice.

Coming over the final hill and looking down into the valley at the village was magical. The hillsides were terraced around the houses and forested with prickly pear cactus, eucalyptus, almond, argan, carib, apricot, and fig trees. Most houses were painted bright colours and were huge.

It was a Soussi village. Aziz described the Soussi as hard workers who make lots of money but don't spend it, except on their houses. In the village there were mainly women and children; the men were all off working somewhere else and sending money home.

While there, our local tour guide was a lovely young woman who not only gave us a tour of the village, but painted hennas on our hands and ankles. Khadijia was twenty-nine; she married at thirteen and had her first child at fourteen, followed by three more. Although she only went to grade three, she said all her kids would go to school. Children in the village can only go to school until they are twelve years old and then they have to leave for boarding school. Although Khadijia married young, she told us the government had changed the law and people must be eighteen before they marry. She said she would let her daughters get married at eighteen, but her boys would have to be at least twenty-three.

Aziz arranged for me to interview Fatima, a woman from the village.

~

Fatima – 50ish

Aziz brings Fatima to the house we are staying at, and when they walk in I can hardly see her behind him. She is a tiny woman, barely reaching four feet tall. She is dressed in a black jelaba (long robe), with her head and face covered, making it hard to tell how old she is. She says she is "almost" fifty. Aziz explains that many people in her generation and older have no records of their birth and don't know their age. She speaks no Arabic, English, or French, only Berber, and a dialect that Aziz knows only some of, so we proceed hoping to have few "lost in translation" moments.

Fatima has outlived two arranged marriages to husbands who were both thirty-nine years older than her. She was brought to this village by friends, after her first husband died, to marry the second one. He was a Hajjis, which means he was a Muslim who has done a pilgrimage to Mecca. This is a revered position in their culture, so he was considered a great man. His first wife had died, and it was considered lucky for Fatima to be able to marry him. I am not sure she felt that way, because when I ask her if she would marry again, she quickly shakes her head and says, "No." She says she had wanted children, but wasn't able to have them. She has an adult stepson from the second marriage, but they are not close.

She is telling Aziz something and trying to puff herself up, in an effort to make her tiny body look bigger. He tells me she is saying she feels young and healthy, and that she can climb all the mountains around the village. I ask if she ever sees a doctor, and she admits she has never seen a doctor or a dentist. Aziz tells me that if the villagers have a toothache there is a man in the village who will take the tooth out. He is not a dentist, just someone who takes out teeth. I see Fatima has seen this man many times, because she removes the scarf from her face and shows me her teeth—or, I should say, lack of teeth, as she has few left.

"I used to work in the fields where we grew barley and wheat, but we have had little rain in the last few years and those crops no longer grow here. I now collect the Argan nuts and rent out rooms to tourists, but there aren't many coming to our village. I cannot read or write, but I am good with numbers," she tells me. Aziz explains that her husband's family helps her out financially. "The giving of alms is one of the Pillars of Islam, and Muslims help each other out," he says proudly.

Fatima is quiet and timid, but when I ask if she has travelled anywhere other than her village, she says she has been to festivals in Tangier with her husband's family and she loves the party atmosphere. Her face, uncovered again, lights up as she rattles on about it. She adds, "We have festivals in this village too and I love them."

I am getting to the menopause questions and I don't think we can go there, but I say to Aziz, "There are some questions I don't think I should ask. I am worried about crossing cultural barriers." He wants to know what the questions are, and when I use the word "menopause" he looks confused. So I say, "It comes when a women stops having her monthly period." More confused looks. I try "monthly bleeding," knowing I have gone too far. He blushes and quickly says, "No, you are right, I can't ask about that." I am tempted to say, "I told you so," but hold my tongue.

During the interview she doesn't make eye contact with me. She seems to relax for a minute, uncovers her face, and then remembers where she is and covers up again. I am not sure if it is being around Aziz or me. Finally, I ask if she is happy and she says, "Yes," but I don't hear conviction in her voice and have to believe Aziz has translated correctly. I thank her for coming to speak with me and give her a little money. She brightens up at this.

Later in the evening, Carita and I are walking around the village, and we come upon Fatima at her house. It is three storeys tall. She seems more at ease with us now, and is proud and excited to show us her home. She shows us her TV, which she had told me earlier she rarely watched, and her CD player, which she says she listens to often. She has several rooms furnished for guests, but she says she spends all her time in the TV room and the kitchen. Her house is perched on one of the hills high in the village and has an incredible view of the whole town. It seems strange that this tiny woman lives in this huge home, but I remember that Aziz explained the Sousi people take great pride in their big homes. Fatimia is a proud woman who seems to be able to carry on without a husband, and I am happy to have met her and had a chance to visit her home.

~

I will definitely return one day to see more of Morocco. I was thrilled to meet so many locals in the smaller villages and towns. They were all wonderful and friendly. I was humbled by how they live out their lives with very little, but work so hard and appear so happy. The homes we visited and the families we met were all generous with the little they had—to complete strangers. Aziz explained it is a Berber custom to keep one room for guests and outfit it with the family's best items. The space is only used for guests, no matter how few possessions they may have in the rest of the house.

On leaving Morocco, Carita said to me, "How are you going to outdo this week? It has been so incredible." I agreed it would be hard to beat, but I had forty-five countries in which to try.

I love to travel, but I hate to arrive.

—Albert Einstein

Chapter 6
Jordan

"You can't be serious?" I asked incredulously. My tour guide had just responded to my comment about "honour killings", and how I had read there were still many of them taking place in Jordan. "Not anymore," he answered. I was relieved for a brief moment, but then he added, "There aren't as many, because women have learned not to dishonour their family."

This was a few days into my tour in Jordan. His response shocked and surprised me. Although I was aware that he was Muslim, he seemed to be very modern and had shown only respect to women since we met him. He wasn't just trying to get a rise out of me; he wholeheartedly believed that if a woman dishonoured her family, by having sex before marriage or marrying without permission, she deserved death. There are many customs in other cultures that I understand, but this certainly is not one of them. It is hard to look into someone's eyes and grasp his deep-rooted cultural beliefs that are so offensive to me. We debated the issue for hours, and he backed down slightly when he admitted he didn't think he would carry out the custom with his own three daughters, but he understood and had sympathy for those who did carry out this horrendous custom. (Although honour killings have recently been declared illegal in Jordan, the punishments for perpetrators are still very lenient.)

That was not the only awkward part of my initiation to Jordan. The first part, however, was my own fault. "How could I be so stupid?" Yes, I was asking the same question two countries in a row. I was getting a bit scared, thinking how early into my journey I had made so many dumb mistakes. I had flown from Morocco to Madrid, where I had to stay overnight, and then flew to Amman, the capital of Jordan, a city of three million, which is half the population of the whole country.

I had done no research and didn't even know what attractions there were to see in Amman. I just assumed there would be tour buses, tour companies, or tourist information booths waiting for dumb tourists. What I learned, however, was that in some countries, that is not the norm. Surprisingly, I realized I think like Albert Einstein—I really don't like the actual arrival in a new place. As much as I like to travel, I always have a nervous stomach when I first arrive in a new city.

The front desk clerk at my hotel had been busy with a tour group when I was ready to go sightseeing, so I just hopped in a taxi, without a map or a plan, and asked to go into the city. The drive in went well and I was able to get my first look at the "white city" (municipal law stipulates that all buildings must be faced with local white stone). Although the traffic was busy, there was not one motorcycle, which was a vast contrast to Morocco, so it didn't seem as crazy. (Apparently, motorcycles had been banned until recently, but the two-wheeled trend obviously hadn't taken hold yet.)

As we approached the city centre, the driver asked where I wanted off. His English was as good as my Arabic, which meant we had no idea what the other was saying. I tried, "Tourist information," but he had no clue and just kept driving. Finally, I saw what looked like the main street and tried, "Stop." That seemed to work.

I then went from one business to another, looking for someone who spoke English and then asking if there was a tourist info booth or a local bus tour. Using the word "bus" had me steered towards two travel agents and a bus depot. None of them had any local tours, just trips out of town, and no one seemed to know of any local tours. It was hot, I was hungry, and I was so mad at myself for not doing my research. I decided to go back to the hotel and sulk. To top it off, I misunderstood the currency exchange and paid forty dollars, instead of four dollars, for the taxi. "What kind of traveller am I? Have I learned nothing?" I found myself muttering.

The moment I entered the lobby the desk clerk called me over, apologized for being busy earlier, and handed me a map and a list of tourist sites. The sheet even had a note about reading the meters in the cabs so you don't pay incorrectly. At least this showed I wasn't the only one who made that mistake.

After a short rest and a quick meal, I stopped beating myself up and tried again. This time the cab driver spoke English, and we had a great discussion about Jordan before he dropped me at the Citadel. The Hashemite Kingdom of Jordan, as it has been called since 1950, has a very long history, and Amman, despite its modern appearance, has many historical sites.

Amman was originally built on seven *jalabs* (hills), which has expanded to nineteen *jalabs*, and at the top of one is the Citadel. The ruins there include a temple from AD 162, a Byzantine church from the fifth century, and a mosque from the eighth century. From the top of the Citadel there is a sensational view of the whitewashed city, and built into the hillside below is a six-thousand-seat Roman amphitheatre from the first century. All that was a small window into the different cultures and civilizations that have helped develop the country into the Jordan of today.

As I was one of only four tourists wandering the site, the tourist police were very bored, and were happy to pose for pictures and then take pictures of me. We had a good time joking around, which helped improve my mood after my morning misadventure.

My second day was better, as I visited with the parents and a friend of a Jordanian friend in Canada. They made me very welcome in a cozy room adorned with family photos, strikingly similar to any of our parents' living rooms. My hosts were Muslim and their friend was Catholic. They made it clear that there was no problem between the Christians and Muslims. (Jordan is approximately 93 percent Muslim and 6 percent Catholic.)

Between them these Jordanians had five adult children and none of them lived in Jordan. One was in Lebanon and the others in the

States and Canada. All their kids had university degrees. There are more than thirty universities in Jordan. Children who don't leave the country often stay at home until (and even after) they are married, if need be. They cited "family" as their most important treasure. It was a lovely visit, ending with a delicious home-cooked meal. Those were few and far between on my trip, so it was much appreciated.

My guided tour started the next day, and the week was spent travelling the length of Jordan and visiting many spectacular sites. During the drives from one place to the next, the tour guide told us more about the country and himself. He was Palestinian, born in Jordan, but his parents were refugees from Palestine. There are close to two million refugees from Palestine who have been given Jordanian passports, and most still hold hope of returning to their homeland one day. He tried to explain the whole Middle East political situation from the Palestinian perspective. There are so many issues I couldn't begin to understand it all, but certainly felt compassion for their struggle.

He also explained that men can have four wives at the same time, although they must have permission from the first wife and inform the next wives of the previous ones. Women can only have one husband. (That's enough, isn't it?)

Despite the many laws which seem to favour men, Jordan is one of the most liberal and modern countries in the Middle East. For instance, women have no specific clothing requirements, and we saw as many women dressed in Western attire as in traditional Arab garb.

Our guide also told us King Abdullah II was very popular and the people were quite happy with the international recognition and trade he has brought to Jordan, but that everyone agreed the prices of goods and services were skyrocketing and it was getting very expensive to live in Jordan.

Our first stop on the tour was not far from Amman, where there are several desert castles, including the one used by Lawrence of Arabia. The castles we visited were built between the sixth and twelfth centuries. Although some have been restored, there are also still original frescoes intact. It was hard to believe the colour, paint, and design can still be seen and recognized so many hundreds of years later.

During the week I swam in the Red Sea and the Dead Sea (at four hundred feet below sea level). Well, I floated in the Dead Sea; you don't swim in it, for fear of getting the high-salt-content water in your eyes. There is an emergency medical clinic at the seaside just for that reason. The salt is so strong it can also sting the skin, especially if you have just shaved your legs, which I had. However, despite that, I still had the "beach boys" rub Dead Sea mud all over me, as it is said to be good for the skin. You are meant to leave the black mud caked on for at least fifteen minutes for the full effect, but it stung too much, so I washed it off after about five minutes. It took a very long time for the mud to come out of my bathing suit.

We also visited Aqaba on the Red Sea, which shares a border with Eilat, Israel. It was there that I experienced my first personal cultural dilemma. All I wanted to do was cool off from the heat (forty-two-degrees Celsius) by having a swim, but while I sat at a table at a beachfront cafe, I was surrounded by men playing cards, drinking tea, and leering at me. Down the beach were a few women swimming, but in full dress, covered from head to toe in their long *abayas* and head scarves. I was wearing a below-the-knee skirt and a blouse covering the appropriate amount of shoulder, but I had my one-piece bathing suit underneath, which in some cultures was conservative, but not there. I cooled off a bit by wading in up to my knees, but just couldn't strip down to that suit. Nor did I want to swim in my clothes. So I forfeited the swim.

I should have followed local custom and gone in fully dressed, however, because that evening I ended up with heat stroke. A night spent in the bathroom followed by a morning in bed had me miss a snorkelling trip. I had no idea that the Red Sea had such good snorkelling and was told by the others that it was sensational. "Better than in the Great Barrier Reef," one of the Aussies said. That will teach me!

One of our days was spent racing around in jeeps in Wadi Rum, a spectacular valley in the desert. Lawrence of Arabia described it as "echoing, spacious, and godlike." I'd have to agree. The bright orange desert sand is accented with mammoth sandstone cliffs eroded into amazing shapes, some towering over one thousand metres. We also explored many of the crevasses between the rocks where we found hidden four-thousand-year-old rock carvings. It was a thrilling day of discovery.

The biggest drawing card for Jordan is Petra, the ancient city carved into the desert mountains by the Nabataeans over two thousand years ago. To find the city you must walk through a 1.25-kilometre, windy, narrow gorge in the mountain (called the Siq), which is spectacular in itself. As we approached the end of the Siq, the Treasury, the most famous monument of Petra, slowly came into view. It was one of those "I can't believe I am here" moments. It is no wonder this building has been designated one of the "New Seven Wonders of the World". The Treasury, intricately carved into the side of the mountain, stands over forty metres tall. Six gigantic pillars of the first floor support the six smaller pillars of the second floor. In the recesses between the pillars are statues of horsemen, a scorpion, a female warrior, and a large urn. The urn was thought to contain a treasure, thus the name.

As we carried on past the Treasury a whole city unfolded before us. All perfectly carved out of the mountains were tombs, caves, churches, and a 3,500-seat amphitheatre. The rock is a stunning orange colour on the outside, but inside some of the buildings a magnificent blend of oranges and pinks in a marble effect shines through the walls. Many children were selling tiny multicoloured stones to the tourists.

A donkey ride up the mountainside led to another magnificent building, the Monastery. It took me a little longer to get up than most, however, because I fell off the donkey. The original donkey they gave me had a saddle with stirrups that broke the moment I got on. I had to be very insistent that I would not take that one, but they got me back, because it turned out the saddle of the second one they gave me was not cinched tight enough. Halfway up the hill the saddle and I went sideways. It was actually quite funny, as I wasn't hurt. Neither was the donkey. But I decided to walk the rest of the way up. I had to stop and rest, since it was very hot, so I plopped myself down with a woman selling jewellery on the side of the trail. She spoke enough English for me to learn she was a Bedouin, who was forty, and the third of four wives. She was thirteen when she married her husband, who was thirty-eight. She had four children with him. He had five with his first wife, one with his second, and none with the fourth. She seemed happy, and we had a few laughs when I tried to help sell her jewellery to the other tourists trekking by. I also bought a beautiful silver and lapis bracelet that she told me her mother had made. I don't think it is real silver or that her mother made it, but I love it anyway.

When I reached the very top, not only was the Monastery another jaw-dropping sight, but the view of the valleys and mountains was stunning. The Monastery stands over forty-five metres tall and fifty metres wide. It is hard to imagine how the Nabataeans carved these buildings with such precision. They had to do it perfectly the first time.

While I was resting before the journey back down, I met another jewellery vendor, a young Bedouin man. I spent several hours with him and we rode his donkey down the mountain. He told me he had written a book about the Bedouin lifestyle. He was of a Bedouin clan that lived in the caves in Petra until 1985, when the government moved them out to a nearby village. He said he was born in a cave.

He had never attended school, yet he was fluent in Arabic, English, and Spanish, and appeared to know much about the world. While I sat with him, he talked to a Jewish tour group that had just been to Israel. He was very respectful and had an informed discussion with them. He said he has learned everything from the tourists, but would rather not have them there, since he didn't care about money, just "his mountains". Three of his sisters attended school, as there is now a law requiring that all children go to school until age sixteen. He told me his mother and father married when they were eleven and sixteen. The first of their nine children was born when his mom was seventeen. As we spoke, I realized his mother was around fifty. So, since I didn't have time to meet her during my tour, I asked him if he would write her story. I was sure he could write a far better story than I could.

He didn't propose, but did ask if I wanted to "stay in a Bedouin village for as long as you want with a nice young Bedouin who was born in a cave." What an offer! These Arab men can sure come up with the lines. He was full of compliments about my beauty and said, "Those Canadian men are stupid to let a woman like you get away." Good for the ego, but I had to decline the invitation; he was far too young and I was sure our cultures would not have blended well. But it was a great day at one of the most extraordinary places I have even seen. I would have loved to spend a few more days exploring the area, but we had to carry on.

Daily, the journey through Jordan brought up memories of Bible stories from my Catholic school days. We visited Mt. Nebo, where Moses lived out the last of his 120 years. From there he could see over to the Promised Land of Jerusalem. Sadly, he never reached it. We could just make out a hillside in the far distance and our guide told us it was Jerusalem.

We also visited Madaba, where the oldest mosaic map of Ancient Palestine was discovered in the late 1800s. The map is said to be from the sixth century and has helped researchers find other archaeological sites that were unknown before its discovery.

For any geology, history, or religious buffs, Jordan is the place to visit. I need to go back and watch *Lawrence of Arabia*, *Indiana Jones and the Last Crusade*, and read the Bible and the Koran before I will get it all. I had as many history lessons and Arab/Israeli/Palestinian political lessons as I could hear in a week. Aside from our one major disagreement, my guide was a pleasure. He was passionate about Jordan and its politics, and was eager to answer my millions of questions.

I really enjoyed the food, dining on hummus, baba ghanoush, yogurts, and a variety of vegetables, olives, salads, spices, breads, and kebabs. Most places served up so many *mezes* (appetizers) that I had no room for the main course.

There were, however, a few things I didn't enjoy in Jordan. The country does not have any smoking bans. People can smoke anywhere, anytime, and they do. Most toilets are squatters that generally lack toilet paper and you still have to pay. I also felt uncomfortable when I walked alone; the leering from men was relentless. Despite those few irritations I really enjoyed seeing and learning about Jordan.

NOTE:

I won't be getting that story from my Bedouin friend. No sooner had I left Jordan than I received the following e-mail:

> *hi. im soory to told you that my donky did yestrday im realy vary sad. its vary sad. i dont know what to do. is the ally thing i maik my living from. i dont know. i dont have noyjing to buy anther one. im resly sad hope to her from you.*

I felt a twinge of sadness until I realized he was probably trying to scam a "rich foreigner". I e-mailed back and asked how his donkey died, assuming that was what "did" meant. He never did explain what happened to the donkey, but said a new one was the equivalent of about two thousand dollars, and then in another e-mail he said it was closer to four thousand dollars. I explained that I would pay him to write the story about his mother, but was thinking of maybe two hundred dollars. He had his sister-in-law, who is American, write me once to get more details, but when he realized I wasn't coming up with the big bucks his last e-mail sarcastically said, "is thes frends? thank you so much my frend."

And that was the last I heard from him. This really bothered me. It wasn't that I fell for all the compliments or had any romantic feelings for this young man, but I had such a good time in such a magical place and thought we had developed a true friendship. Obviously, I had read it all wrong. I do realize that a single woman prancing around telling people she is "travelling the world" is a target, but it still makes me sad that the moment was spoiled.

When you travel, remember that a foreign country is not designed to make you comfortable. It is designed to make its own people comfortable.

—Clifton Fadiman

Chapter 7

Syria

"Why don't you marry me and live in my beach house?" proposed my tour guide, Muti. Sounded enticing, but the problem was, he meant for me to be his second wife. And as is custom in Syria, he would still keep his first wife. So it was another proposal I had to decline; not just because of the second wife idea, but because he popped the question within two minutes of meeting me and learning I was Canadian. As it turned out, his parents and one brother live in Canada, but he hadn't been able to acquire a visa himself. I guess he thought he could marry his way in, and how convenient that a lovely Canadian such as myself should show up.

I first met Muti at the Jordan/Syria border, when we finally got into Syria. Three of us from the Jordan tour carried on to Syria together. Our journey to the border was unsettling, as our driver, who spoke no English, seemed nervous, drove erratically, and had no idea what he was supposed to do once we got to the border. We didn't know what was going to happen to us when we got to the border, and we were promptly turned away. Having no way to understand what had happened, the three of us were completely bewildered as to what we were going to do. We didn't even have the cell number for our Jordanian tour guide, who had left us hours before, to call for advice.

As we were trying to come up with solutions, which included getting out and walking across on our own, the driver drove back into

Jordan and stopped the first taxi he found. Fortunately for us, the taxi driver not only spoke English, but was an expert in taking people over the border. He explained to us that our driver was turned away because he didn't have the right papers. (An oversight on the part of our Jordanian tour guide, who had arranged our ride.) Once back at the border, other than many men with rifles staring in the window, we had no problem getting out of Jordan. We started to get worried again, though, when our new driver stopped the cab and went into the duty-free shop, halfway into no-man's-land between countries, brought out ten cartons of cigarettes, and hid them under the seats. (As we were in full view of both border gates I am not sure who he was hiding the cigarettes from.)

It was at Syrian customs that we met Muti. He was there to take us to Damascus, where we were to meet up with our new group. He asked for our passports and told us to wait in the car. So we handed our passports to a stranger, sat in a car with contraband cigarettes, and had no clear idea what was going on. There were many men with guns and machine guns, not all in uniform, and several men in long robes and chequered head scarves (kuffiye) or crocheted beanie hats (kufis). We were definitely questioning our decision to visit Syria.

We sat for over forty-five minutes before Muti came out, smiling from ear to ear, and handed us our passports. I think he was enjoying a visit with his buddies and drinking tea while we sweated away and imagined all sorts of spooky border scenarios. What was interesting was that we had applied for and paid for Syrian entrance visas long before arriving in the country, and they didn't even compare the photo to the person. Nor did they look in the car to do a person count. All our worrying had been for nothing. We left our taxi driver and his cigarettes and hopped in Muti's van for our journey into Syria.

Our first stop inside Syria was Bosra, about forty-five minutes from the border. Bosra is an archaeological site with ruins from the Roman, Byzantine, and Muslim times, dating back to the second century. The stone of most of the ruins was black basalt, a stark contrast from the brown and orange stone ruins I had seen in Jordan and Morocco. However, in the well-preserved fifteen-thousand-seat Roman theatre, the pillars were sandstone. Muti said the pillars were assumed to be pillaged and carried hundreds of miles from Petra. (I tried to imagine how they moved these massive pillars thousands of years ago.) We were interested to discover that although Bosra is a UNESCO (United Nations Educational, Scientific, and Cultural Organization) World Heritage Site, there is a small community of people living within the ruins. Souks are set up within the crumbling walls and people have built homes throughout the site. We spent a few hours wandering amongst the ruins; visiting the Mosque of Omar, with original facades, minarets, and columns; taking great photos of headless statues, massive pillars, and Roman baths; and singing in the middle of the stage of the theatre to prove the acoustics were as good as we were told they were. And they were! The sound carried to every seat equally. Bosra is one of over 3,500 historical sites in Syria. We didn't get to all of them!

The drive to Damascus was through some of the fertile farmland, which covers about 45 percent of Syria, the rest being semi-desert. We arrived in Damascus and joined our new tour group. It was made up of very experienced travellers, which makes sense, as Syria would generally not be the choice of a new traveller. I enjoyed comparing notes and getting ideas for the rest of my journey from my new tour mates.

Muti was our tour guide only for the day, which was unfortunate, because other than the marriage proposal he was a great guide. Our tour leader for the rest of the week was Omar, who inadvertently helped the group bond quickly. He tried to scam us, by collecting his tip at the beginning of the tour.

The kind of tours I signed up with for most of my trip are called "Adventure Tours". There are usually ten to twelve people, the transportation and accommodations are covered in the initial payment, but there is a local payment, which is detailed in the paperwork when you sign up. Everyone brings the money to pay the tour leader on the first day and it is expected you will tip the leader and driver at the end if you feel they did a good job. Omar started our first meeting by trying to get us all to pay the local payment plus his and the driver's tip. I think he believed we would not figure it out because we had to pay in Syrian pounds, but he was unaware he had a group of savvy travellers. He tried to talk his way out of it, but only dug himself in deeper. This resulted in the group bonding over uncovering his con, but created an unfortunate tension with our new leader.

The tour turned out great, though, and we all warmed up to Omar by the end of the week. We did a round trip between Damascus and Aleppo, stopping at many incredible sites, and learning more about the history of the area. There are twenty million Syrians, with five million in Damascus and five million in Aleppo. For me, Aleppo seemed a little less crazy than Damascus, but only slightly. Both cities claim to be the oldest constantly occupied city in the world. Both have massive souks (markets), and in both, the skills of a magician and the patience of a saint are both needed to cross a street without losing life or limb. It really is like playing chicken with cars, buses, trucks, and motorcycles every time a crossing is undertaken. It was truly frightening. The locals don't even stop at the curb; they just start and weave in and out of the various vehicles. I would find a big man, or group of people, and place myself so that they were the buffer between me and the traffic. I decided they knew what they were doing, or if they got hit first, it might at least soften the blow. I worked it out, or Mom was watching over me, because I survived unscathed!

As in Jordan and Morocco, the people are very proud of their country and happy to show it off. We were welcomed everywhere and invited to share tea with many. Tea is generally made at a teahouse and brought on a silver tray by a tea boy. Even in most restaurants, the tea is brought from the teahouse, freshly minted and loaded with sugar.

Everywhere we went we saw groups of men lounging at cafes and sitting in front of the shops or in front of their homes drinking tea, smoking *sheeshas* (water pipes), and playing cards. Women were seen, in most cases covered from head to toe, working or on the move, but rarely just sitting about.

The souks in both cities were for the locals more than the tourists, which gave us an insight to how the locals carry on their daily lives. Twelve kilometres of streets and alleys make up the Aleppo souk.

Shops of fabrics, carpets, antiques, hardware, household trinkets, jewellery, clothing, and foodstuffs filled the streets. We found the clothing was the most surprising, as there were hundreds of dress shops selling the fanciest evening and wedding dresses I have ever seen. Those, along with all the sexy lingerie shops, seemed the opposite of anything we had seen on any woman. The secrets of what women wear under the abayas, or to a party or at home, are revealed in these shops. As well, the younger generation has started wearing non-traditional clothing, and it appears the sleazier the better. We saw many teen girls dressed in tight jeans, low-cut shirts, and spike heels.

We could smell the spice market long before we found it. Thousands of barrels of colourful spices, herbs, gooey filled phyllo pastries, nuts, olives, and candies lined street after street.

We almost managed to leave the Aleppo souk without getting harassed, until a young vendor came up to me and said, "You look like Diana, before the accident." After we stopped laughing, we explained to him that his declaration was not the best way to find customers. (At least he said, "Before the accident.") After we were spotted talking to him, several others tried to get us to their shops, and we were finally persuaded to follow one man to his jewellery shop "just around the corner." Five turns and many streets away, we came to his shop and decided we had made a good choice of who to follow, because one of the other gals and I bought a few pieces of unique handcrafted jewellery.

The tour was also a journey of historical lessons about Arabs, Romans, Greeks, Christians, and Crusaders. We visited mosques, churches, castles, citadels, monasteries, fortresses, amphitheatres, and museums with artifacts dating back five thousand years. At the Omayyad Mosque, said to be the third-largest mosque in the world, we were provided with abayas to go in and observe hundreds of men on one side and women on the other, worshipping. Prayers were being read, and what looked like a choreographed dance took place as the worshippers stood, knelt down, and bowed with perfect timing. The mosque was built on what once was a Christian basilica and there is a shrine that is said to contain the head of John the Baptist.

We stopped to explore several ruins of Crusaders' castles, including Crac des Chevalier (I like saying the name). This massive stone castle, perched on a hilltop, dominated the countryside below. The stories we heard about the battles during the years of the Crusaders were awful and gruesome.

We also visited St. Simeon Monastery, built over one thousand years ago. The story of St. Simeon says he stood on a pillar for forty years and would offer advice to people below. The church and several arches, including part of the pillar, still stand.

Our last stop before returning to Damascus was Palmyra. It was once an Arab metropolis along the Silk Road dating back to the second century, and there are still many pillars, temples, arches, and a fortress stretching out in the middle of the Syrian Desert. We had two days of exploring, riding camels, and enjoying the ancient ruins.

The week was almost over and I did not yet have an interviewee. I had asked Muti, the first day, if he could arrange someone for me if I didn't find a lady before we returned to Damascus, and I was happy when he told me he had lined up an interview for me. He took us on a tour of the city and then I left with him to do the interview. I wasn't afraid to go off with him because everyone on my tour had met him, but I had him leave his phone number and license number with them before we left, for reassurance.

Being in a car, rather than a van, brings you closer to the craziness on the roads, and it was like a carnival ride. I had my eyes closed most of the time, not wanting to see the vehicles barely missing us or us barely missing the pedestrians scrambling across the streets. The truth came out as we drove. Muti didn't have anyone lined up, but did have a few "ideas". We stopped at a pharmacy, but the woman he had in mind wasn't there. Next, we stopped at a little grocery store, walked through the courtyard with its typical group of men sitting around, and went into the store. The owner was obviously a good friend of Muti and he went and got his wife to join us. Between them they didn't really explain my story very clearly, but even though she was tutoring a student in the next room she said she could give me a few minutes to answer my questions. Once she realized, however, that I really wanted more time, she said, "My husband knows all the answers. I have to go," and out she went. This was not what I had in mind, but had to make do with her quick answers and her husband's elaboration's.

~

Mona – 56

Mona is fifty-six and has been married thirty-six years. Her husband is her cousin, but she didn't know him until university. They dated for two years. She is a biology teacher and tutor. Both her parents finished grade twelve. Her mother, who is eighty-five, speaks four languages. They have a son, thirty-three years old, who has two children, a degree in business, and works for the government; and a daughter, twenty-eight years old, who is married with no children, has a degree in fine arts, and works in the private sector. Mona had a hysterectomy at forty-eight and has had no menopausal symptoms since then. She says that none of her friends have had problems or take any medications. They are Christian, their children married Christians, and they all still go to church. As in Jordan, they feel there are no issues between the Christians and the Muslims. Mona has done quite a bit of travelling; she has a sister in Montreal and has spent lots of time in Europe.

~

It was too bad she didn't have more time, as she seemed like a nice woman and I would have liked to talk to her more. She seemed like an ambitious and busy woman, like most of the others I have interviewed.

From there, Muti and I picked up some take-out chicken, done in slices with lots of spices, and went to his apartment. I only agreed to go because he told me his mother, who was visiting from Canada, was there. When we got there, the apartment was dark and no one appeared to be home, and he was chuckling. I stood at the door and said, "I am not coming in, you jerk. Where is your mother?" I didn't really have a Plan B, but I was going to at least stay outside. He started laughing, went out to the deck and brought his mother into the apartment. They both were laughing and joked that he was just teasing me. I told him I didn't find it all that funny, and when he explained this to her, they both laughed more. His mother, dressed traditionally and with her head covered, had been doing her evening prayers. The call to prayers was being called from a mosque nearby.

His mother spoke no English, even though she had been living in Canada for years. We ate dinner on the deck as the lights of the city were coming on. We had sliced chicken, chips, coleslaw, tomatoes, green beans, yogurt, bread, and a yogurt drink, all without benefit of utensils. They showed me how to use the bread to wrap or scoop up the food.

During dinner Muti continued to try to persuade me to stay, or at least spend a week at his beach house. He said, "You are the whole package: good body, good face, good laugh. You are perfect." I just kept laughing at him. His mother was in and out, and she apparently liked my laugh and was all for the second wife arrangements being proposed. He tried to explain that it didn't matter what his wife thought. I asked him, "What if your wife did this?" He said, "She couldn't, because legally she can only marry once and I can marry many times." I finally broke the spell when I told him I don't like to cook. My perfection started to fade and he took me back to the hotel not long after, but as he dropped me off he asked me to seriously consider returning when my trip was over. As I thought about the whole evening, I realized it was quite comical but also sad. The polygamist unions were another cultural aspect of the life in an Arab country I will never understand.

Getting out of Syria was not much easier than getting in. The airport was under construction and I was alone, with no translator to help. Even the woman at the information booth, who spoke some English, did not know where I was supposed to be. After going back and forth between terminals a few times, dragging my luggage in the exhausting heat, I finally worked out where my gate was. The flights from that terminal were going to Saudi Arabia, the United Arab Emirates, and Turkey, and I was the only non-Arab in a room of about a thousand Arabs. I was on the way to Istanbul. Most of the people were dressed in the most expensive abayas, burkas, and robes, but under the robes of the women I caught glimpses of highly fashionable dresses and shoes, and jewellery, and they were all carrying brand-name handbags and sunglasses. I was extremely out of place in my khakis, T-shirt, and runners, and my little bit of luggage was dwarfed amongst their ten pieces of luggage each.

Eventually, I started talking to a modernly dressed girl, who was the daughter of the Syrian ambassador to somewhere. She introduced me to another woman, whose dress was even more modern, who turned out to be fifty-one. She was on her way to Istanbul, spoke perfect English, and was happy to answer my questions—a much better candidate for my survey than Mona. So I did a second interview.

~

Dunya – 51

Dunya is in perfect shape and is dressed like a rich Westerner, wearing expensive red velour pants, a tight white T-shirt showing a surprising amount of cleavage, and sporting dyed blonde hair. She looks nothing like I would have expected a Syrian Muslim woman to look. She was born in Homs, in western Syria, but lives in Damascus now.

Dunya is at the airport with her husband. They are on their way to Istanbul. I didn't even realize they were together at first, because he has been wandering around, talking on his cell and doing his own thing. He was on his way back to sit with her, but when he saw her talking to me, he just turned around and walked away.

She starts off telling me about her first marriage, which happened when she was eighteen, because her parents wanted her to marry "this good man with a good future." She says they made her quit school and marry him, and she was completely naive and knew nothing about sex. "I thought you just took your clothes off and laid together," she said. I could hear the sadness in her voice when she explained that they moved to London right after the wedding, where she was lost and confused because she spoke no English. They stayed for five years while he finished his education and she had two of their four children. "But," she says, "I learned English and grew up very fast."

Dunya stayed in her first marriage for nineteen years. She says, "For the last three years my husband kept a woman in another house. This is common in my country and many women accept it, but three years was enough for me and I finally left him." She laughs and continues, "He has married her now and she is from the village. She doesn't speak well and has no class. I believe it is karma and God is letting me watch his pain."

As for her second marriage, it isn't going much better. She has been married to her second husband for six years, but explains, "He has already had an affair and I kicked him out. We even started proceedings for a divorce, but in the end I let him back in, but there is no real love." She doesn't seem terribly upset about her current situation.

She has two girls and two boys between the ages of nineteen and thirty-one. Dunya has made sure all her children were able to go beyond high school, still resenting the fact that she was made to leave early. The older three are in university or finished, the fourth is writing exams to get into university. If students get high marks on the entrance exam their university education is free. Her father, who passed away seven years ago, had a university degree, and her mom, who is eighty-seven, has a high school education.

Although her English is great, when I ask her about menopause and mention symptoms, like problems sleeping, she thinks I am asking her if she sleeps with her husband. She says they don't have sex anymore. By this time he is sitting about two metres from us, and I am not sure if he doesn't understand English or if she doesn't care if he hears us. I am surprised how open she is being with me.

As far as menopause goes, she says she is just starting. She does get hot flashes and sweats, but says she works out two hours a day to help get the sweats out. Her doctor wanted her to take HRT, but she refused, although she knows many women who do take it.

She says they go to Istanbul once a month for four days on their buying trips. She also goes to Lebanon once a week to visit a friend, but hinted that she sees a plastic surgeon there as well. (This explains her unusually high cheekbones and full lips.) She loves Lebanon and says she likes their spirit. I ask, "What do you mean?" She says, "Well, after each time there is a bombing they just rebuild and carry on." I tell her that I can't relate to having to consider such a thing.

I ask her what women wear under their abayas and burkas, and she says, "All the latest fashions." We were surrounded by Saudis, and she says when they have parties they are separate for men and women. The women are just dressing up for each other; the men don't see them in the fancy dresses.

She only goes to the mosque during Ramadan and her kids don't go at all. She agrees that Christians and Muslims get along fine, and says you often don't even know if people are Christian until you find out they are celebrating Christmas.

Our flight is called and she gives me her number in Istanbul in case I have any problems. We hug good-bye, and as we part ways she says, "I will see you on Oprah."

This was a surprising end to another enjoyable week, and I was pleased to get an interesting interview with a very modern, non-traditional Syrian woman. I am glad I went to Syria, and found it extremely interesting, both in history and culture. I felt safe with a group, but I knew that it is still a very unsettled part of the world and I would definitely not want to travel alone or venture too far from the tourist areas.

Turkey, one of my all-time favourite countries, was next. I hoped to be able to rest up for the five following weeks with Joanne, as I knew that we would be on the go every waking moment.

Tourists don't know where they've been, travellers don't know where they're going.

—Paul Theroux

Chapter 8
Turkey

"I have the week planned out for you. I am so happy to show you my country," said Mazhur. He had just picked me up at the airport in Bodrum, a lovely beach town in the southwest corner of Turkey. Normally these are the words I love to hear, but this time I had hoped to just relax on the beach and regroup after almost four weeks of constantly moving and never spending more than two nights in the same place.

I had arranged a house in Bodrum, through Fatih, a Turkish fellow I knew from home. He said the house was empty, but he had a housekeeper. He also had an English-speaking neighbour who could find me an interviewee. Mazhur was that neighbour.

I imagined a lovely little beach house and a housekeeper. What a great deal! In reality, the house was not in Bodrum and not on the beach, but eighteen kilometres out of town, in a village two kilometres off the main road, with no available transportation to get back to the beach. The house was rustic, which wasn't a problem, but there was no air-conditioning, which meant I had to leave windows open, letting in many mosquitoes. Also, there was very little lighting, so I couldn't read after dark. The mosquito net over the bed was the best feature in the house.

The few times Mazhur left me alone at the house, the housekeeper and an elderly neighbour would come by to visit with me, but we just sat and stared at each other. I have been to Turkey three times before, but have not picked up any Turkish and they spoke no English, making our visits very awkward. I finally came up with the idea to show them my pictures of the countries I'd visited up to that point. They seemed to enjoy that, nodding and smiling as I took them through my journey.

Except for those rare moments at Fatih's house, Mazhur and his wife, Catarina, kept me busy day in and day out. The week of lying around, reading, going to the beach, and catching up on my e-mails was not to be. Mazhur had spent his retirement years studying the history of the area and took much pleasure in showing me all the ruins for miles around, which was great, except that it was forty-eight degrees C. It is amazing I didn't melt. Mazhur was in his seventies, but was apparently in much better shape than I was. He did take pity on me, though, and took me swimming at a beach not far from the village.

We did go into Bodrum, which is a beautiful town on the Aegean Sea, where a medieval castle guards the entrance to the bay. It is a popular tourist town, on what is now called the Turkish Riviera, where you can find many historical sites as well as shops, restaurants, white sand beaches, and fantastic sailing and diving. Along the coast are many other small towns and villages.

Mazhur and Catarina took good care of me. They cooked for me, took me out for dinner, toured me all over their area, taught me many historical facts, and even took pictures of all the sights we saw and made a disk for me. They wouldn't let me spend a penny. All this for a woman they had never met. Their hospitality was amazing. To top it all off, they also found a woman for me to interview.

Nukhet lives on the sailboat that she and her husband use to charter sailing excursions. Unfortunately, I came for an interview only, and not a sailing adventure.

~

Nukhet – 52

Nukhet has the most pleasant smile and we hit if off immediately. She is dressed in casual boat clothes and would fit in with my group of girlfriends easily. I can tell she is busy getting ready for her next excursion and am grateful she has agreed to sit for a while to answer my questions. I think it was the mention of menopause that caught her interest. She gives us a quick tour of the four staterooms, crew cabin, and wide galley, and I really wish I could go for a sail. We have Turkish tea, of course, served by her niece who helps out on this beautiful wooden boat.

She blushes when she tells me she has been with her husband for over twenty years, but only married him a few months ago. They decided on New Year's Eve to get married and had the wedding January 8. I ask her why they waited so long, and she answers with a laugh, "It is not an easy decision." Neither had been married before and they have no children, nor at this point are they planning on having any. As we sit at the dock, the ocean breeze helping to keep us cool from the heat of the day, I understand their decision. They have a very nice lifestyle going on this boat.

She tells me she has lived in a few places in Turkey, but has been settled in Bodrum for the last eleven years. She is now in her "dream job" after working for years as a travel agent. She says their charter business runs seven months a year, but admits they are only really busy for three months. Since the boat is wooden, their off months are spent on upkeep. Unfortunately, she feels that business is dropping off this year, as Europeans (who are their best customers) are staying closer to home. (Remember, this part of Turkey is Asia.)

She sadly tells me that both her parents passed away in their sixties from lung cancer. They had high school diplomas, while Nukhet has a university degree. She says she was raised as a Muslim, but does not practice any of the customs. She said her parents' "heart" was Muslim, but they did not practice much either, although her grandparents were more devout.

She has been having night sweats, hot flashes, and trouble sleeping for a few years, she says, and although she knows many women who take HRT, she has chosen not to take any medications for her menopausal symptoms.

I hardly have to ask, because I can tell by the way she smiles, but when I ask if she is happy her smile only widens. "Yes," she says. Again, another ambitious, happy, fifty-something woman. There is a definite trend emerging.

~

Before I arrived in Bodrum, I had a few days in Istanbul, which is one of my favourite cities. Turkey is the only country in the world on two continents. Istanbul is on the European side of the Bosphorus Strait. On the other side is the Anatolia region of Turkey, which is part of Asia. Only since 1973 has there been a bridge across, connecting Europe and Asia. So in one day I was in the Middle East, flew to Europe, and could see Asia from my hotel room. Not bad for a day's travel.

After four weeks of travel through deserts and dusty ruins, a Turkish bath could not have been more necessary, and Istanbul is a place to experience the best, in an original hammam. After receiving a small towel and choosing the texture of the cleansing loofah mitt that would be used, I was led to a changing room; then, to the steam room, to open all the pores. Once sufficiently steamed, I was led to a room with moon and star-shaped openings in the dome to admit light, and was told to lie on a marble bench. So I stretched out totally nude, in a room full of other nude female bathers and female attendants. (There was no room for modesty.) Using the loofah mitt, the attendant scrubbed every part of my body, from head to toe, removing layer upon layer of dead skin. She spoke little English, but knew enough to say, "You dirty girl." I was a wee bit embarrassed, but didn't know enough Turkish or Arabic to explain my past four weeks. After the scrubbing, she used a soapy cloth that she managed to blow up to a large cloth bubble and then whip me with it, until I was covered in a soapy mess. It was hilarious, as I almost slid off the marble bench many times. She would just casually push me back and continue washing off the soap. This whole process took about forty-five minutes and finished up with a fabulous oil massage. I left feeling cleaner than I had in a very long time.

I stayed in Sultanahmet, which is the "old city", In my past visits to Turkey, I have come to know this city's narrow streets and alleys well. Many of the main attractions of Istanbul are within the walls of the old city. I spent two days visiting a few shopkeepers I knew from past visits, wandered through some of the three thousand shops of the Grand Bazaar, enjoyed the aromas of the Spice Market, and took in the ambience of the city with its many incredible sights. Within minutes of each other are the Blue Mosque, built in 1616; Haiga Sophia, built in 537; and the Topaki Palace, the home of sultans beginning in 1453.

I also visited Isiklal Caddesi, the pedestrian-only street, in the more modern part of the city. They may call it "pedestrian-only", but that is only if you disregard the tram running down the middle, the delivery vehicles, and the motorcycles that freely travel the street. Lining the road are Western and European fashion stores and fast-food chains like Starbucks, McDonald's, and Pizza Hut. (I prefer the old city.) The street was packed with locals and tourists alike, although it's hard to tell the difference, as most Turkish, in the city especially, do not wear traditional clothing even though it is a Muslim country.

My four Muslim countries were finished. I knew I would miss the call to prayer, the aroma of the spices and the sheesha, the tasty cuisine, the invitation to tea, and the pleasant welcomes. I will return to all these countries one day, especially Morocco and Turkey.

Our truest life is when we are in dreams, awake.

—Henry David Thoreau

Chapter 9

Back in London

"I need to rest," I told Gail and Joe, as I shuffled back into their home in London. How lucky I was to have this "home away from home" so I would have a respite between countries, work out more details for the coming months, and wait for Joanne's arrival. It was great to have time to research flights, tours, and cruises for the next two months. I wasn't sure where I was going after Joanne left, so I sent out an e-mail asking if anyone wanted to join me on a cruise in the Baltic. There was never enough time while I was on tours, and in Turkey I had no e-mail access.

I did actually rest for two days, I slept in and read and visited with Gail, Joe, and Harry. But two days is really my limit and then I had to go out and explore. As luck would have it, the Wimbledon Tennis Championship was on and I joined the queue with thousands of others keen spectators. I spent more time in the queue than inside the grounds, but I thought it was worth it. The queue is as much a part of Wimbledon as the event. There are actual signs up with "Etiquette of the Queue" rules—no reserving spots, no leaving something to mark your spot (except for washroom breaks), no jumping the queue, and so on.

If you want tickets to the three main courts, where the higher-seeded players play, you can enter a lottery ahead of time, get up very early to try to get one of the five hundred tickets they sell daily, or wait until after three p.m. to get tickets people turn in when they leave. Alternatively, you can line up in the queue to get a grounds pass to watch any of the matches in the sixteen other courts for only fourteen pounds (about twenty-eight dollars). Although I was in the line for roughly four hours, the time seemed to fly by while visiting with others. Everyone was happy and knew the wait would be long, so there was no complaining.

I got in at five p.m. and wandered around to get my bearings. The grounds were decorated with hundreds of beautiful flower baskets. There were many different food venues, including the famous strawberries and cream—a Wimbledon tradition. There were eighteen courts plus center court, some with bleachers, some standing room only. I watched a few matches between players I had never heard of and then came upon Serena and Venus Williams playing a doubles match against a couple of girls from Poland. I was thrilled to be able to watch the Williams sisters, but felt so sorry for the Polish girls. They didn't stand a chance against the power of the siblings.

It would be hard to calculate how many people it takes to carry out this event. There were so many stewards, door people, security people, and camera people, and on each court there were six ball boys or girls, four linesmen, one service linesman, a referee, and at least one scorekeeper—it is hard to believe there was room for the players. Everything was done with precision, including how they stood and how they picked up the balls and handed them over. It was a well-choreographed dance of sorts, and a great event that I never thought I would attend.

On another day, I went on a cruise down the Thames to Greenwich with one of the gals from my Syria tour who lives in London. Seeing the city from the river gives a great perspective of the varying architecture from old to new.

Gail was kind enough to drive out to Heathrow to pick up Joanne, who arrived realizing it is quicker to get from the east coast of Canada to London than it is to get from Canada's east coast to its west coast.

We only had one day together in London so we hit the ground running, as only Joanne and I can do. We took the tube into the city and walked for hours. We visited Hyde Park, Knightsbridge, Harrods, and then Green Park and Buckingham Palace. We had lunch at the Bag of Nails pub; then went off to Leicester Square, Piccadilly, Oxford Circus, and Covent Garden. We also did a Thames cruise to Westminster. By the time we decided it was time to rest, we learned that the London premier of the movie *Mamma Mia!* was taking place in Leicester Square. The chance to see Meryl Streep and Pierce Brosnan was too much to turn down, so we stood for about ninety minutes and they all came out—Meryl, Pierce, Tom Hanks, Colin Firth, and the rest of the cast. Meryl was in a gorgeous red dress and looked spectacular. Pierce was as good-looking up close as he is on the screen. Colin seemed like a really nice guy, coming over to some elderly women beside us to make sure they had received the tickets he had put aside for them. Apparently, they were his biggest fans.

We still had time to see a play and went to *Joseph and the Amazing Technicolor Dreamcoat*. I had seen it several times before, but Joanne had only heard the music so she was very excited to see it. It was a fun day, and just a hint of the high speed Joanne and I are capable of. By the time we arrived back at Gail's house we were completely exhausted.

A journey is best measured in friends, rather than miles.

—Tim Cahill

Chapter 10
Poland

"We will show you where to get off," three people assured us, sensing our confusion, on the bus from the airport in to Warsaw. That was our first indication of how friendly the Polish people were, and with their help we found the way to our hotel on the local bus. Warsaw is an odd mixture of Communist Block apartments, ultra-modern buildings, and Western chain-stores, as well as an Old Town totally rebuilt after the war.

Over 80 percent of Warsaw was destroyed during WWII. The Old Town (Stare Miastro) was completely reconstructed with amazing accuracy to resemble that of thirteenth-century buildings. The city has many parks, statues, churches, wide sidewalks, and streets. We found it quite easy to get around by tram, and we walked for hours. We found our Lonely Planet had a lot of useful information for a self-guided walking tour.

From Warsaw we travelled north by train to the city of Torun. Joanne had contacted our hosts through a friend of hers in Nova Scotia. Not only did they pick us up, but they fed us, housed us, toured us around, bought us gifts, and treated us like royalty for five days. Maria and Krzysztof, their daughter Julia (who lived in Canada with Joanne's friend as an exchange student fifteen years ago), and her husband Pawel took us to their incredibly beautiful home in the country outside Torun. It truly was a magnificent home, furnished with antiques, some of which they had restored themselves. The garden was lovingly cared for by Maria, a perfect place to relax and enjoy our limited downtime.

Maria prepared a delicious dinner of Polish specialities our first night. Their cousin Anna and her friends, Joanna and Dariusz, joined us. Joanna had agreed to be my interviewee.

Joanna and Dariusz had planned a trip away for the weekend we arrived, so they just took us with them. Simple as that. They picked us up on our second day and we went further north to attend an art exhibit of one of Dariusz's artist friends, Gosia. On our way there we got lost once or twice, and it wasn't even my fault. The drive gave us a chance to get to know each other and to hear some Polish history. Joanna is an English teacher, translator, and teacher-trainer, making her a perfect person to interview. She was very passionate about Poland, its history and politics. She was a wealth of information, some of which reminded me how lucky I am to have been born in a country with no strife. Communism, strikes, martial law, and the fall of Communism have made life a challenge. I can hardly imagine all the emotional and financial turmoil they have lived through.

Poland joined the European Union in 2004 and things appear to be progressing. They are supposed to be getting new roads, but they say it is a slow process. There are very few highways in Poland; most roads are still small country roads that have had little repair over the years. But as we drove through the countryside, Joanna noticed new construction and plenty of restoration and painting of older homes that she hadn't noticed the last time she was there. During Communism most buildings were old and grey.

The art exhibit was in a parthenon, on the property of an aristocrat's home, that had been turned into a museum. Manicured lawns, an apple orchard, and a lovely pond made a beautiful setting for the opening, and the property was the inspiration for many of Gosia's paintings. After a champagne reception we joined a group of Gosia's friends in the guest house. In the evening we had a bonfire, roasted Polish sausages, and had a sing-along. It was a delightful day! We stayed the night in a guest house on the property.

The next day, on the way back to Torun, we stopped to see what I call "Catholic Disneyland". In the village of Lichen, two hundred years ago, a vision of the Virgin Mary was reported. Since then people have come on pilgrimages to the village. From 1994 to 2004 the Sanctuary of Our Lady of Lichen was built, apparently funded by donations from the pilgrims. It is the largest church in Poland, the seventh largest in Europe, and eleventh largest in the world. It seats seven thousand and has room for ten thousand more to stand. The church is surrounded by acres of parkland, and amongst the trees are hundreds of shrines to every saint, soldier, and war you can imagine. Thousands of people were at the site and the parking lot was full, with at least one hundred buses. There were hotels, and tourist souvenir booths to complete the experience.

Joanna told us that Dariusz was an artist, but until we arrived back in Torun we hadn't realized how famous he was in their city. We visited his studio and saw his whimsical-styled ceramic sculptures of people and animals, and then learned that the City of Torun had purchased many of his pieces. It was exciting the next day, while exploring the city, to seek out and find all his pieces, and there were many placed in windows, sitting on ledges, and installed in front of buildings all over Turon's Old Town.

After our two days with Dariusz and Joanna, we again joined Maria, Krzysztof, Julia, and Pawel. Julia and Pawel are in their early thirties and are both doctors. He is a surgeon and she is an internist (recent PhD), now working on becoming a nephrologist as well. The whole family made sure that we were always looked after and that we saw as much as possible in their beautiful town. Torun has about two hundred thousand people, of which forty thousand are students. University is free in Poland if you pass certain exams, and it appears that many people take advantage of this. Most of the people we met were very highly educated. Maria has a teaching degree and is an extremely talented artist and Krzysztof is an ophthalmologist. Somehow, between those extremely busy people, we were taken care of night and day.

Torun, unlike Warsaw, was not damaged too much during WWII, so the Old Town was incredibly preserved. Several Teutonic knights' castles are still found, as well as many Gothic red-brick churches and burgher houses. We explored many of the churches and climbed the tower in the City Hall, where we had a great view of the city, the Vistula River, and what was left of the thirteenth-century city wall around the town's perimeter.

When Anna, who is an actress and singer, took her turn being our tour guide, she took us inside several of their beautiful theatres, some new and some old. She then surprised us with a private concert. She lined up her pianist, and together they performed four wonderful Polish songs for us. We were truly spoiled!

When our train left the station, our new Polish friends were all standing on the platform waving white hankies in the air. They were fabulous hosts, and we were lucky to meet them.

Our train ride to Krakow took seven hours. We both enjoyed it, as we had time to read, catch up on our journals, and see more of this lovely country. Getting closer to Krakow, which is near the southern part of Poland, the countryside is not as flat as we had seen in the centre and further north. Most of the trip to that point had been through farm country.

Krakow is another beautiful city which we explored for a few days. The first day it was raining on and off so we weren't as enamoured as with Warsaw and Torun. But then the sun came out and we realized what a lively, vibrant city it is. We spent our time in Old Town and did not see any of the modern district. I found a new favourite church, St. Mary's Basilica, which was built in the fourteenth century. The inside of this Gothic church was a feast for the eyes. Massive colourful mosaics, beautiful stained glass, magnificent sculptures, and incredible woodwork covered every inch of the altar, the walls, and the windows. It was spectacular.

The Polish people are very proud of the late Pope John Paul, and everywhere we spotted pictures, sculptures, and references to him: where he lived, where he attended school, and where he visited.

We loved Poland. There was so much to see and we didn't cover half of it. There are rivers and oceans and mountains we didn't get a chance to explore. Next time! We found the contrast of old and new fascinating.

~

Joanna – 54

I have learned a lot about Joanna before we sit down to finish off the questions. I know she is fifty-four and that she was married at twenty-three to her first husband. That marriage lasted eleven years. She doesn't elaborate about him. She says she has known Dariusz for many years, but they only started dating four years ago and married after a year of dating. He was living in another town and moved to Torun after the wedding.

She has a degree in English literature. She not only teaches English, but also does teacher-training and translating. Her first experience as a translator was in the 1980s, when she worked in Iraq for eighteen months. Her twenty-eight-year-old daughter has followed in her footsteps and is an English major working on her thesis. Her daughter is married and has a five-year-old son.

Joanna now tells me that she gets her interest in language from her parents. Her mother had a degree in Polish literature and her father had one in Polish linguistics. Her mother was originally from Lithuania, which had been annexed to the U.S.S.R. After the war, she moved to Torun, where she met Joanna's father.

When Joanna was a young child they lived in the country, in an old house with no hot water, but she says she loved it there. When the Communist Party offered apartments, with all the amenities, in the city, her mother jumped at the opportunity and they moved to a flat in the city. "I wish we had kept that house," Joanna laments.

When Communism fell, people who lived in the flats were given the chance to purchase them at a very low price, so Joanna and her husband were able to buy his family flat. She says this set them up financially and feels it allowed her to have a better quality of life than her parents'.

While we are talking about Communism, she explains, "I enjoyed my childhood. I didn't lack for anything, or maybe I didn't know I lacked for anything. Even though my parents had to line up for hours to buy things, and sometimes got to the end only to find the item sold out, we as children didn't suffer."

When we start talking about the time during martial law her demeanour changes and she becomes sad. From December 1981 to July 1983 martial law was in effect. During that time curfews were enforced, borders were sealed, airports were closed, roads were restricted, telephones were disconnected, mail was censored, and classes in schools and universities were suspended. Joanna says, "That was a horrible time for me. My daughter was very young at the time, and although I helped type pamphlets, my role as a mother prevented me from getting too involved." I could tell she really wanted to have a bigger role in the movement, but it was a good thing she didn't, as she had friends arrested during that time. "I really haven't completely dealt with all the issues from that time. It is something I am still working on," she says sadly.

Joanna says she was brought up Catholic, and although Dariusz attends church, she and her daughter do not.

She has lived in Torun all her life, but since the fall of Communism has travelled throughout Europe, Russia, India, Australia, and the States, and plans to continue to travel as much as possible. She is very knowledgeable about the world. At first she says she doesn't think she could move to another country, but then thinks she would consider Barcelona.

She tells me she wears a hormone patch, which has stopped the hot flashes she had for fifteen months. She doesn't seem to have any other menopausal symptoms.

She describes herself as a stork. "I am like a bird that loves adventure and loves to take challenges, but always comes back." Then she adds, "And a cat, because I love my home." Is she happy? "I am happy. I have always been happy," she answers confidently.

∼

I really enjoyed meeting Joanna and Dariusz, and found her to be another lovely, ambitious woman. They just keep coming!

Chapter 11
Slovakia

"The tenth country and the tenth currency. I'm really starting to get confused," I complained to Joanne. We were in Bratislava, the capital of Slovakia, and although the country had joined the European Union, it was still using the Slovakian koruna as its official currency.

My whining was probably due to fatigue. We decided to take the overnight train from Krakow to Bratislava to save a night's hotel and keep the day open for sightseeing, but it really was not one of our better decisions. One toilet on the train was broken, the other one didn't have toilet paper most of the time, and they both stank. The ride was very noisy, the train stopped frequently, the compartment walls were paper thin, the beds were hard, and the pillows were dirty and tiny. Sleep was but a dream.

We arrived in Bratislava at six a.m. and discovered that nothing opens until eight a.m. We spent our wait time learning a little history of the city. Bratislava was once the capital of Hungary. It then became part of Czechoslovakia in 1918, and when that country split up, it became the capital of Slovakia. I wonder if there are many other cities that have been part of three different countries.

When the tourist bureau opened we booked a hotel and hoped to get a little rest. However, when we arrived at the hotel, it was too early to get in the room. Fortunately, they let us leave our luggage and we headed out to explore the city.

High on a rocky hill above the town loomed a massive castle and, as is my nature, I asked no questions and we just marched right up there, only to find the building closed for renovations. All was not lost, however, as we found the view from the top was a great reward for our long trek up the hill. We could see the historical buildings of the Old Town and the meandering Danube River in one direction, and in the other, the area where most of the people live. It did not look nearly as inviting with its multitude of concrete Communist apartments.

Despite the temperature soaring to thirty-eight degrees Celsius, we enjoyed our day. The Old Town, where most of the tourist action is, was lovely and immaculately clean. It is much like other old European towns, with the main square, churches, sidewalk cafes, palaces, museums, and great architecture. The city is also dotted with quirky statues. We almost tripped over the one of a man coming out of a manhole and got some great pictures of us sitting on a park bench with Napoleon.

From our table at a sidewalk cafe in the square we took in all the activities and watched the world go by. We had a mini fashion show parading past our table, from women in European high-fashion couture to young girls dressed in almost nothing. Their short skirts were the shortest I have ever seen. This, of course, might explain why the marriage proposals, coming fast and furious in the first countries I visited, had dried up. In the Arab countries many of the local women were completely covered; in the last few countries they were barely covered.

Unfortunately, we did not find a woman to interview, despite Joanne's enthusiasm to help. Our stop in Slovakia was brief and planned mainly so we could catch a day cruise down the Danube, which had come as a highly recommended way to get to Budapest in Hungary.

Chapter 12

Hungary

"I have a sore mouth," Joanne blurted out, on our second day in Budapest. I thought she meant she had a toothache and started asking her what her symptoms were. She laughed and said, "No, my mouth hurts from smiling so much." She was absolutely enchanted with Budapest. The only trouble we had was working out yet another exchange rate. We were carrying thousands of Hungarian forints, because one dollar was about 175 forints.

We both agreed that the only way to see Budapest for the first time was from the Danube. The cruise from Bratislava took three and a half hours, sailing past small towns, summer homes, and a castle, and navigating through a lock. As we got closer to Budapest, the Parliament Building, with its 365 turrets, came into view on one side, and the Royal Palace loomed large on the other side. Together they made a stunning first impression.

Fortunately, Budapest was not damaged too badly during WWII, so many beautiful, historical buildings still stand. We were constantly saying, "Look at that. Look over there. Look back. Look up." On a bus tour around the city we heard the terms Baroque, Classicist, Romanesque, Gothic, and Art Nouveau many times. I couldn't distinguish them all myself, but I sure liked what I saw.

Budapest is divided by the Danube, with one side being Buda, and the other, Pest. On the Buda side, on Castle Hill, sits the Royal Palace. It was originally built in the thirteenth century, but has been destroyed three times over the centuries. The current palace was built after WWII. From the hill we took in the magnificent view of the city and the Danube.

The Pest side has the city centre, amazing parks, museums, shopping streets, and public baths. We had sore necks from turning our heads so often, sore feet from walking so long, and sore mouths from smiling. We could have spent days, if not weeks, in Budapest and still not seen it all. It is definitely another place to return to one day.

In the middle of our sightseeing Joanne pushed me in the door of a small hair salon and made me arrange for a haircut. She was tired of listening to me whine about my hair, which was long overdue for a cut. I tried in my very best sign language to explain I only wanted a trim around the front. After watching the hairdresser back-combing her current customer's hair for over twenty minutes, I should have realized she was a little obsessive-compulsive. But I sat in her chair anyway, and as she started clipping inches off the back, I realized she didn't understand me at all. When she finally got around to the front, and had cut the bangs away from my eyes, I tried to tell her that it was enough. She wouldn't stop! She kept clipping and clipping. I tried as pleasantly as possible to make her stop, but eventually I had to just stand up and walk away from the chair. She was a little shocked, but I was able to escape with a decent hair cut—shorter than I had wanted, but not as short as she was headed. It took so long that Joanne, who had ordered our dinner in a nearby restaurant, had finished her meal and mine was cold. But Joanne didn't have to listen to me whine about my hair being in my eyes anymore.

On our last day in Budapest we decided to find the train station to book our train to Szolnok, where we were going to be visiting relatives of a friend from home. The distance looked a lot shorter on the map than it actually was, so we were weary by the time we arrived at the chaotic station. It wasn't in the nicest part of the city and really reinforced our thought that it is best seeing Budapest first from the Danube.

Just getting information at the train station was a trick in itself, as there were local info desks, international info desks, and tourist info desks, as well as schedule counters and ticket counters. It took about half an hour to find the correct line for the tickets we needed, and after about fifteen minutes in that line we arrived at the front, only to have the woman behind the ticket counter look past us and, in Hungarian, ask if there was anyone in line who could speak English. Someone piped up, and she told the person to tell us that train was on strike. Not all trains were on strike, but those for the direction we were headed were. We were absolutely deflated and had no idea what we were going to do next.

We walked up the stairs, out the main doors, around the corner and sat down, bewildered. As we were trying to develop a Plan B, a young couple came up and said, "We heard what happened and we can help you find the bus station." They appeared to come out of nowhere. They must have made a great effort to follow us through the crowd from the ticket counter, and we couldn't have been happier. They helped us get the right subway to take us to the bus station. When we arrived the station was closed, but we found out what time the bus left the next day, from a schedule posted on the wall. Although it was a hassle at the end of a long day, we realized how lucky we were that the couple had come along to help, and we saw a little more of the city and learned how easy the subway system was to navigate. I am sure Mom was up there watching over us.

Back at the bus station, after a good night's sleep, we were somewhat confused with more signs, counters, and line-ups. Again, a woman volunteered to help us and made sure we were in the right place at the right time. However, because of the train strike the buses were overextended and it didn't look likely that we were going to get on the bus. Joanne was determined to get us on it, so after she watched a little old lady pushing and elbowing her way in the crowd, she just did the same amount of jostling and managed to get us two seats. I stood back in amazement. I would have never guessed she could get so pushy.

The bus ride took us southeast to Szolnok through a countryside planted with corn, wheat, and bright yellow sunflowers. Our next hostess, Aniko, was waiting for us when we arrived. Aniko is the cousin of Eszter, who is a friend of my cousin Ann—another collaboration of friends who helped me find connections.

We spent several days with Aniko, her mother Marta, and her niece Lilla. (Marta's husband was away fishing.) Marta spent our whole visit in the kitchen making us every Hungarian treat we could have ever imagined: goulash, pancakes filled with homemade cottage cheese, Hungarian camembert, cauliflower soup, sausages (many kinds), homemade applesauce, and many pickled things, just to name a few. To add to the traditional food, we had to have a taste of all the traditional drink. We loved the palinka (like schnapps), and tokaji, which is a very popular Hungarian wine, but didn't like the unicum, which was more like cough syrup.

During our visit we discussed the time during Communism and the struggles now to balance the new life. One thing we heard in both Poland and Hungary was that during Communism no one worried about the future, since everyone had a secure job. The fall of Communism brought much worry over job security. I sensed that, while no one wants to go back to Communism, a fine balance has not been reached, and that scares them a little. Joining the European Union has increased prices, but not wages. Aniko, who was only home in Hungary for a visit, works in Qatar as a teacher, because in Hungary she would be lucky to make about eight hundred dollars a month.

Aniko was a great tour guide, showing us as much of her area as we had time for. We again travelled past miles of sunflowers, wheat, corn, tomatoes, and peppers. The area is a big paprika producer. (I didn't know that paprika was made from red peppers.) The roads are mainly two-lane country roads, very similar to Poland. Many of the utility poles have been rigged with platforms on the top for storks to build their nests on and we passed many full nests with the babies' heads peering out. One day we took a pulley bridge across a river. Four cars drove onto the floating deck and then two beefy men turned a wheel, pulling the platform slowly across the river. Who needs machines? Those men did a great job, and we couldn't keep our eyes off their arms!

We went as far south as Szeged, which is near the Serbian/Romanian border. Szeged, the fourth-largest city in Hungary, with its beautiful architecture and an outdoor theatre, is also the home to yet another of my favourite churches, the Dom Cathedral. All the inner walls, coves, and ceilings are painted with the most intricate frescoes, each a colourful masterpiece.

We had a great time seeing the countryside and, while driving, we also helped Aniko adjust to some of the new road laws Hungary was about to enforce. Very soon it would be against the law not to stop at pedestrian crossings if a pedestrian is waiting to cross. So every time we approached a crossing, we would have to remind her. She got better as the week went on. The drinking and driving law was also being changed to zero tolerance, but she had no problem following that law.

During our visit, Aniko introduced me to Hajnalka, whom she had picked for my interview.

~

Hajnalka – 48

We meet up with Hajnalka at her boyfriend's restaurant. Although she is forty-eight, she looks much younger, dresses fashionably, and sports a stylish haircut. I feel a little frumpy in my travel-worn clothes, but my hair looks good after the recent cut. Joanne and I are not really dressed appropriately for this fancy place, but we didn't pack clothing for fine dining. At least it is only lunch; I don't think we would have been allowed in at dinnertime.

After we are seated, Aniko says she will translate because Hajnalka is worried that her English is not good enough. I assure her that her English will be a lot better than my Hungarian, but we let Aniko translate. Instead of asking the questions in order, I decide to ask her to describe herself first. She says, "I am an average woman, cheerful and open-minded. I live with my boyfriend of ten years. I have never been married and have no children of my own, but my boyfriend has a daughter and she works here at the restaurant."

As we enjoy a delicious lunch of minestrone soup, pork with mushrooms and rice, and a lovely rosé wine, we continue to discuss lifestyles, and she explains that her life would be completely different if she lived in a village. Even though she says she is average, she also says she isn't a "typical" Hungarian woman. She describes "typical" as a housewife who stays home and cooks and takes care of the household, usually living in a village, not the city. "I love theatre, concerts, and travelling," she is happy to say.

Hajnalka has a degree in education and special needs and is a kindergarten teacher. She says, "I chose to only have one job, so I don't make much money." Lucky for her, by the look of the crowd at the restaurant, her boyfriend's business seems to be doing well.

Her parents are still alive at seventy-six and seventy-five, and have been married fifty-two years. They both finished school in grade eight. She thinks her life has been better than her parents', but that would go without saying considering the era they have lived through.

We talk about Communism and she says, "During Communism everyone felt secure, and as a child life was good for me, but I feel the freedoms we have now outweigh the insecurity of jobs and money. I have been able to enjoy travelling around Europe since we were given our passports back."

We talk about menopause briefly. She is in the early stages and has been experiencing some emotional swings. I sense she does not want to go into that too deeply. She is not taking any HRT. Then she surprises me and asks, "Why don't you ask about my sex life?"

I explain, "I don't even ask my closest friends about their sex lives, so I can't go around the world asking strangers." She did tell me from the start that she was open-minded!

She has no hesitation when I ask if she would move to another country if she could. She says, "I would love to live in Spain, on a beach."

The final question, is she happy? "Yes!" she answers in English.

Chapter 13

Austria

"We have to go back to looking after ourselves again," I whined to Joanne as we left Hungary, sad and full. We really enjoyed our stay with Marta, Aniko, and Lilla, and were now on our own again for the next two countries. I was just getting used to being in a house and eating scrumptious home-cooked meals. We took the train from Szolnok, changed trains in Budapest, and arrived in Austria in the late afternoon.

As we enjoyed the countryside flying past us from our seat on the train, we noticed almost the moment we crossed the border into Austria that we were in a more modern and organized country than the three previous countries we had visited, that had all once been Communist ruled. I don't know how Austria managed to avoid being taken over by the Communists, when it was surrounded on three sides by Communist countries. There is so much history to learn, but I realized I wouldn't learn it all on this trip. Fifty countries' worth of history lessons was too much for me. Instead, I resolved to simply learn a little about each place.

We arrived in Wein (Vienna) to pouring rain, so it was fortunate for us that we had booked a hotel across from the train station. We ate in a pub close by and had an early night to rest up for a full day of sightseeing the next day.

We got up early and were soon out on the road, to see as much as we could in our one day in Austria. We visited the summer home of Queen Maria Theresa, the Schonbrunn Palace, built in the 1700s. Maria Theresa was the first female ruler of the Hapsburg Empire. She was Archduchess of Austria, Queen of Bohemia, and Queen of Hungary. By marriage, she was Grand Duchess of Tuscany and Holy Roman Empress. Now there's a title and a half! Maria Theresa was the mother of Marie Antoinette, as well as fifteen other children, eleven of whom lived to adulthood. Napoleon also lived in the palace for two years. The Hapsburg name comes up in the history of many of the countries in Europe, and they lived a grand lifestyle by the looks of this one "summer home". The grounds surrounding the palace were spectacular and the palace itself was magnificent. We spent a few hours roaming from room to room viewing masterpieces, from the artwork to the beautifully crafted furniture.

The pieces of information I seem to retain are the silly things, and from the Summer Palace I learned a handy entertaining idea. During festivities in the grand ballroom one thousand candles would be lit. The festivities would be declared over when the candles burned out. So, if they liked who was coming they used tall candles; if not, the short ones were lit. The other story—although I am not sure it is true, it seemed believable—was from a beautifully stitched tapestry wall hanging depicting a market scene with a man and a monkey. The monkey is taking fleas from people's hair and the man is collecting money. Our guide told us that is where the term "flea market" comes from.

The Ringstrausse surrounds the city, and a bus tour around the ring gave us an overview of the city's history and the significant sights. In the afternoon we wandered the city checking out all the beautiful, historic architecture, the hundreds of street performers, and the high-fashion stores, but we just weren't into the city. We were both tired. I guess we couldn't have perfect days every day. Or maybe we just didn't know how to look after ourselves anymore, having been so spoiled in the last few countries. It was too bad we couldn't find more energy, as there was a film festival going on and lots of activity in the city. Instead, we went back to the hotel, collapsed on our beds, and read.

Joanne was not going to let another country go by without an interviewee, so she asked every clerk at our hotel if there was a woman around fifty working somewhere in the hotel. She was told the night manager was in that age category, and in the morning she found her and convinced her to be my Austrian interviewee.

~

Elisabeth – 55

Elisabeth seems somewhat sceptical about this, but has agreed to see what questions I am going to ask. Her English is perfect and I don't think there will be any misunderstandings. We have to go into the smoking room, a lounge off the main lobby and front desk, so she can combine our interview with her break. She lights a cigarette, grabs a coffee, and I explain in further detail what I am doing. She is more intrigued now that she realizes she will be one of fifty women I will be talking to. She is dressed in a black skirt and a white blouse, probably requirements of the job, but has the collar of the shirt turned up to make it more stylish and wears a lovely pearl necklace to complement the outfit. Despite the fact that she is at the end of a night shift, she seems remarkably awake. She is the first woman, since Debbie in California, who is as tall as I am and probably about the same weight. Finally, I don't feel like a giant, as I have with several of the women I have interviewed.

She tells me that she has worked her way through most of the jobs in the hotel to finally become the night manager, a job she loves and is very proud of. "I started at this hotel when I was eighteen, attended university at night, had three children, and have continued to work here for thirty-seven years," she explains. I do the quick math in my head and work out she is fifty-five. No one had known for sure how old she was when telling Joanne about her, and I hadn't actually asked. I would have guessed between forty-nine and fifty-three.

She says she met her husband when she was in her late twenties, they lived together for two years before they were married, and have been married twenty-four years. Their three children are all currently attending university.

Her father passed away at eighty, but her mother, who is seventy-seven years old, still lives in Vienna. She was raised as a Catholic and attends church. "But not every Sunday," she admits.

"I have lived in Vienna all my life and wouldn't want to move anywhere else. I have travelled a little bit around Europe, but don't see the need to go far, as I love it here so much," she says. She lights another cigarette and quickly checks on the girls at the front desk. Her shift is almost over, but she is definitely still in control. She loves to read in her spare time, she says, "Especially books about history."

I ask if her life is where she expected it to be at this age, and she says, "I take life as it comes and have no expectations." She is very exact with her answers, and although she is smiling, she doesn't seem comfortable. I am not sure if she is worried about her co-workers hearing her, or it is just her personality. I think maybe a little of both and decide to avoid the menopause question altogether, because the girls at the desk can hear us and a few other guests have come in to have their morning cigarette. She has to go back to work, and I am happy to leave this room now full of smoke.

When I ask the final question, I expect the answer to be positive, since she presents herself with such control, so I am not at all surprised when she answers, "Yes, I am very happy."

Chapter 14
Czech Republic

"And then they burnt his eyes out," explained our tour guide. That was from the story of the clockmaker in the 1400s who built the astronomical clock, which is one of the features in Prague's Old Town historical centre square. The gigantic clock, which shows the position of the sun and the moon and has medallions representing the months, was so unique that the king did not want it recreated anywhere else. Consequently, he had the clockmaker's eyes burnt out. Years later, when the king felt it was safe, he let the clockmaker go back inside the clock to work on it. Two stories emerged from there: either the blind man intentionally disabled the clock, or he touched something wrong, which killed him and disabled the clock. Either way, the clock stopped working, and it took seventy years to find someone who could make it work properly.

Years later, the "Walk of the Apostles" was added to the top, and now, on the hour, the clock opens and little statues of the apostles go around in circles. When we visited, the square was jammed with people in anticipation of the event. The clock is beautiful, but I found the apostle walk to be a little anticlimactic. Joanne and I decided to watch from one of the cafes close by and have a beer, which was not one of our smarter decisions—the beer was eleven dollars a glass. Other than London, Prague was the most expensive place I had been to so far on this trip.

Despite the prices, I love Prague. This was my second visit to this delightful city. There is a reason this is one of Europe's top tourist destinations. I couldn't wait to show Joanne around. We arrived in the city at four p.m., checked into our hotel in the middle of the Old Town, and were on a bike tour by four thirty. We may have been tired the day before, but Prague was rejuvenating. We were the only ones on the bike tour, so had the complete attention of our guide, a really nice young man who had studied history. When we weren't consumed with dodging the crowds of people, we really enjoyed our ride and history lessons.

Prague is another city that did not suffer too much damage during World War II, leaving many historically amazing buildings standing. Again, we heard about Art Nouveau, Baroque, Renaissance, Cubist, Gothic, Neoclassical, and Ultra Modern. In 1992, the historic centre of Prague was added to the UNESCO list of World Heritage Sites, and it really is no wonder.

Our bike tour covered more territory in two and a half hours than I saw the last time I was there for three days. It was a great way to get an overview of the city. Like me, our guide liked quirky facts, and besides the clock story he had this one. During WWII the Germans made one of the music houses into Gestapo headquarters. Along the roofline of the magnificent building stand statues of all the popular composers and musicians. The story goes that the Germans did not want Joseph Mendelssohn represented, as he was Jewish. They didn't know which one he was, but decided it was the one with the biggest nose and took it down. Hitler showed up the next day to find they had destroyed the statue of his favourite composer, Richard Wagner.

Amongst all the historical architecture and museums, modern and contemporary art is also represented in museums and throughout the city. On the bank of the Vltava River, which divides the city, we came upon twelve yellow plastic penguins, standing over a metre tall. Behind them was a cement chair at least ten metres high. I don't understand modern art! Down the road was the John Lennon Memorial Wall, which was started in 1982. In a tribute to Lennon and the peace movement, students started painting graffiti based on lyrics by Lennon and the Beatles. The Communist police used to whitewash it, but the next day it would be covered again. The tradition has continued to this day. On the day of our visit, the memorial comprised a small bust of Lennon, a large peace sign, the word *IMAGINE*, and plenty of graffiti.

Because we spent more time in Poland and Hungary than we originally anticipated, our time in Austria and the Czech Republic was very limited. This crunch for time meant that we didn't experience some of the real highlights of Prague or Vienna; namely, the food and the music. But I understand both are amazing. There are frequent musical performances in many churches, opera houses, and theatres of these cities. The great music of Mozart, Beethoven, Bach, and other famous composers can be heard day and night. The Vienna Boys Choir would have been great to hear, but we just couldn't fit it all in. Last time I was in Prague, my brother and I were able to catch a few choirs practicing in local churches, which is another great way to spend a few hours and not spend money.

We would have loved to spend more time in Prague, but had already booked a flight to Ireland. We flew with easyJet, one of Europe's budget airlines, to Belfast. Although their prices are incredibly inexpensive, (one hundred dollars from Prague to Belfast), the restrictions can make travelling with them stressful. EasyJet Airlines has a twenty-kilogram limit on luggage, and the cost of overweight baggage can sometimes run higher than the cost of the flight. So we spent the night before the flight rearranging all our clothes, souvenirs, books, and shoes, trying to find the right combination between our checked luggage and carry-on bags. We were still not sure if we were within the limits since we both, especially Joanne, had bought so much. Luckily, we came in at forty-one kilograms between our two bags, which satisfied the airline clerk, but we could barely lift our carry-ons into the overhead bins.

As our plane lifted off, I reflected on how lucky I was to get my interview in Vienna, but not so lucky in Prague. Joanne had almost lined up another night desk clerk at our hotel in Prague. She was the right age and seemed slightly interested, but after she gave it some thought, decided she wasn't ready to share her life with me. She used the excuse that she was too busy at the time, and Joanne suggested I get up in the middle of the night to talk to her, but I sensed she didn't want to do it once she realized I was going to write a book. It was too bad, because when she started talking about being a single mom and working so hard, I could sense she had a story to tell.

Chapter 15
Northern Ireland

"I like a bit of crack," said Pat, my Northern Ireland interviewee. It was day three of our visit to Northern Ireland, so I knew she meant "fun" when she said *craic*. Joanne and I were looking forward to re-entering the world of English-speaking people, only to find we could barely understand a word they said. It took us days to catch the accent and the different expressions. We were constantly saying, "Pardon? Could you repeat that, please?" Or thinking we knew what they were saying and then responding incorrectly. This made for plenty of laughs, at our expense.

Upon our arrival in Belfast, we were greeted by Joanne's cousin Alistair and his two children, Alex (ten) and Tom (four). I use "cousin" loosely, as he is Joanne's grandmother's sister's great-grandchild. Alistair and his wife Gillian live in Templepatrick, about twenty-five kilometres outside Belfast, in County Antrim. They live on the family farm, which in the past had been a dairy farm, but now they grow wheat and barley, and Alistair also bales and wraps hay for other farmers' fields. There was a lot of heavy equipment in and out of the farm when we were there and we learned about most of it from Tom, the four-year-old. He was well beyond his years and was great at explaining how everything worked. One day Alistair phoned to ask Gillian to get a certain tool out of the shed. When she hung up and looked puzzled, Tom piped up, knowing exactly what it was and where to find it.

Our first night on the farm, Gillian had a delicious roast beef dinner waiting for us. Soon we were part of the family, playing Monopoly and a fun card game with a name I will not repeat. In this game I was the s---head, three times running. Some card shark I turned out to be!

Templepatrick and the surrounding area is vast farmland, divided by stone dykes and hedges, rolling hills and green, green glens. Ireland is called the Emerald Island for a reason. The fields are dotted with cows, horses, and sheep by the hundreds. When we visited, the heather was starting to bloom, which added a glorious splash of purple to the already beautiful landscape.

One day we travelled into Belfast on the local bus with Alex and her friend, and Joanne realized how much things have changed in Northern Ireland. The last time she came to Belfast (in the early '80s), the bus was searched, bags were checked, people were frisked, and then they would have to go through security again in each place they entered. That was during "the troubles", when the Unionists (mainly Protestant) who were pro-Britain were in conflict with the Nationalists (mainly Catholic) who weren't big fans of Britain.

The Good Friday Agreement was signed in 1998 when the paramilitary groups involved in the conflict agreed to stop fighting. There are still incidents, but they are not as severe or as frequent as they used to be. On our city tour of Belfast some of the areas of conflict were pointed out. The Peace Wall that was built to divide the city still stands in some areas. Memorials and murals dot the city. The tour guide was very careful to say, "Both sides carried out atrocities against the other side."

Belfast itself is a bustling city, with a great blend of old and new. On the "new" end of the spectrum, we stumbled upon a mall that had only opened in the last week. Alex and her friend were happy to get a chance to see that.

We drove past the huge port of Belfast. Ferries, cruise ships, freighters, and cargo ships all share this very busy port, and hundreds of cranes crowd the docks. Our guide was proud to tell us that this was where the mighty *Titanic* was built and where the Wright Brothers built their first plane.

The parliament buildings, called Stormont, came with a few more quirky stories. They call it "buildings" because originally they planned to build three buildings. They only built one of the buildings, yet still use the plural. The second story was about the building itself. Sitting at the top of a massive well-manicured lawn is a large white Greek-styled building. Our guide told us that during WWII, Stormont was covered in dung and a mixture of other materials to camouflage it from enemy planes, and that after the war it took seven years to clean it up.

We heard the term "the troubles" many times during our visit. From what I was told, most of "the troubles" centred around Belfast and the border towns. The people I spoke to in Templepatrick said their lives were not affected and they only knew one person killed, in a drive-by shooting at a local pub. They also said they rarely went into Belfast. So to me, this meant they certainly were affected. They couldn't travel far from home without worry or police checks. They simply adjusted to how life was, and they lived with it. I did not speak to anyone who had family in the military or who lived in the troubled areas "during the troubles", and I am sure their stories would have been far different. This was another reminder of how lucky I felt to have been born in Canada.

Besides enjoying the country life, and taking our trip into Belfast, we also spent some time on the northern coast. The drive through towns called Ballymullock and Ballygalley was scenic and intriguing. We stopped at a cemetery and found headstones with Joanne's family name, and tried to find Joanne's mother's first house. We were unsuccessful in our search, but had fun driving up the narrow country roads and venturing into a few private driveways. (Joanne's mother was born in the area, but moved to Canada with her family when she was a child.) At the coast, we made our way to the Giant's Causeway, which is another UNESCO World Heritage Site. Those UNESCO people sure know how to pick them. The geological story is that the forty thousand interlocking basalt columns are a result of ancient volcanic eruption. Most of the columns are hexagonal, although there are also some with four, five, seven, and eight sides. The tallest are about twelve metres. The thousands of columns form uneven hills, which make a very unique site and were great fun to hike and climb around.

While I respect the geological explanation of its creation, it does not explain why it is called a *causeway*. The columns do not cross over the water, but hug the coastline. For the answer to that I prefer the folkloric tale that comes with the name. From this coastline you can see Scotland, and the legend is that the causeway stretched all the way across. There was a Scottish giant and an Irish giant. The Irish giant, Finn MacCool, challenged the Scottish giant to come over, but as he approached, Finn got scared and jumped into his mother's arms. When the Scottish giant saw the size of the "baby" he feared that Finn might be even bigger. So, the Scottish giant ran back to Scotland, breaking the causeway as he ran, making it impossible to cross again. Gillian had to repeat the story many times, because Tom just loved hearing it over and over again.

It was another fantastic week. Gillian took such good care of us that I started calling her Mom, even though she is at least ten years younger than me. She was constantly cooking and cleaning and making sure we had everything we needed. One of her specialities in the kitchen was an Ulster fry: fried potato bread, bacon, eggs, beans, sausage, and tomato, all mixed together. It was tasty, but even better were her gypsy creams, scrumptious biscuits with gooey chocolate cream sandwiched inside. We left hoping that Alistair's sister Ann, who we were going to visit next, would be just as welcoming.

The weather was perfect and sunny. In fact, during our whole Northern Ireland visit we were fortunate to have great weather and none of the misty Irish moments we expected.

Gillian arranged for me to interview her good friend Pat.

~

Pat – 53

Gillian has invited Pat over early for the interview. Her husband will join us later to party the night away. I ask her to describe herself and she says, "I like a bit of craic." We can't stop laughing—good start! I know I am going to like this lady. Sitting in Gillian's kitchen, drinking wine and snacking on gypsy creams, we four ladies keep jumping from story to story. The interview is secondary to the fun and I am fine with that. Gillian and Pat say they have been friends and neighbours for many years.

Pat has just returned from being a model in a charity fashion show. Admittedly, she is not the model type, but she says, "I had a grand time and feel quite important, modelling one minute and being interviewed the next."

She tells us she is fifty-three and her birthday is next week. "So is mine!" I shout, and we realize our birthdays are days apart and we are both Leos. No wonder I like her so much. It already feels like I have known her for years. We celebrate with more wine.

She has been married twenty-seven years and has two sons, one daughter, and one granddaughter. She knew her husband for five years and lived at home with her parents until the day of her wedding. I tell her I can think of only one friend who did not live with her husband before she was married.

She says she is Presbyterian, but does not attend church.

She says her parents, who both passed away in their eighties, were married for sixty-two years. They were both born on farms and had to quit school at fourteen to help out on the farm. Pat tells us that she and her husband have moved out of farming, as it is a very tough business these days. Pat has two years of technical college education. Her children finished high school and her sons work with her husband in a plastering business. Her daughter is a care assistant.

I ask her if she is where she thought she would be at this age, and she answers "Basically, yes, but I didn't think I would be a granny yet." When she is not looking after her grandchild she works at the Hilton Hotel, in the golf shop. Joanne's and my eyes light up when she tells us this. She catches our delight and invites us for a round of golf tomorrow night. Now there's a bonus I wasn't expecting. My dream of spending time with my interviewees just keeps getting better and better.

Pat admits she has not travelled far up to this point of her life, but she is ready now. She has always lived in Templepatrick and doesn't think she would want to live anywhere else, but if she had to move, she thinks Australia would be nice. "Our constant rain does get tiring," she says.

I ask about "the troubles", telling Pat and Gillian that our impression was that everywhere in Northern Ireland had been unsafe and people lived in fear for their lives. But she says, "We were not affected in the least. We just didn't go into Belfast. We didn't get involved in the politics, we had no bombing in our area, and we were not bothered."

Pat is one of the lucky ones; she says she is already over menopause, and even when she was going through it she only had "a glow" from time to time. The most polite description of hot flashes I have heard. She insists she didn't have any problems with memory. In fact, she says, "I have a good memory." Meanwhile, I am trying to think where I put my glasses and Joanne is searching for her camera.

Even though I asked her earlier to describe herself, I ask again, and she surprises us when she says, "I am a kind, generous person, but I am not easy to get on with. I have my own views and am not afraid to share them." We certainly don't see that and have not had a hard time getting on with her—we think she is great. I didn't need to ask if she was happy. I just knew she was.

Alistair and Pat's husband John arrive, and we spend the rest of the evening sharing stories and having a good craic. The men bring out the poteen, which is Irish moonshine, but by now we have had our share of wine and only take a "wee" sip, to please them. Even that burns on the way down! Time for bed. What a great night!

Chapter 16
Ireland

"You must have it backwards," I insisted to Joanne, when we were looking at a map and planning to visit her cousins in Ireland. She said Ann lived in Southern Ireland and Alistair lived in Northern Ireland, but when we looked at the map, Ann's town of Carndonagh was further north than Alistair's town of Templepatrick. She was right, however. When they split the country in 1921, they left the northwest portion of the island to Southern Ireland, which is now the Republic of Ireland, but usually simply called Ireland.

So, after leaving Northern Ireland we travelled north to Ireland. Our first stop was on the Northern Ireland side of the border in Londonderry/Derry, where Ann (the other "cousin") picked us up. I write Londonderry/Derry together because that is how it appears on signs in the train station and that is what the announcement says when you approach the station. It is a political issue that indicates all is not quite settled when it comes to Unionist and Nationalist issues.

The only hint we had that we crossed the border into Ireland was a sign indicating the change from miles to kilometres. Although Great Britain, which includes Northern Ireland, uses the metric system, it still uses miles on signs. Ireland is part of the European Union and does everything metric. Northern Ireland uses pounds and Ireland uses Euros. It all made our heads spin, going from one Ireland to the other!

Our drive to Ann's home in Carndonagh, on the Inishowen Peninsula, was a lovely trip through countryside of picturesque green rolling hills. We arrived on Ann and Stuart's 180-acre dairy farm to the persistent ringing of a phone. Ann is a veterinarian and her clinic is on the property. From then on, there wasn't a quiet moment.

It was breeding season for horses, so if Ann wasn't checking on horses to see if they were pregnant, she was inseminating them and then flushing them. All this had to be done on the horse's ovulating schedule. During our time there she also had to do surgery on a dog, stitch up a puppy, check an injured cow, and continually drive her four children wherever they needed to go. Stuart kept busy either feeding and milking their two hundred cows, giving the cows their medication, letting the calves out for their first run, fixing fences, or cleaning out pastures. These two did not sit still. Somehow, Ann also managed to bake fresh bread daily and feed everyone. Joanne joined in on the action (of course). She helped stitch up the puppy, held down a dog which went into shock during treatment, and read out the ear tags on the cows and calves as they received their medication.

As for me, I tried to get involved too, when Ann ran into the house and asked in an excited voice, "Do you want to watch me scan a horse?" I jumped up and followed her into the clinic. When I saw her pull on rubber gloves that went up to her armpits, I realized what came next. Sure enough, her arm went in the back end of the horse, and at that moment, I realized that I am not much of a farm person.

I have never spent time on a farm, and I now know that there is never a dull moment. There is always something to be done, from very early in the morning until late in the evening. Stuart has dairy farming in his blood. He is the fourth generation of his family on that very farm, which was built in the 1860s.

With all the work to do on the farm Ann still found time to show off some of their part of Ireland. Driving to the northern coast took us through many small towns and a patchwork of farms. Many farms were as old as Stuart's, with rock fences, whitewashed stone buildings, lopsided barns, and rooftops of moss and plants. We drove along the coast, with a stop at a beautiful golden sand beach, which looked surprisingly tropical. The water was not a tropical temperature, however. Joanne, not one to miss a water opportunity, ventured in, along with two of Ann's kids, six-year-old Mark and ten-year-old Jill. Ann and I preferred to watch them from the comfort of the shore. It was a great day, topped off with a brisk walk along the rugged coastal hillside at Malin Head, the northernmost point in Ireland on the North Atlantic Ocean.

During our stay in Ireland, my fifty-first birthday rolled around. One year since I heard about my mother's diagnosis. One year since my life as I knew it changed. I was struck by how much I missed her! I knew she and my daughter Carly were up there, having a good laugh every time I lost something or got lost. But in the end they always helped me out. They were my guardian angels!

Our time in Ireland was another fantastic visit with great people who managed to find time in their hectic schedules to welcome us into their home and show us some of their region. I loved the countryside, the small-town atmosphere, and the community spirit. I am not sure I could live on a farm and be involved in all the work that it entails, but it sure was fun to visit.

For my birthday, Ann found time to bake a Swiss roll for my cake. She also invited three of her friends to join us to celebrate and we had a great evening of laughter. I decided to interview all the women: forty-seven-year-old Ann, fifty-year-old Bernie, fifty-six-year-old Helen, and sixty-year-old Jean.

~

Ann – 47, Jean – 60, Bernie – 50, Helen – 56

The women have all arrived and Bernie brought champagne to celebrate my birthday. What a nice thing to do, considering she has never met me, or even heard of me, until this afternoon. Out comes the cork and the party begins. The laughter starts before the first sip; this is going to be a fun evening.

I explain to the women about my journey and they all agree, without the slightest hesitation, to become my "Southern" Irish interviewees. We agree that although Ann was born in Northern Ireland, not Ireland, she has been here close to thirty years, so she can be included. Ann lived in Northern Ireland until she started university in Dublin. She says, "I would never move back. I didn't 'think' life was different in the North, until I moved to Ireland. I could see the differences right away. In the North people would ask, 'Where did you go to school?' and by the name of the school, we would know if they were Protestant or Catholic. Those questions just don't get asked here, and no one would care anyway." Proving her point, Bernie says she is Catholic, Jean is Protestant, and Ann and Helen are Methodist.

Ann goes on to say, "We never sat around talking about politics in my home, but my father did have one rule about who he would allow me to marry—he could not be a football (soccer) player, he had to be a rugby player. We are a rugby family."

The other ladies have lived in this area their entire lives. They all married young and lived at home until the day they were married. Bernie pipes up, "There was no nonsense until the wedding night, either." Jean says the same for her.

I ask if they would move to another country if the opportunity arose and immediately they all say no. But then Bernie declares she might consider somewhere with better weather. "We love the community spirit we have here. We all are involved in activities, through our churches or the community, and we support each others' efforts. Even though everyone knows everyone else's business, we still love it here," says Jean.

This is a farming community and all the women have farming in their background. Jean and Ann are still on farms. Jean's children are all still involved, and Ann's oldest son is eager to stay in the business. The rest of the sixteen children among this group are either enrolled in postgraduate education, have completed degrees, or will be going to university when they are old enough. One of the sixteen lives in England, a few attend college or university in Dublin, but the rest are still in Carndonagh. None of the women are certain how many of their children will stay in this area and how many will move to bigger cities in the future.

They tell me that they all follow their religion and attend church regularly, except Jean, who can't attend early mass because she has to milk her cows. (She is a widow.) Proudly, they say that most of their children also attend church with them. "This is a church-going community. You won't find many that don't attend a church around here," Helen tells us.

Hot flashes and night sweats are a common symptom amongst the group. Helen says she is over them now, but remembers her "power surges" well. That gets a good laugh. Ann goes to her cupboard and brings out a bottle of a natural HRT called Ayuda with soya isoflavones and we all write the name down. She says it seems to help. We also exchange stories of lost items and forgetful moments, but no one mentions any emotional or mood swing problems.

The phone rings, of course, and it is a local policeman, to say a puppy has been hit by a car. "Can we bring it over?" he asks.

"Sure," says Ann. Despite their nice clothes, Joanne and Ann head over to the clinic. "I have big aprons to keep the blood off our clothes," Ann says as they walk out the door. The rest of us finish up the champagne. After they stitched him up, they bring the limp puppy back to stay warm by the AGA stove. I will say it again: never a dull moment!

Ann brings out the Swiss roll birthday cake that she made in her "spare" time; it is scrumptious. I tell her how amazed I am at what she can accomplish in a day. Her friends agree that she is a whirlwind.

We finish the night laughing and reminiscing about their marriages, children, husbands, careers, and life in general. I tell them that I don't think I could find a group of four of my women friends, in their fifties, and find they all attended church, had never been divorced, lived in the same area all their lives, and had no emotional upheaval during menopause. To me, they are a unique group.

Embrace the detours.

—Kevin Charbonneau

Chapter 17

Scotland

"My guardian angels have been at work again," I said in relief, as we got on the ferry in Larne, heading to Scotland. This was because we almost didn't get on a ferry at all that day. We were supposed to be on a ferry out of Belfast. Ann had dropped us off in Londonderry/Derry, where we caught a bus to the Belfast bus station and then took a taxi to the ferry terminal. Much to our dismay we learned the passenger ferry had broken down, and although they were letting "walk-ons" on the car ferry, that was full by the time we arrived. Joanne tried pleading for them to let us on, but they weren't listening to her pleas.

As we sat down, deflated and wondering what to do, I remembered there was another ferry to Scotland in a place called Larne. I didn't know how far away that was, but asked the clerks and one said, "Oh yes, that is about half an hour away, and there is a ferry going this afternoon." Why they didn't volunteer that information when they said their ferry was full is beyond me.

We overheard a couple in the same dilemma, asked them to join us, hopped in a cab, and made it to the ferry terminal, with time to spare. At the Larne terminal they were more than helpful, even telling us how to find the bus driver on the ferry to get a ride into Glasgow. We were back on track and thankful for the wheels on our bags after we had hauled them through the bus, train, and ferry terminals. I was also thankful to my guardian angels, who must have slipped that memory of the Larne ferry into my head.

We almost didn't go to Scotland. Although we had decent weather during our trip, Joanne was longing for a trip to a beach-and-sun destination to complete our trip together. We had been on the go every day, and lazing around a beach resort appealed to us both. We tried to find a last-minute deal to a sunny destination in southern Europe, but couldn't find anything that worked into our time-frame or budget. So we continued with our original plan and headed to Scotland. And despite the rain, we loved it!

I am part Scottish. My father was born in Scotland—by accident. His parents were Scottish, but had immigrated to Canada in 1910. Then, while pregnant with my father, his mother and her two young children went home to Scotland to visit family. The year was 1914, and they arrived the day the First World War broke out. Grandma couldn't leave for four years. I wonder now, what made her go home without her husband, taking two small children and carrying a child? The boat trip alone must have been tumultuous. My grandfather did eventually go back to Scotland and joined a Scottish regiment for the duration of the war. My grandparents died before I was born, but it was nice to see where they grew up.

I am not sure if it is in my blood, or just a lovely place, but Scotland was the first country I have ever been in that I thought I could move to. It might have been because it is similar to home in many ways. The people are friendly and down-to-earth, and there are oceans, rivers, lakes, and beautiful green countryside.

Scotland was another country where Joanne had contacts. A few years prior to our trip she billeted a couple of women from Scotland who were visiting Nova Scotia on a women's curling tour. She must have treated them well, because both Fiona and Bev invited us to stay a few days in their homes.

Fiona and Bob picked us up in Glasgow and we drove to their home in Killearn, a small village about an hour from the city. Again, we were treated like family. We were wined, dined, and toured around their region. They even took us golfing at a course on the banks of Loch Lomond. I surprised myself by outdriving them all on the first hole. That was it, though; not another good swing all day. However, we had lots of fun until we had to stop at the seventh hole due to rain. Surprise!

On a day without rain we visited the local distillery, explored Stirling Castle, and spent time in the "garden". I explained to Fiona that if I told someone at home I was sitting in the garden they would think I was sitting amongst the flowers or plants, as we call the grass part the "yard". She thought this was amusing, and by the end of our visit they were calling it a yard.

At the Glengoyne Distillery, originally started by monks, we learned that whisky is the lifeblood of Scotland. Callum, a very funny young man in a kilt, whose father was the distiller, explained all there is to know about single malt whisky. Water, barley, mashing, fermentation, distillation, and ten—or more—years of maturation in sherry oak barrels; we heard it all. The funniest part of the visit was that one of the fellows that worked there is the uncle to someone I know from home. It's a small world after all. I also learned that in Scotland the name *whisky* is spelled without the *e*, unlike Irish and American *whiskey*.

Stirling Castle is one of the largest and most important castles, both historically and architecturally, in Scotland. It sits atop a hill looming over the town of Stirling. It is an imposing sight as you drive towards it. The one piece of historical fact that I remember from my visit to the castle is that when King James VI of Scotland also became King James I of England, Great Britain became the "United Kingdom".

Fiona was kind enough to drive Joanne and me to our next destination, St. Andrews. This is the hometown of Bev and Iain, who took over spoiling us with more home-cooked meals and tours of their area. St. Andrews is on the North Sea coast, on the east side of Scotland, and it has become another of my "favourite places". It is a town of about twelve thousand, and for those who love golf, St. Andrews is basically the birthplace of the sport. It has one of the oldest courses in the world, coincidentally called "The Old Course at St. Andrews". I say, "one" of the oldest because there are conflicting reports on whether it is actually the oldest.

There are now seven courses included in The Links Courses of St. Andrews, and if you are a resident, it is obscenely cheap to golf there. If you are a visitor, it is the opposite—very expensive. And to golf on the Old Course you have to enter a ballot every day to see if you actually get a tee time. You must also have a registered golf handicap—no duffers like me would be allowed on.

Most of the courses in St. Andrews are "links" courses, meaning they are located in coastal areas, on sandy soil, amid dunes, with few water hazards and few, if any, trees. That is the case with the Old Course, right on the coast. It is an idyllic setting. Although we couldn't golf on the Old Course, we did walk on its "hallowed" grounds. There is a walkway right through the eighteenth fairway. On Sundays the course is closed and it is used as a park for walking and picnicking. We also visited several other courses in the area. They were all beautiful, although I think the wind and the ocean breeze would make them very cold places to golf. We didn't get the chance to golf in St. Andrews, but I don't think I would have wanted to show off my limited golf abilities in the "mecca of golf".

The town of St. Andrews is a great place to explore, from the golf shops to the University of St. Andrews, to the medieval and Romanesque ruins of the St. Andrew's Castle and Cathedral that sit prominently on the coast. The university is where Prince William attended, as did Bev, so we wandered the grounds of the oldest university in Scotland, built in 1410. We also learned about some of the university traditions when we saw one of the students in town with his red robe hanging off both shoulders. It turns out that first-year students wear their robe over both shoulders, second-years off one shoulder, third-years off the other, and fourth-years off both. They wear these robes when they attend the rectory, do their traditional "pier walk", and when they are touring new students, which must have been the case when we saw the student in town.

Bev and Iain also took us to the Pittenweem Arts Festival in a burgh not far from St. Andrews, along the coast in the district of East Neuk. This is a charming seaside village with white stone houses lining the shore. Fishing boats, lobster traps, cobbled roads, and wynds (very narrow, winding roads) make it a very picturesque place.

There were over one hundred venues of art, jewellery, pottery, sculpture, and woodwork. Most of the venues were in people's homes, which was great because we got to see what the homes looked like inside and their back gardens, full of flowers and ancient stone walls.

We said good-bye to our new Scottish friends and headed to Edinburgh. We only had about ten hours there, which was at least three days short of what you would need to enjoy it properly. The Edinburgh Fringe Festival was on, and what I am sure is already a crazy city was absolutely wild. The Fringe Festival is apparently one of the biggest performing arts festivals in the world. There were people, in every kind of costume you can dream up, doing street performances, playing music, marching in parades, and, of course, doing theatre in hundreds of venues. The event's program was almost an inch thick.

Edinburgh's Old and New Town are on the UNESCO World Heritage List. It is a fantastic city full of beautiful Georgian and medieval architecture; another city with a huge castle looming over it. We had a great day wandering the streets and taking in all the sights. We even found time to take in a fringe performance. We really loved Scotland!

While we were with Fiona, she found her friend Karen to be my interviewee. She had just celebrated her fiftieth birthday.

~

Karen – 50

Fiona introduces us, takes us into the sun room, brings us tea, and leaves us to get on with the interview. Karen and I seem to connect the moment we sit down. She has a great spirit about her and we are gabbing like old friends in seconds.

She is interested in my trip and we discuss travelling for a while. She has travelled through Europe and over to the States, working in Corfu, Paris, and London before getting married. But she says, "I love Scotland and would not want to live anywhere else." She still lives in her hometown, about twenty minutes outside of Glasgow.

She has been married twenty-two years. Her husband is trained as a chartered accountant, but has returned to his family business and is a fishmonger in Glasgow. They have three children: twenty-one-year-old twins (a boy and girl), and an eighteen-year-old daughter, all of them in university. Karen says she feels lucky to be able to be a stay-at-home mother.

Because both her parents died in their fifties, Karen says, "I am a bit of a fatalist. I am always a little worried I could meet the same fate, so I appreciate every day as it comes. My life has been far better than my parents'. They had many worries and money issues." She says she was brought up Protestant but does not attend church now.

As far as menopause goes, Karen's story is a new one to me. She started having symptoms at thirty-nine, was crying all the time, and had migraines. Her doctors were baffled. She demanded to go to a menopause clinic, had to wait six months, and when she was finally checked, her hormone levels were sky high. She had every symptom in the book, from hot flashes to headaches. To relieve some of her symptoms she took black cohosh, red clover, and evening primrose oil. She is over it all now, but unfortunately still has the odd migraine. Imagine, thirty-nine! That is early! She says her mother was early as well.

It always challenges my interviewees when I ask them to describe themselves, and Karen hesitates until I tell her, "Just say the first thing that comes to mind." She says, "Bubbly on the surface, but more to me underneath." And lastly, "Are you happy?" Another yes. I tell her that all the women so far have responded positively, and we decide that when you get to fifty you realize that life is much easier to handle with a positive attitude. I really like Karen and feel we would be good friends if we lived in the same town.

~

Joanne and I left Scotland doing something we later vowed never to do again—we got on an overnight bus to London.

Chapter 18

Estonia, Russia, Finland, Denmark, Germany, Netherlands

BALTIC CRUISE

"I can meet you in London and join you on a cruise, just give me the dates," read the e-mail from my friend Linda. She not only agreed to join me, she organized the trip while I toured around with Joanne. I have great friends. She even arranged a terrific hotel in London where she, Joanne, and I could stay. One friend in, one friend out. It worked very well.

Joanne and I survived the overnight bus ride from Edinburgh better than we thought, and we easily hooked up with Linda. The three of us had a great visit, a tasty Italian dinner, and even had time for the theatre, where we saw the play *Billy Elliott*.

The day was not without its troubles, however. First, Linda lost her balance in the tube. She fell, arms extended out in front of her, right into a fellow passenger's crotch. While trying to right herself, she fell into another fellow's lap. It was all made funnier by the fact that the next tube stop was Cockfosters. We were giggling like schoolgirls. Then, at the end of the night, as we headed back to the hotel, we were talking so much that we went right instead of left in the subway. We ended up going the wrong way. Normally this isn't a real problem, because you just get out, cross over to the other side of the tracks, and get on the train going the right direction. But the train we missed was the last train of the night. We got out and had no idea where we were. We wandered awhile, found a cab, and eventually decided that other than the forty-five dollars it cost, our subway goof-up was quite funny.

I must admit I was tired at this point. Seventeen countries complete, not many rest days, and so much history and politics were whirling around in my head. The cruise was just the thing to do. Not having to pack and repack every few days, being able to go to sleep and wake up somewhere new, without having to work out how to get there, was going to be a nice rest.

The cruise was with Carnival Cruise Lines. I had cruised with Norwegian Cruise Lines in the past and wanted to try a different line. Our ship was brand-new, so it was very clean and modern, but whoever decorated it must have been on some wild drugs—it looked like a pink Vegas nightmare. Everyone joked about it, including the staff.

"Two and a half days at sea is enough. Where is the land?" both Linda and I said on the third day of our cruise, though we had known it would be a long journey from England. We were excited to reach Estonia, our first destination, and were ready to get off the ship, even though we had taken full advantage of all a cruise has to offer. We went to the spa, the gym, the art auction, played a trivia game, did a wine-and-food pairing, swam, had some great meals, and watched the entertainment in the main theatre. Neither of us really worked out how to relax for long, but we did manage to get in a nap or two as well.

Carnival has set dinner times with set dinner companions. That can be a problem if you don't like them, but we were very lucky, as our dinner mates turned out great. At our table was a fun group, including Ralph and William from New Jersey (neither were candidates for Mr. Right—they were gay), two sisters from Ontario, and another woman our age and her daughter, also from Ontario.

Looking around at the other tables, all of which appeared to be filled with couples or families, we were very happy with our seat assignments.

~

Estonia

"The Old Town of Tallinn is a UNESCO World Heritage Site," boomed the announcement as we were sailing into our first port. (I wondered how many more UWHSs I would see this trip.) Tallinn is on the southern coast of the Gulf of Finland, in northwestern Estonia. Sailing into town, the red roofs and church spires of Old Town come into view first. Then the magnificent Russian Orthodox Church and Alexander Nevsky Cathedral, with its gilded black onion-shaped cupolas, rise up in the middle of town.

The city has been attacked and pillaged many times. Although extensively bombed by Russians during WWII, much of the medieval Old Town still remains. Tallinn is the capital of Estonia, which has apparently become the Silicon Valley of the Baltic. In fact, Skype was developed there.

The medieval Old Town of Tallinn is well preserved and we enjoyed walking the narrow cobblestone streets, venturing into some of the churches, salivating over some of the high fashions available, and relaxing over an Estonian beer. It is a very touristy area, with plenty of cafes, restaurants, souvenir shops, and tours available. We had wanted to do a bike tour, but arrived too late.

Wanting to get away from the tourist area, we wandered over to the other side of the train tracks and into an area that appeared not to have changed since Communism. Many kiosks and small shops— cluttered, untidy, and not very clean—filled the local square. Some of the products looked like they might have been there since the time of Communism too. Several drunks were sleeping up against a wall, and other locals who were wandering around and working in shops just didn't seem happy. We felt quite uncomfortable and not welcome. As we were hightailing it out of there, we were sure we were being sized up to have our purses lifted; but we held on tight, walked faster, and made it back to the tourist area safe and sound.

Even in the tourist area we didn't find the locals very friendly. I can imagine they get tired of cruise ships full of English-speaking people invading their town, but I would have expected a friendlier welcome. I have talked to many people who loved it there, and to be honest I was a little "Old Towned" out, so I probably didn't give it a fair chance. I also didn't find anyone who was friendly enough to even approach about an interview, so that didn't help my opinion.

~

Russia

"This is where Rasputin was poisoned, and this is where Emperor Alexander was assassinated, and this is where Paul the First was murdered." That seemed to be the theme of our tours during our two days in St. Petersburg—alias Petrograd and Leningrad. There really is some ugly history there.

We were a little unsettled before we got off the ship to visit St. Petersburg, because we had heard on television that morning, "Russian aggression will not go unnoticed, and continued aggression will bring repercussion from the U.S.A." This was a result of the Russia and Georgia conflict over Ossetia. We had to hope the "repercussions" didn't happen in the two days we were there. Worried about our American friends, we considered lending out our extra Canadian flag pins to them so they didn't have any problems while we were on tour. The world over, people love Canadians!

St. Petersburg streets were immaculate, but when I mentioned how impressed I was to our guide, he seemed surprised. So I was not sure if it is always clean or maybe the street cleaners had just been through. Either way, what we saw was virtually litter-free.

St. Petersburg has been called the Venice of the North. The Neva River winds through the city, but the buildings are not built right out of the water, as in Venice. Since the 1700s with Peter the Great, followed by Catherine the Great and all the monarchs into the 1800s, St. Petersburg has had the best European architects build an incredible city. The city is chockablock with summer palaces, winter palaces, year-round palaces, churches, museums, and plenty of magnificent bridges.

Our first tour guide was Sasha, who also taught Russian at a local university. A city that has had so many names and so much history gave him plenty of facts to share with us, but I found it interesting that there was no talk of anything since WWII or perestroika.

Our first stop was the Hermitage, consisting of the Winter Palace, the Old Hermitage Museum, the Small Hermitage, the Imperial Residence and the New Hermitage. Building started in 1754 to 1762 for Elizabeth Petrovna, continued for Catherine the Great between 1764 and 1768, and was further developed until 1851.

Sasha said, "The Communists may have killed off the Russian royalty, but did not destroy any of the masterpieces or artworks or the buildings." Thank goodness for small miracles. We went through most of the buildings at breakneck speed, or at least as fast as you can go with wall-to-wall people. We did see Rembrandts, Goyas, and a Michelangelo sculpture, as well as beautiful rooms with gold fixtures, parquet floors, solid marble pillars, huge urns of malachite and lapis, and many more works of art and sculptures. Over one thousand rooms and three thousand artifacts—not bad for about an hour and a half. I guess we may have missed a few rooms.

Next up was another favourite church, the Cathedral of the Resurrection. Construction began in 1883 and it took twenty-four years to finish. It was built to commemorate Emperor Alexander II, who was assassinated on the very site upon which it stands. It is better known as "Church of Our Saviour on the Spilled Blood." It features glazed bricks, coloured tiles, marble, mosaics, fancy-shaped stone detail, and onion-shaped cupolas. It is truly a spectacular building. We saw many wedding parties having photos taken in front of the church. Sadly, one of the things we also saw was that everyone seems to smoke there, and even most of the brides were smoking during their photo shoots.

We had different tour guides each day and they were like night and day. The first fellow obviously did not like what his country had become and I think would have been shot twenty years earlier for the things he said. The woman the second day could find only positive things to say. Our first guide pointed out a sailing ship on the shore of the Neva River and told us it was just an expensive restaurant that we shouldn't visit, while the second guide told us the ship was a gift from President Putin to the city to celebrate its three hundredth birthday. While the first guide spoke of it disdainfully, the second guide was very proud of it.

We had lunch in the city both days and tried the potatoes, cabbage, fish, borscht, and, of course, caviar and vodka. I don't understand why caviar is so special; it is way too salty for my taste buds, and I love salt. They brought around the Russian vodka more than coffee. Our tour guide noted, "The afternoon tour is always more fun than the morning tour!"

Again, this is a small view of a huge country, and as our first tour guide said, "You can't judge Russia by what you see in St. Petersburg." For a historical view it was great to see, but in terms of the people, I am really none the wiser.

Our female tour guide became my Russian interviewee. She was a little older than my target (fifty-eight), but spoke perfect English, and we really didn't get an opportunity to talk to anyone else. Because we were with a cruise and did not have an entrance visa, we had to stay with the tour at all times and were not allowed to stray on our own.

~

Ludmilla – 58

Ludmilla appears to be a little older than I am looking for, but as the day goes on I am guessing she is a little younger than I think. It isn't really her features that make me think she is older, but her mannerisms. She has a little trouble getting up and down the stairs of the tour bus and is constantly red in the face and wiping her brow. Hot flashes, maybe, but she doesn't seem that healthy. Finally, I ask her how old she is and she says she is fifty-eight. I ask if she would be willing to be interviewed at a break or at the end of the tour and she agrees.

It turns out to be the end of the tour before we can start and she tells me she doesn't have too long, as she has to leave soon, so I ask her as many questions as I can.

She tells me she has been married for thirty-eight years and has two children, a thirty-seven-year-old son and a twenty-two-year-old daughter. I wonder if the daughter may have been a bit of a surprise, but Ludmilla is much too proper for us to discuss the matter. Her son still lives at home, although he has a girlfriend who owns her own apartment. Her daughter was recently married.

Ludmilla lives in a state-owned apartment, where they pay very little rent. She says they could pay a fee to "privatize" the ownership, but if they did, they would become responsible for all upkeep. As it is a very old building that needs a lot of repairs, some of which are being done now, they prefer to rent.

She tells me that she and her husband and her parents helped her sister buy an apartment. They even sold their Swedish refrigerator to help out. I ask how her life has changed since, and she says, "It is still perestroika. People in the world believed no one owned anything, which is not true. Many people owned places in the country." I take this to mean she doesn't think much has changed for people like her. She still has to rent a run-down place, while the rich still have the luxuries.

Ludmilla is very proud of her degree in psychology and literature. For thirty-seven years, she was a tour guide for Russian tourists, guiding them on tours throughout Europe. I didn't think Russians were allowed to leave Russia, and yet she was taking them on tours. She said again, "People around the world have no idea what was going on here. People with money could go wherever they wanted." She is extremely knowledgeable about Russia and on the tour said only good things about her country, but the more we speak, the less I believe her patriotism.

Because her father was in the military, her family travelled a lot, and her mother did not work. Her parents passed away in their seventies. She says both her children have university degrees, which she made sure they finished, as education is free, but neither of them uses their degree for what they are doing now.

It seems that she must be going through menopause because she is constantly wiping her brow and getting extremely flushed. As it turns out, she has a thyroid condition that causes this. She had a hysterectomy after her daughter was born and has had no menopausal symptoms since then.

She says she believes in God, but does not have a religion or attend any church. She has always lived in St. Petersburg and loves it, but if she were to move, she says it would be to Nice, France, or anywhere in the countryside, even in Russia.

She was very aggressive on the tour, pushing her way to the front of every line we were in, telling the driver how to drive, and even taking us into the road against busy traffic, putting out her arm to stop it and leading us across. She knew how to get her way! I am surprised, then, when I ask her to describe herself and she says, "I am fond of animals, nature, flowers, my daughter, ballroom dancing, and I am very soft. Make sure you say 'very soft'."

Ludmilla breaks the "yes" cycle. When I ask if she is happy, she says, "I am only happy fifty percent of the time."

"Because of the government?" I ask.

"No, because of people." We run out of time for an explanation, but I think she really follows the "party line", and I am not sure that she would find many like-minded people to connect with. I am grateful she had some time at the end of our tour to talk, and only wish we had more.

～

Finland

"I feel like I am home sailing the waters around Victoria," I said to Linda as we sailed around the Helsinki Archipelago. We found ourselves on a harbour cruise shortly after the cruise ship docked near Helsinki. The likeness to home was phenomenal. Helsinki covers numerous islands, peninsulas, and bays. The city is on the southern part of Finland, and the rest extends to the small islands across the sea.

The city centre is a mixture of historical and modern buildings and is dotted with several parks. Aleksanterinkatu is the main street and is lined with fashionable shops, cafes, and restaurants.

Many people were dressed in high fashion. The people we encountered were happy and friendly. We didn't think of it at first, but realized later that we were just walking up to people and speaking English, and everyone answered back in English without hesitation. It is a very cosmopolitan city.

The Market Square, bordering the harbour on the Baltic Sea, is a lively market with rows of kiosks selling fur clothing, jewellery, paintings, handicrafts, souvenirs, fresh produce, fish, and Finnish specialty foods, including pickled herring. (We didn't try it.) It was a great place to people-watch. We enjoyed Helsinki. It probably helped that we had sunshine for the first time in days, and I can't help but love a city by the sea. Despite the fact that we were only in Helsinki for five hours, we found an interviewee.

~

Paivi – 51

I found the perfect small black leather purse and my Finnish interviewee at the same market kiosk. Linda and I are both buying purses from this woman. We look at each other, nod our heads in agreement without saying a word, and decide she is the right age. I shamelessly ask her, "Do you mind if I ask how old you are?"

She looks a little surprised, but says in perfect English, "I am fifty-one."

"Perfect!" I say, and explain what I am doing.

She asks the young girl working for her to take over and offers me a seat. The kiosk is not very big, but there are not too many customers at the moment, so we are free to talk until more customers arrive. "My name is Paivi and this is my kiosk. I have been selling leather goods here for over sixteen years." She says she is here seven days a week from April until December.

"Don't you get tired?" I ask.

"Yes, but I travel when we are closed, so it is worth it," she says.

Paivi was married for twenty years, but has been divorced for about eight years. She is in another relationship now. She has one son who is twenty-six and attends university. She tells me that education is free in Finland. Both her parents received degrees, and she has a business degree.

Paivi's parents were divorced when she was thirteen. (This is the first woman I have interviewed whose parents were divorced.) They are both still alive and in their mid-seventies. Her mother still follows their Lutheran religion, but Paivi stopped practicing when she was thirty. She doesn't explain why she stopped then. I ask if she feels her life is better than her parents' and she says, "No, I think we have all had a good life."

Paivi has lived in Helsinki most of her adult life, but would love to move to Spain when she retires (at least for the winters). She says Helsinki only gets about six hours of daylight each day in winter and it is very cold. "That explains all the fur coats and hats for sale around here," I comment. She has done lots of travelling in Europe, India, Brazil, and the States, and she worked in Thailand before she started her leather-selling business.

She has been taking two hormone medications for three years. She started taking them six months after all the classic symptoms started. She is symptom free now.

She says she doesn't have time for hobbies during her working season, but in the off-season she loves to travel and has learned how to sail. She can't come up with a description of herself, saying, "I'm just who I am. That is a very hard question."

"Are you happy?" I ask. Another yes to add to my list.

The kiosk is getting crowded as I thank her for her time, and we part with a hug. I leave thinking how lucky I am to keep finding these women willing to share some of the stories of their lives with me, and thinking she fits right in to the mould that is shaping up of ambitious, busy ladies.

~

Germany

"How can we stop in Berlin? It is not on the coast," I said, when we were reading the itinerary for the cruise. The cruise line advertised Berlin as a stop, but what it meant was that it stopped at Warmaden, and then you took a three-hour train ride into Berlin. The clincher was that the train ride was $215. I remember vividly watching on TV as the Berlin Wall came down and realizing what a significant historical event it was. I really didn't want to miss it, so we dug deeper into our pockets and off we went.

The train ride was through the countryside, passing many farms and small towns. We arrived at the train station, took a metro to the centre of town, and were on a bike tour within a half hour of arriving, just like Joanne and I did in Prague. I told Linda that bike tours are my favourite way to see a city. Our tour guide was from New Zealand, was well-informed, and was just full of fun anecdotes about the history of this extremely diverse city.

Berlin now has the third-largest gay community in the world, next to San Francisco and Sydney, Australia. It also has the second-largest Turkish community outside Turkey. It is a vibrant city both day and night. We weren't there for the eclectic nightlife, but I am told there is something for everyone, from opera to outrageous.

Stopping isn't always an option when on a bike tour, so we missed taking pictures in the nude sunbathing area of the Tiergarten Park. The Tiergarten was once the hunting ground for Prussian kings and is now one of Europe's largest inner-city parks. It is a beautiful park of gardens, forest, paths, lakes, and, of course, a beer garden, where we stopped for lunch. We sampled the bratwurst, sauerkraut, pretzels, and beer, giving enough nourishment to fuel us on our afternoon ride.

The city is full of Russian and German monuments, reminders of the division of the city, and stunning new architecture. Any signs of Communism have been torn down or renovated. There is new construction everywhere. Although there are cobblestones on the road to show where the Berlin Wall once stood, it is hard now to distinguish east from west. The new government buildings are all glass, apparently to represent "open government". There is also plenty of graffiti.

The area around Checkpoint Charlie and what remains of the Wall are a stop every tourist to Berlin would have to make. It is hard to imagine what it must have been like for the people living there when the wall went up overnight in 1961. Families were divided, and people who had jobs on the opposite sides were out of work. An open-air exhibit is there now, with an overview of life in Berlin while Germany was divided.

A two-man watchtower still stands, where the no-go zone was watched over. Our guide explained that if the two men in the tower collaborated, a person could escape. Over the years that the wall stood, twelve men did escape that way. He also showed us a building where a man attached a hammer to a rope and threw it to the other side, where someone waited to secure the rope. He and his family were able to escape, inching their way along the rope.

Then we rode our bikes to the Memorial to the Murdered Jews of Europe, a huge complex covering more than four acres. There are over 2,700 concrete grey bare slabs of various sizes and shapes. It is a foreboding exhibit. There is also an underground "Place of Information" displaying the names of all known Jewish Holocaust victims. Having an exhibit only for the Jews caused some controversy. So after it was completed, a Memorial to Homosexuals has opened, and one for the Gypsies is being considered, thus representing more of the victims of the Holocaust.

We also rode over the spot where Hitler's bunker once was. It was almost completely destroyed by the Russians. This was where Hitler and Eva Braun were married and within forty hours committed suicide. There is no memorial plaque; it is just a parking lot now.

Our bike tour was a great ride through an amazingly interesting city with so much history. I knew I was coming back to Germany in a few weeks, so we didn't look for an interviewee on this short visit.

~

Denmark

"Has everyone on the cruise decided not to take a tour?" we wondered, when we arrived at the local bus stop outside the cruise terminal. We were trying to save money by taking the local bus, but also not willing to waste time in line, so we decided to take the "Hop On, Hop Off" bus. Most big cities have these and they are a great way to see a lot of a city in a short period of time. Unfortunately, we spent too much time at our first stop, the city centre, and missed the rest of the stops. A twenty-five-dollar one-way trip to town. So much for saving money.

Copenhagen is a vibrant city. But for a busy, crowded city, it is surprisingly not very noisy. I was amazed to see how many people rode bikes. There are bike lanes everywhere, and people of all sizes, shapes, and ages, in every kind of fashion you can imagine, ride bikes. I don't think I heard a horn honk while visiting, and that is very unusual for a European city.

Much of the architecture is from the seventeenth and eighteenth centuries, with Renaissance palaces, parks, and colourful merchant houses lining the canals that run through the city. It reminded me of Amsterdam. One of the longest pedestrian shopping streets in Europe was good for a few hours of our time. Copenhagen is a very high-fashion town with many upscale boutiques and stores. Linda even picked up some designer gum boots, in black and pink.

As much as we liked it, we found it extremely expensive. Our lunch, consisting of a chicken Caesar salad, a cheese plate, one beer, and one glass of wine, was seventy dollars. It was very good food, though, and we enjoyed resting our shopped-out bodies in a delightful sidewalk cafe while watching the world go by.

We couldn't pass up the Ice Bar, where the walls, the chairs, the bar, and the glasses are all made of ice. At the entrance we were given warm ponchos, gloves, and snow boots, and in we went to enjoy a choice of a variety of vodka drinks. Another expensive decision. One drink and entry for one was thirty-two dollars. But you have to try it once, don't you?

We had an enjoyable day in a beautiful city, but might have been better off on a tour, considering how much money we dropped. It didn't help that the sales tax was 25 percent. Yikes!

I didn't hook up with my Danish interviewee in person, but thanks to my brother, and the magic of the Internet, I did get to know a fifty-year-old Dane called Brigitte. She and her daughter were buying Converse shoes at Baggins, my brother Glen's store in Victoria, while I was travelling in Scotland. Glen told her about my journey and she happily volunteered to meet me when I got to Copenhagen. Unfortunately, our dates did not line up like we hoped they would. Instead, she and I got acquainted online.

~

Birgitte – 50

Birgitte has just celebrated her fiftieth birthday. She has been married for twenty-three years. She writes that she and her husband lived together before they were married, which is the custom in Denmark. She has a twenty-two-year-old son and a twenty-year-old daughter. Both children did a year-long international exchange during high school, her son in Australia and her daughter in the States. Her son is now in second-year economics and her daughter has just finished high school. Denmark is another country where higher education is free.

Her parents, who are in their mid-seventies, are both healthy. Her mother was a nurse and her father owned a furniture store. Brigitte is a trained nurse and continued her education by taking management and consultant courses. She is now a job advisor/consultant for PricewaterhouseCoopers.

Brigitte worked as a nanny in London for a year when she was twenty. She has lived in a few different places in Denmark and has done quite a bit of travelling in Europe, Thailand, the USA, and Canada. She would move to another country, but only for a few years; she can't decide which country.

In answer to the question, "Do you feel your life is better than parents'?" she writes, "Perhaps not better, but easier, as we don't have a shop with long working hours. We have longer holidays, and especially my childhood was far easier than the one they had growing up during WWII."

She hasn't started menopause, or at least has no symptoms and takes no medication.

She is Protestant, only attending church at Christmas. She is an active woman who enjoys reading, gardening, rowing, running, tennis, and bicycling. She says her family, friends, and her great job give her joy. She describes herself as "open-minded, generally happy, helpful, and easygoing, without a lot of prejudices." I'd say she is helpful and easygoing, helping a complete stranger she has not even met. Another very active woman.

∼

Netherlands

"Can I have your chair for awhile? My pins are killing me," asked the tall blond "woman" in spike heels. Linda and I were surrounded by transvestites, in a tiny bar. We arrived in Amsterdam on "Heart

Day", which was originally the one day the common folk could hunt and bring the heart of their catch to town. Now it is just an excuse to have a holiday, and it seems that the gay community does it up big. In front of many bars, contestants for the "best transvestite" strutted their stuff, while onlookers cast votes for their favourites. Amsterdam is a city where anything goes.

In the Red Light District, the smell of marijuana wafted out of many cafes and bars as we passed by sex shops, sex shows, and windows full of scantily clad women. I was puzzled that these women make any money; we didn't see an attractive one in the bunch.

The bars were full of guys on their "stag weekends". Because airfare is so cheap in Europe, on most weekends the big cities are invaded by groups of guys and girls coming to party like there's no tomorrow. It has become a problem in some cities, as the groups have become crazier each year, but they fit in well in Amsterdam.

I have been in Amsterdam several times, so was able to give Linda the quick tour once we left the area of debauchery. No trip to Amsterdam is complete without taking a canal cruise to get an overview of this unique city. We travelled along several of the one hundred canals and under some of the one thousand bridges. Most of the tourist attractions and old houses are within the city centre, so the canal tour passed many great sights. Colourful old canal houses that cling to each other, some crooked, all tall and narrow, line most of the canals. I was told the reason the houses are so narrow is because the taxes are calculated by how much land they use. Most have hoists at the top, to bring furniture through the windows, because you couldn't possibly get the bigger furniture up the narrow stairwells. Many of the narrow roads only have a small eight-inch-high rail at the edge of the canal. Apparently, there is a special branch of the fire department just for getting cars out of the canal. Wouldn't it be cheaper to install higher railings?

Walking around the narrow streets is dangerous, and it isn't because of cars. It is bicycles that are the hazard. Amsterdam has been declared "the most bicycle-friendly city in the world." More than 40 percent of the traffic movement is by bicycle. Instead of horns, you hear bells. The interesting thing is that most bikes are old, one-speed bikes. So many bikes are stolen that no one wants an expensive one. In fact, most people pay more for their locks than their bikes. The only safe places for pedestrians are the several pedestrian-only areas around the city, which are lined with shops, including every brand-name fashion shop I have ever heard of.

I didn't get an interview, because the only "women" we talked to were men.

Our twelve-day cruise went by very quickly. When Linda and I weren't touring a city, we enjoyed great dinners on the ship with our new friends, sang a few tunes at the piano bar, played mini golf, read, napped, saw most of the shows in the theatre, and caught up on the last few years of our lives, since Linda moved away from Victoria. I also spent some time working out the last weeks in Europe and the next leg in Asia. I was so glad Linda could join me.

Journeys, like artists, are born and not made. A
thousand differing circumstances contribute to
them, few of them willed or determined by the will
—whatever we may think.

—Lawrence Durrell

Chapter 19

Spain

"One hundred and fifty-three people died in a plane crash after takeoff at Madrid Airport," stated the TV report on the night before I was to fly to Madrid. I felt sick and devastated. People just like me, going on a holiday, now dead, I thought. Will the airport be open? How do they deal with the aftermath? Will I see the families of all those who died arriving at the airport? I had never been afraid of flying, but that was too close—less than twenty-four hours before I was to take a flight.

I had said good-bye to Linda at the airport and spent another night with my cousin in London. After a sleepless night I headed to the airport. As it turned out, my flight went as scheduled, and if I hadn't heard what happened I would never have known about the crash. There must have been a section closed off somewhere at the airport, but things were running normally. I didn't see an excess of police or reporters anywhere. I still had a queasy stomach from thinking about the crash, and couldn't help but wonder how the staff was dealing with the whole shocking event.

So there I was, back in Madrid after twenty-nine years. For the rest of the European portion of my journey I was on my own. I didn't remember liking Madrid as much as I did this time: I found the drivers much politer than in many big cities; the city was cleaner than I remembered; the architecture, both old and new, was beautiful; the people were friendly; and it was easy to get around.

The Metro (subway) is easy to navigate, but to see the best parts of town I didn't need to use it, as most of the main attractions are within walking distance of each other. There are lots of tree-lined boulevards, colourful gardens, parks, and plazas to sit and watch the world go by. There are also many monuments and museums. The world-famous Prado Museum is the second biggest museum in Europe and only has a ten dollar entrance fee.

Fewer vendors appeared on the streets than in most big cities. Many of the ones I did see were Chinese people selling fans, and they were constantly dodging the police. I saw one elderly Chinese lady running away and getting caught, while her friends rushed off, hiding their fans under bushes and watching her pursuit from a safe distance. I felt bad for the woman, but I think they just took her fans and let her go.

On my first day in the city I did a bike tour. It was quite an interesting experience, as there are no bike lanes in Madrid and cycling is not the norm. Luckily, in many areas of the city, sidewalks are very wide and we rode along them. (I don't know whether it was legal, but no one stopped us.) This worked fine early in the day, but as lunchtime rolled around it got a lot busier and was like an obstacle course as we tried to avoid the pedestrians. I only clipped one old guy and I don't think he went down. I didn't stay to see.

I booked the tour through a company called Like a Local, which had a variety of tours and cooking classes in Europe. In fact, my guide wasn't truly a local. He was married to a Spanish woman but was from Amsterdam, and of course had grown up riding a bike there. We stopped for coffee at one of the many cafes. In cafes and tapas bars it is cheaper to eat and drink while standing up at the bar; sit down and you pay more. I chose orange juice because the coffee was the strongest espresso I could ever imagine. I didn't want to finish off the bike tour on a caffeine high. No pedestrian would have been safe.

The next day I found a walking tour that was free, except for the tip at the end. Apparently, there are others like it in many cities in Europe. Our tour guide, who was from Buenos Aires, had a lively way of explaining history that made it sink in more than with the guide from the bike tour. The tour took over three hours and we saw all the things I had seen the day before, but from the opposite direction and, obviously, at a slower pace. It reminded me of one of my own travel rules that I'd forgotten: always turn around to see what you missed behind you. I saw many things I missed the day before.

Both tour guides explained that the king, Juan Carlos, is the "People's King", who can be seen dining at local restaurants and has no problem chatting with people while he is out and about. The grand Royal Palace in the centre of town is only used for state ceremonies, while the king and his family live in the outskirts of the city. Open for viewing, it is the biggest palace in Western Europe, with over two thousand rooms. It is still furnished with many masterpieces.

Next up, I spent a week at Pueblo Ingles, where the rules are: "Never utter a word of Spanish; talk, talk, talk in your own raw, natural and authentic style of English; and be on time," according to Davy, our MC for the week. Easy for me, I thought. I don't speak Spanish, I love to talk, and I always try to be on time.

Pueblo Ingles, which translates as "English Village", is what I like to call a summer camp for adults. Twenty English-speaking people from around the world (called Anglos) join twenty Spanish business people for a week of fun and conversation. For the Anglos, the accommodations and meals are free. For the Spanish people there is a fee, often paid by their employers.

There are several Pueblo Ingles locations, the one I stayed in was in Valdelavilla, a small town in the highlands of Soria, about four hours north of Madrid. Originally built in the eighteenth century and abandoned in the 1960s, Valdelavilla was redeveloped as a rural tourist complex in the late '90s. Twelve traditional stone-walled houses, linked with cobblestone streets, overlook sweeping panoramic views of beautiful hills and valleys where we hiked for miles throughout our week.

Each day started with a wake-up call at eight fifteen, followed by breakfast at nine. We were encouraged to sit with two Anglos and two Spaniards and then to switch dining partners at each meal. Following breakfast four hours of one-to-one sessions took place. A

Spaniard and an Anglo spend one hour together talking. We often hiked around the area surrounding our villa while we talked. Lunch, with all the "red or white medicine" (wine) we could drink, was at two p.m. Then, as it was Spain, a two-hour siesta followed.

The evenings started with a group activity, two more hours of one-to-ones, and an entertainment hour, with dinner finally at nine p.m. Dinner, which again included the "medicine", was a little late for me, but almost early to Europeans, who always dine late. Group activities included various assignments. We came up with inventions, drew posters, created jingles, and presented our projects. At other times we were preparing for our skits. The entertainment hour was always fun; some of the participants brought guitars, or we performed our silly skits. (Remember I mentioned summer camp?) After dinner we were encouraged to meet up at the bar for a few more hours of conversation and two evenings we had theme nights.

The first theme night was a "Disco Night". We all put on our best clothes and danced like we were still in the '70s. Before the dance, we watched the chef go through all the steps it took to prepare paella (a Spanish rice dish, usually made with a variety of seafood). It was delicious and fuelled us for hours of boogie-woogie good times!

On another night a *queimada* ceremony took place. In this ancient ritual from Galicia, in northern Spain, a magic potion is brewed, set alight, and then poured into glasses while an incantation is read in Galician, Spanish, and English. The whole ceremony was dark and mystical, and after we drank, we sang songs from our home countries. There was one other Canadian, but he and I could only come up with "O Canada". A bit lame, I'm afraid. The Spanish had a greater repertoire and it was fun listening to them all singing so proudly.

The evening of the *queimada* was one of my latest nights of the whole trip. I was exhausted, but turned on the computer to check my e-mails. One e-mail subject line shocked me to the core: "Donna call home as soon as possible, Lynda (my sister) has had a heart attack." I couldn't believe what I read. My sister was only sixty-one, I called my nephew Grant, who informed me that Lynda had not been feeling well, so her husband Jim took her to the emergency ward at their local hospital in Vernon, British Columbia. She seemed well enough to walk in on her own, so he dropped her at the door and went to park. In the meantime, she had a heart attack in the waiting room and was flat on the floor. When she went down she banged her head. They were putting the heart paddles to her as Jim walked in the door. I don't know how he managed not to have a heart attack himself.

She couldn't be put on blood thinners because of the head wound, so they flew her to a bigger hospital in Vancouver, an hour away, where she could get specialized care. On the call, Grant explained they might need to do brain surgery and heart surgery. He said Jim had flown down with Lynda, and he and his brother Paul were on the way to meet them, and that I should call in the morning.

I didn't sleep that night. I was trying to get my head around it all. There had been no hints of anything wrong. She hadn't been sick. I couldn't lose my mother and sister in one year. She and I were best friends. It just couldn't happen. How could I get home fast? I had things at my cousin's in London and I was four hours out of Madrid. There wasn't transportation out of Valdelavilla until the end of the week.

The morning couldn't come soon enough. I tossed and turned and worried, and then one of my recurring nightmares happened. In my nightmare I can't use the phone properly. It won't work, or I dial wrong and just can't get through, and that actually happened. Skype on my computer was not working, I did not have a cell phone, and the front desk wasn't open. I tried Skype again, and was on the verge of tears when one of the girls came out of her room and came to the rescue by lending me her cell phone.

"She is awake and talking," Grant told me with relief. The doctors said they would do tests, but the bleeding in her brain, from her head wound, had stopped and they were able to put her on the blood thinners. As far as her heart, time would tell, but things weren't looking too bad there, either. Grant told me to carry on with my trip and he would keep me updated as the test results came in.

I was relieved, but felt like I had been hit by a truck. I bowed out of the one-to-ones and got some sleep, but walked around in a bit of a daze for the rest of the day. Later, Grant e-mailed that things were looking better and Lynda probably wouldn't even need surgery. Selfishly, I was not only happy for her, but also that I was able to stay in Valdelavilla. I spoke to her four days later and she was out of the hospital, still feeling tired, but not needing surgery. She was going to be treated with medication and would be fine. I carried on with my week and truly enjoyed every minute of it, but in the back of my mind I was working out a plan to cut short the European portion of my trip and return home a few weeks early.

During the week I was fascinated by how people of different age brackets and backgrounds came together and interacted. We would have a girl or guy in his or her twenties having a one-to-one with a man or woman in his or her fifties or sixties, from a different country, finding lots to talk about and bonding. This kind of opportunity does not come up very often. One Spanish doctor in our group admitted having spent his life on his career, working day and night, and rarely travelling. He had written and published many papers and done speaking engagements along with his day job. He was flabbergasted by the "travellers". He had no idea people could be so free-spirited. My journey left him speechless. He said his "eyes were opened" by all of us, although he did admit he would probably just go back and continue his life in the same manner as he always had.

"More than English". This is the phrase on the paperwork when you sign up for Pueblo Ingles. On the last day of the week, I heard Julian, one of the Spaniards, say, "Now I know what that means. To explain our week together you have to remember what it was like at summer camp: camaraderie, games, songs, laughter, and just plain fun. Add to that a chance to learn more English for the Spanish and to learn more about Spain for the Anglos."

I was lucky not just to learn more about Spain, but to find Paloma, my Spanish interviewee. All the Spanish women at Pueblo Ingles looked too young and I was disappointed that I wasn't going to be able to find an interviewee while there. It wasn't until the third day that I sat at the same table as Paloma. She didn't want to tell me her age at first, but finally admitted she was fifty and agreed to be interviewed. I would have guessed she was in her early forties.

~

Paloma – 50

We are spending our one-to-one doing the interview. Paloma and her husband are both doctors with a specialty in allergies. Paloma tells me that she has been married twenty-two years. She goes on to explain that although they were living together, they had made no plans to get married until he found out he was accepted to a doctor's fellowship in New Orleans and invited her to join him. It was going to be easier if they were married, so they planned a wedding and had the ceremony within two months. She says in Spain this is unheard of, as it is usually a big event that takes lots of planning, but they accomplished it and left for the States, where they lived for a year.

They have two children, a twenty-two-year-old-daughter, who is already in her third year of medical school, and a seventeen-year-old son, who is in his last year of high school. Paloma's parents were teachers. They have both passed away, her mom at eighty and her dad at ninety. She feels she has had a better life than her parents'. Her parents were Catholic and so is she, although she doesn't attend church all the time.

Paloma lives in Madrid, but has done a lot of travelling. When I ask if she would move to another country, at first she says, "Maybe to the U.S., as it is an easy country." But then she says, "Or somewhere in South America. But I love Spain."

Despite her busy schedule, she says she loves skiing, reading, and travel. She describes herself by saying, "I am comfortable with people, friendly, active, like to be a leader, am reserved about myself, and am a worker woman." I take her Spanglish "worker woman" to mean "hard worker", which has described almost everyone I have interviewed so far. Her answer to the last question surprises me. "Are you happy?" I ask.

"More or less," she answers. She seems much "more" than "less" to me.

She is your mirror, shining back at you with a world of possibilities. She is your witness, who sees you at your worst and best, and loves you anyway. She is your partner in crime, your midnight companion, someone who knows when you are smiling, even in the dark. She is your teacher, your defense attorney, your personal press agent, even your shrink.

—Barbara Alpert

Chapter 20

At Home with My Sister

After my week in Valdlavilla, I had planned to go to Germany, Switzerland, and Iceland, before going home for three weeks and then continuing on to Asia. As I sat in my hotel in Madrid, I decided that after a week of fretting about my sister I should go home sooner, so I could have time to visit with her before I left again. I e-mailed my friends in Germany and Switzerland and told them I wasn't coming. I still planned my final week in Iceland, but would then be home for five weeks instead of three.

Just as I was trying to change my flights to Iceland, the e-mail lit up. It was from my niece, telling me, "Lynda has had another heart attack and is on the plane back to the Vancouver hospital again." When I called, that was all the news she had. I was devastated, and immediately changed my flights to fly to London the next day and back to Canada the day after.

That was the longest flight I have ever been on. I couldn't focus on any of the movies, and my mind was racing too much to sleep. I was not ready to lose my sister. When I finally arrived home in Victoria, I called and found out that Lynda was out of surgery, but had not yet regained consciousness, and that she almost did not make it out of surgery because she had a torn ventricle. She also had a clogged artery, but the danger was from the torn ventricle. However, she did come through the surgery. Her son Grant said she wouldn't be waking up that night, and told me to get a good night's sleep and come in the morning. (I live in Victoria and she was in Vancouver, which is a ferry ride away.)

The next day, my friend Gail and I caught an early ferry and arrived to find Lynda, still unconscious, with a breathing tube sticking out of her mouth, hooked up to a dialysis machine and another twelve different lines of tubes. She had a rash from some of the tape holding the lines on, and her face, hands, arms, ankles, and feet were swollen. Most of her toes were black. I felt sick just looking at her. What a shock! I couldn't believe she looked so bad. The good news was a scan of her head showed her head wound was a non-issue.

We just sat with her and talked to her. I have watched so many movies where people sit beside someone in a coma and talk to them. Now it was me, doing just that. I kept looking at her and wondering when she would wake up, how she would feel, how she would heal, and whether she would become a "cardiac cripple", a term I had never even heard before that week. I also wondered how much pain she would be in from all the punctures and rashes and tubes and those poor black toes.

Gail and I tried to bring a little laughter into the ICU, and after visiting twice a day for four days we were soon called the giggle sisters. Not everyone enjoyed our humour. An ultrasound tech came in to do a liver check. We had just arrived for a visit, so the nurse asked the tech how long she would be. She said, "It depends on the patient." As Lynda was still unconscious I said, "She won't be putting up much of a fight." All the nurses laughed, but the tech didn't.

By day four, Lynda started squeezing our hands, by day five she opened her eyes, and by day six she showed shock and laughter on her face when I told her, "One of the doctors thought you were my mom." She still had the breathing tube in, so she couldn't speak, but from that look on her face, I knew she was going to be fine. The mother/daughter thing has been a joke with us for years, as she has chosen to let her hair go grey and I haven't.

To make the rest of it a short story, she got better and better every day. She spent almost a month in the hospital, but has now recovered fully. It was a tough first week, but she is healthier now than she has ever been. Her toes took the longest to recover. The doctors had told us she might lose a few, but all are completely healed. I would like to think the foot rubs we gave her twice daily helped them along. She doesn't remember much from the first three weeks, but she does remember the foot rubs.

I am not religious and have been uncertain about God since I lost my daughter, but our mother was very faithful and I always think of her as being "up there" with Him. I think she was as close to a saint as possible, so I "talked" to Mom many times and asked her to help out. I don't know what I would have done if I had lost them both in one year!

Lynda's husband Jim and I took turns in Vancouver with her at the hospital after that first week. Then I went to Vernon for a week after she was discharged. I still found time to organize my next three months in Asia and arrange for visas to China and India. I even managed to get in some visiting with friends. It was a rough six weeks, but I am so glad I was able to be there for my sister. I was also selfishly glad she was doing so well that I could continue my journey. Asia was next!

To my mind, the greatest reward and luxury of travel is to be able to experience everyday things as if for the first time, to be in a position in which almost nothing is so familiar it is taken for granted.

—Bill Bryson

Chapter 21

Thailand

"I have to tell you, Laura, I have been talking about you with all my fellow travellers. I've been telling them about my friend who is going to be in for a big surprise when she realizes the kind of tour we are taking. We'll be staying in lower-budget hotels than you are used to, and I hope you know Asia is not like Hawaii."

Laura and I met when we were thirteen. Now she is married and has three great sons. Although we have both been busy with our own lives, we have always managed to get together once in awhile and have stayed friends all these years. She has been there for me during some very pivotal moments in my life. She was my maid of honour, even though she correctly assumed I was making a mistake —the marriage lasted only five years. Twice, she has been given some reprehensible news about men in my life and has had the unenviable task of breaking that news to me. She was also with us in the hospital at the very moment my daughter passed away in my arms.

Laura and her husband had recently been planning a twenty-fifth anniversary trip to Southeast Asia, but in the end they made other plans. So when she heard about my trip, she asked if she could join me. I was a little surprised she wanted to go to Asia, as most of her holidays have been to Hawaii and on cruises, so I really didn't think she would be into a trip consisting of travel every few days and staying in low-budget hotels. This is a woman whose house is impeccable at all times, who dresses well and always looks put together. I didn't think she knew what she was getting into, but I was happy to have her join me. She has been there for some really bad parts of my life, so I wanted her to share one of the best parts.

"I really had some good laughs at your expense," I told Laura, as we got on our first of several planes to Thailand. She informed me that she was totally prepared, had read all the paperwork from the tour company, and was fully informed. I have to admit, her luggage was smaller than mine and she didn't pack her blow-dryer or flat iron. She also knew more about what we were going to do on our four-week tour than I did. Day one of our trip and she had already surprised me.

Victoria to Vancouver to Hong Kong to Bangkok took over sixteen hours of flying and many more hours of waiting. We had a few hours in the Hong Kong airport, but the shopping available was way beyond our budgets. On the first day of the trip we just couldn't see purchasing any Prada or Versace.

Arriving in Bangkok in the middle of the night should have found us exhausted, but we still had some energy left. Thank goodness, because we were in the customs line for over two hours. One of my travel rules is to always know the exchange rate before I get to a bank machine. However, I don't always follow my own rules, and when we were finally out of the customs line I went to get some Thai bhat, and realized I didn't have a clue of the rate. I had to guess and took out five hundred bhat. That turned out to be only fifteen dollars. But that was more than enough for the forty-five-minute cab ride to our hotel, which was only twelve dollars. We also learned another valuable travel rule to add to my list. Although we had the name of the hotel written down, it was in English and not in Thai. Their alphabet is completely different from ours; the letters don't look anything like ours and the driver could not read the name. We had to stop and ask directions twice before he found our hotel, on the outskirts of Chinatown. From then on, we needed to get things written down in the local language.

Here I was, with a great friend, on a new continent. What fun! "Let's get massages before we head out," I said to Laura, once we crawled out of bed after our first night in Bangkok. The hotel advertised a two-hour massage in your own room for only eighteen dollars. This was an offer we could not resist after all the hours of travelling. It seemed the only thing to do.

Within minutes of our call, two tiny young Thai women and an older woman arrived at our door. The older woman asked for our money in advance and left. I felt like I was paying a pimp. The two girls came in and started pointing at Laura, who was wearing a skort (a skirt with shorts underneath). We kept asking if we were supposed to take our clothes off and acted out taking them off. They kept shaking their heads no and pointing at Laura. Finally, one of the girls went up to Laura, lifted her skirt, and showed her approval that there were shorts underneath. We realized they want us fully clothed. So down on the beds we went, and had what I like to call a "full-body contact massage". All we could do was laugh when we weren't grunting from being stretched beyond where I ever thought possible. The girls crawled all over us, twisting us into some very strange contortions. The funniest moment was when I was lying on my stomach and the girl was kneeling on my butt and shaking her knees. (Just picture it.)

We were stretched and ready, and big, overwhelming Bangkok was out there waiting for us. With a few suggestions from the tour desk we decided to start with Chinatown and Little India. Both were within walking distance, which was good because the traffic was unbelievable. The problem is not crazy drivers or fast drivers, but there are curb-to-curb cars with everyone going nowhere fast. There are said to be twenty million registered motorized vehicles in Thailand and 80 percent of them are motorcycles. The motorcycles and *tuk-tuks* (auto rickshaws) weave their way in and around the traffic, but the driver of a car, bus, or truck must be very, very patient. What surprised me, though, was that despite the gridlock, there was not that much horn honking. Perhaps it's the Buddhist faith that keeps everyone calm.

In Chinatown we squeezed and weaved our way through the hundreds of alleys of clothes, shoes, knickknacks, fabrics, sewing accessories, jewellery, exotic spices and remedies, toys, and rows of intriguing foods, from unknown meats to nuts and everything in between. Just trying to identify some of the food was a challenge, and we were still wary of trying anything unknown, so we just took in the aromas and sights. The alleys were jammed with people, so, like the cars, everyone had to go slow.

Starting out as a big, foreboding city to us, Bangkok became a bit easier to negotiate once we became comfortable using the taxis, buses, and tuk-tuks. Surprisingly, many signs were in English, and once we worked out where we wanted to go, it was cheap and easy to get around. Tuk-tuks can be fun, but negotiating the price is not always easy. We had to be really careful, because the drivers would offer rides almost free as long as they could drop us at a "few" shops first. After stopping at a tailor's and a jewellery store, I had to yell at one driver to take us where we wanted to go. I hated doing this because they don't like to "lose face" in front of their peers, but he just kept saying, "One more, one more." I felt bad after I did it, but he finally took to our destination. Later we realized—rather sheepishly, when we worked out the exchange rate—that it only cost about one dollar and fifty cents, and we were trying to get it cheaper.

From the culture and craziness of Chinatown we caught the local bus to a very modern mall that could have been anywhere in the world. Every brand-name store could be found inside. We really wimped out and ate in the comfort of this mall, but at least we ordered Thai food. It was tasty and cheap—my budget loved this country.

Being in the modern mall, we almost forgot where we were until we walked out, and directly across the street we came upon Thais and tourists placing their offerings of incense, candles, flowered garlands, and rice at the Erawan Shrine. Seated inside a shrine gilded with beautiful coloured tiles was a gold statue of the four-headed, eight-armed Hindu god Brahma. Those giving offerings make a wish and if it comes true, come back and give a further offering. I realized I have much to learn because from what I knew, Thais are Buddhists and Brahma is a Hindu god. The obvious mixing of the cultures, I was sure, was only the first of many lessons I was about to learn. We saw smaller "spirit houses" or shrines in front of almost every building in Thailand, surrounded by fresh incense, flowers, and rice. We even found a cat cuddled up on one, but I don't think he was an offering; rather, just a feline seeking a good place to rest.

Bangkok was overwhelming at first, but it didn't take long before we really enjoyed all it had to offer. The Royal Palace and temple of Wat Pho, one of over twenty-five thousand temples in Thailand, are spectacular. We found the biggest reclining Buddha at one and the biggest emerald Buddha at the other. The intricate, colourful gilded decorations on the stupas, pagodas, and temples are remarkable. And colour fills the streets of the city, with most taxis brightly painted in pink or purple or green or blue, and many of the big trucks are decorated in very bright, colourful designs.

We saw the city from a different vantage point by taking a Khlong tour. A long-tailed speedboat took us down the Chao Phraya River and *khlongs* (canals) of Thonburi. We drifted past temples, houses on stilts, kids swimming off the porches, people washing their dishes and bathing, and, of course, several statues of Buddha. We even fed the catfish that stay near the temples, where they are not allowed to be caught.

Another day Laura and I took a tour to a floating market about an hour and a half out of Bangkok. There were so many tourist boats crowding the canals that we literally had to pull our boat, using the vendors' stalls, to manoeuvre any distance. Also crowding the canal were the vendors' stalls lining both sides, as well as boats loaded with wares. Some boats even carried coal stoves for preparing food. Bargaining was hilarious, because vendors went from asking eight hundred baht for something to easily settling for fifty. I imagine that years ago this was probably just a local market, but now it is full of tourists and touristy junk, along with locals trying to wind their way through to buy their fruits and vegetables. This is where I struggle as a tourist who wants to see more than just monuments and museums. Opening local villages and traditional ways of life to tourists ultimately changes the very traditions you want to experience. Tourism is a great way to make money, but then I wonder, at what cost to their heritage? Selfishly, I decided to see as much as they had to offer and hoped that a fine balance between maintaining their way of life and showing it to the world could be found. I hoped that my tourist dollars would help them with enhancing their lives in a positive way.

Included in the tour to the floating market was a stop at an elephant park. The offer to ride elephants seemed exciting, but we could see that the area wasn't very exotic. However, it was inexpensive, so we joined the group. The platform-saddle tied to the elephant wasn't the most comfortable seat, but we had fun being jostled along the path, even when the elephant walked into a deep swamp and our feet were hovering just above the waterline. We were sure the elephants wanted to dump us in the murky water. It was good for some comical pictures and a few laughs.

After a few days on our own we joined an Intrepid tour for the rest of our trip. Intrepid is an Australian company that advertises local guides, taking passengers to places regular tourists don't go, having small group sizes (usually twelve), and following guidelines for "responsible tourism". They also try to support local business as much as possible and teach local customs.

Our tour had ten passengers and our twenty-two-year-old tour leader, Daisy, from Australia. Although she was young and not local, as advertised, she was well organized and very knowledgeable about the area. She had been in Asia for several years. It was a fun group, but did not include Mr. Right; only three guys, with two already taken and one aged twenty-four. He was a great young man, but that is a little too young! My friends would have to wait for any romance news.

Daisy informed us of some of the customs and gave us some helpful hints:

1. Cover your shoulders and knees, especially in temples, shrines, and palaces.

2. Take shoes off in temples and most homes.

3. Women should not touch monks. "Try not to look them in the eye," Daisy said. And if you are on a bus or train do not sit next to them.

4. Don't touch anyone on the top of the head, even children—no matter how cute they are. Buddhists believe the head is the holiest part of the body.

5. The feet are the lowliest part of the body. Do not point with your feet and don't point the bottom of your feet at anyone or any religious statues.

6. Try to make yourself lower than a monk. If you are near one, duck down. (This can look very silly.)

7. Shaking hands is not done often, but if you do, only use your right hand. Also, only touch food with your right hand. This one is very important. (The left hand is reserved for other functions, including all things toilet related.)

8. Don't give beggars, including children, anything. This is a hard one for me, but I understand that it only encourages the behaviour.

9. Learn some of the language.

10. Try not to yell or embarrass the locals. They do not like to "lose face". (Whoops! Already broke that one!)

Our first group adventure was to Khao San Road, a backpacker's and budget traveller's mecca. This one-kilometre road is lined with budget hotels, Internet cafes, restaurants, travel agents, bars, bookshops, tailors, massage parlours, neon lights, and a night market that fills the street. In a word, wild. We ate, drank cheap beer, shopped, and fed our new addiction for massages. They were even cheaper than at the hotel: four dollars and fifty cents an hour.

On our plane trip to Bangkok, Laura had said, "If it looks like I'm going to buy something that I won't wear at home, stop me." I agreed, so when she tried on harem pants at Khao San Road, I reminded her of our conversation. She bought them anyway, and when she showed Ian, our twenty-four-year-old British tour mate (the same age as one of her sons), he said, "I will laugh in absence of your sons." She realized her folly, and we had a good laugh.

From Bangkok we travelled thirteen hours north to Chiang Mai, on an overnight train. We had fun visiting and getting to know the group a little better, but my opinion of overnight transportation has not changed. We were all exhausted when we arrived. Too many stops and too much noise meant no one slept well.

I was disappointed to discover, upon arriving, that we really had only one day to see the area. (I should have read the itinerary.) With no time to spare, we deposited our bags at the hotel and departed for an elephant trek within minutes of arriving in Chiang Mai. I was captivated on the drive to the elephant park through countryside of terraced rice paddies and beautiful rolling hills. The elephant trek was another hilarious event. We bought bananas to feed the elephants, but when we ran out they started shoving their trunks into the backs and necks of the people on the elephant in front of us, to find more. I was surprised the squealing from those accosted didn't scare the poor elephants.

On the way back into Chiang Mai, while most of the group had lunch, three of us went rafting. We floated on bamboo rafts down a calm river, enjoying the wilderness while passing small villages, kids swimming, and a group of elephants that crossed our path. We were the only raft on the river. It was fantastic.

I had hoped to get to see one of the Long Necked Hill Tribe that day, but it wasn't on the agenda, which is one of the downfalls of a group tour. There often is not enough time to do things that aren't in the plan. Daisy also discouraged us from finding our own way, because she felt that the nearby tribe was becoming much too dependent on the tourist dollar and was losing their culture.

We did have time to visit the Dol Suthep Temple high on a hill above Chiang Mai. The orange-clad monks of the monastery have an evening ritual we took part in. They led us in a procession around the grounds and into the temple. We knelt, as they did, while they began chanting in front of a huge gold Buddha that was surrounded by many smaller gold Buddhas. We joined them for awhile, but our knees gave out long before theirs did.

We took part in another tradition where we were given a narrow bamboo container full of numbered sticks. We had to shake the container, trying to have only one stick fall out. It took a few tries. The number on the stick had a corresponding fortune card. Mine read: "You will have good prosperity and your love life is looking up." That was great news. Laura's read: "You will have medium luck." We decided that was better than bad luck.

We arrived back in town in time for the night market in Chiang Mai, where we spent hours trying to decide what we could carry, what we might find somewhere else, and what we just couldn't live without. Of course we found many things: jewellery, bamboo, and rice paper lanterns, to name a few.

We ate at our first street stall that night. Daisy told us there shouldn't be any food safety issues, so we ordered a soup called kao soy with yellow wheat noodles in a curry broth. We had no idea what else was in it, nor could we guess, but we loved the spicy dish. When we were finishing, however, Laura spotted the "cleaning up area": a few plastic basins of dirty water, with no soap and lots of filthy dishes. We just had to hope the water had been cleaner when they washed the dishes we ate off of.

On our way back to the hotel, we stopped for a leg massage, even though we had already had a massage between rafting and the temple. Did I mention we were addicted to the massages?

While we found our accommodations in Bangkok good, the hotel room in Chaing Mai was minimal and the beds were hard. We were happy that both rooms had proper toilets. Although most stops outside hotels were squat toilets, Laura never once complained. And thankfully, our street food sat well in our tummies and we had no need to spend hours on a toilet, as we had feared.

Dogs and cats run freely throughout Thailand, as much in the city as the country. The odd thing was that most of the cats had crooked tails. The tale we were told was that Buddhists believe, "If something is perfect it will reach Nirvana. Since cats are perfect, their tails are broken so they don't take up space in Nirvana." The truth is more logical, of course, and it is that the strange tail is a genetic trait.

Laura and I enjoyed the food, as it was not only delicious but inexpensive. We also appreciated the hospitality of the warm Thai people, who constantly greeted us with, "*Sawatdee Kaa*" (hello), hands pressed together in a prayer-like fashion and a slight bow of their head.

We had a small view of Thailand, leaving so much to see another time. The southern beaches and islands are a completely different kind of trip, and I planned to see at least one at the end of our tour after Laura left. I also arranged to interview a woman who worked at the hotel in Bangkok at the end of the tour.

And so, with all that set up, we were off to Laos.

Chapter 22

Lao People's Democratic Republic

"My twenty-fifth country. I am halfway through!" I announced, as we boarded a long boat to cross the Mekong River into Lao People's Democratic Republic, better known as Laos. We had just spent seven hours travelling from Chiang Mai to the Thailand/Laos border at Chiang Khong. The boat trip across the Mekong to Huey Xai, in Laos, took only a few minutes. Once in Laos we filled out the paperwork, paid forty-two dollars to get our visa, and walked into my twenty-fifth country.

I reflected on how lucky I had been up to this point. I had completed half my dream journey and everything had gone almost perfectly. I had been so fortunate to have such good friends join me, and Laura and I were having a fantastic time together. The sounds of laughter from our room every night had our tour mates wondering what we were up to. Our mantra was T.I.A. (This Is Asia) and our motto, "Every day is a glass-half-full day." When the beds were too hard, the bugs too plentiful, the food service too slow, or the weather too hot or too rainy, we would find the humour in the situation and laugh through it.

Laos is just slightly less than half the size of Thailand, but has only six million people, compared to Thailand's sixty-five million, which would explain why we found everything slower and quieter. As we had been driving on the left side of the road in Thailand, we were happy to see that we were back on the right side in Laos. It just makes for fewer mistakes when crossing the road.

Most prices were even cheaper than in Thailand, which was hard to believe, considering we found Thailand so inexpensive. The fun part about the money was that we became millionaires in Laos. The currency is the Laotian kip and 8,500 kip is one dollar. That made two hundred dollars about 1.7 million kip. Our millions went a long way, as most meals were two or three dollars.

We spent the first few days cruising down the Mekong River, and the nights in villages on the banks of the river. Huey Xai and Pakbeng reminded me of Old West towns, with unpainted wooden buildings lining the dirt roads, but that's where the similarities ended. In front of every home was a little store or restaurant. Most people were cooking their meals outside as well. Many doors were open and we could see how stark the insides of the homes were, with bedding on the floor and very little furniture, although many had TVs and huge satellite dishes. There were few cars, but many bicycles and motorcycles darted everywhere to avoid all the cats, dogs, chickens, and kids running around in the streets. In Pakbeng we left the market a little squeamish after seeing some of the meat that was for sale. We hoped the rat and squirrel we saw at one stall did not end up on our plates at the next restaurant.

We enjoyed a peaceful two days slowly floating down the river, passing villages, beautiful green tropical jungle mountain ranges, fields of sticky rice, and sandy shorelines covered with peanut plants. Conical hats topped most of the farmers working in the fields, making for some of our favourite photos. We spotted cows, water buffalo, and elephants. The river was an uninviting dirty brown, but many people were fishing, washing laundry, and swimming. We learned that sticky rice is a different plant than regular rice and peanuts are planted in the sand banks.

Although our itinerary said we would stop at an authentic Laotian village, Daisy tried to talk us out of it. She explained that on her last trip the villagers appeared to have abandoned their culture and way of life to accommodate the tourists. As we hoped to experience the way of life, as much as see the countryside, we asked our boat captain if he knew of a village that didn't mind visitors, but was still living an authentic Laotian lifestyle. He said he had the perfect place, and pulled up to a tiny isolated village not long after we asked.

We were greeted by a group of ragged but beautiful, excited children, who grabbed our hands and brought us into their little village of rickety bamboo houses, built high off the ground on stilts. Dogs, pigs, and ducks outnumbered the villagers. The men were working in the fields, and the women were busy weaving on looms, placed in the shade under their raised houses. The women seemed shy, but they were happy to show off their delicate woven fabric and pleased when we each bought a piece. We played with the kids and one of our tour mates thrilled them with his magic tricks. We left feeling we had not disturbed their lifestyle, perhaps helped a little with our purchases, and enjoyed spending time amongst the villagers.

Further down the river, we stopped at a Buddhist sanctuary to visit two sacred caves high in the cliffs, filled with four thousand statues of Buddha. So ended our fantastic two-day introduction to the Laotian people and their serene river.

Our river journey ended in Luang Prabang, a city located in north central Laos, where the Nam Khan River meets the Mekong River. The city is another UNESCO World Heritage Site. There are no billboards, no neon, no fast-food joints, and everything has been kept historical. It is a truly charming town, with a mixture of Buddhist temples and French Indochina architecture. It was definitely another "favourite" city.

We stayed in bamboo bungalows, surrounded by beautiful gardens, overlooking the river. The peaceful setting only enhanced the sound of our laughter. The bungalows were lovely, but built with little support and shook if we moved too fast or walked too heavy. Laura felt it was a perfect opportunity to teach me the art of walking softly. As I rattled the furniture, our peals of laughter echoed out to the garden.

At the Ethnology Museum we learned a little about the Laotian culture. Laos has four main ethnic groups with forty-nine registered tribes, but it is believed there may be as many as one hundred tribes. Weaving and embroidery are some of the traditional types of handiwork done by many tribes.

We heard about one tribe that matches up their young folks with future mates by dressing them in their best clothes and lining them up, with one village's boys facing a line of girls from another village. (People can't marry a fellow villager.) The boy throws a ball at the girl he wants. She goes home with him for a week, and if the parents agree on a dowry and the girl does not run away, they are married within ten days, during the Laotian New Year. The guide told a story about a friend of hers who had a more modern version, where the young man asked her to go to the market but started heading to his home instead. Unimpressed, she dropped her shoe from the motorcycle, and when he stopped for her to get it, she bolted.

My favourite story was about the colourfully decorated hats that children wear in Laos. Their hats are designed to look like flowers. Their theory was that when the spirits looked down at the children they would think they were flowers and wouldn't take them away. Most of the hill tribes believe in animism, which is the worship of the spirits of the earth, the skies, and their ancestors.

The night market was our favourite to date. The Hmong villagers start setting up in the late afternoon. Several hill tribes bring their unique and intricate handicrafts and lay them out on the street for blocks. Scarves, table runners, quilt and pillow covers, silver jewellery, embroidered clothing, pants, artwork, rice paper products, and various bamboo items fill the stalls. Thinking about how many weeks we had left and how heavy our bags were already, we planned to only buy small trinkets, but Laura could not stop herself from buying a fantastic appliquéd duvet cover for only seventeen dollars. I had to resist, having almost two months left before going home.

The day market was another story entirely. Set up mainly for the locals, we were not tempted to buy anything we found there, especially the dog and lizard meat on display.

One day while in Luang Prabang, we went on a hike that started out in a small village outside the city and took us up through fields of sticky rice, corn, hops, and pineapple; into a forest of teak, rubber, bamboo, and poinsettia trees; and finally down to a waterfall. We spent time at the school in the village, talked to the kids, took pictures with some of the local farmers, and enjoyed all the different vegetation. Even the downpour that made the trail slippery and treacherous didn't dispel our good mood. We slipped and fell and were soaked from head to toe and caked in mud by the time we reached the waterfall, but a natural shower from the falls was a perfect finish to the day.

Another morning we were up before sunrise to take part in a morning ritual. Orange-robed monks fill the street in front of the monastery, as locals and tourists fill their brass donation bowls with food. As it is encouraged that Theravada Buddhist men become monks for at least three weeks of their lives, and each family has one son who becomes a monk, it wasn't surprising that there were hundreds of monks and some were as young as six. These alms are the only food the monks have each day. The locals bring food from home, and a smart local has set up stalls to sell food to the tourists, who in turn donate it to the monks. As the monks approached we knelt down, made sure we didn't look in their eyes, and placed the food in their bowl. (Similar to Halloween, without the "trick or treat".) Most of the locals contributed sticky rice from bamboo containers. At first I thought they would hand over the whole container, but they actually would pick out a small handful and mix it amongst the other foodstuffs in the monks' bowls. Each bowl must be a heck of a mess by the time they get back to the monastery.

I spent one afternoon in Luang Prabang looking for an interviewee. I met a female journalist from Vermont who was doing a story on the fabrics of Laos for a textiles magazine and she told me of a weaving shop where I might find someone. After wandering along the frangipani-lined streets, past gleaming temples and along the river, I found the shop, but not a woman to interview. One of the clerks thought I might have better luck at a weaving centre just outside of town. I took a tuk-tuk, as it was a little far to walk in the afternoon heat. There were many women there, but no one in the right age category. It was a shame that I didn't get an interview, but

I enjoyed my wander through town, learning more about weaving, and my tuk-tuk ride was fun. The driver kept picking up other people, squeezing them into the little cab, and then dropping them off without having them pay. I didn't mind at all; in fact, I enjoyed getting to meet more locals.

Although we had our lovely bungalows to relax in, we didn't spend much time in them. Besides the markets, the hiking, the temples, and the monks, we fed our massage addiction, went bowling, and even visited the local nightclub.

Next up was Vientiane, the capital of Laos, a city of close to two hundred thousand. Despite being the biggest city in Laos, it is a quiet town that reflects the "simple life" we had seen elsewhere. Many rustic temples line the riverbank and crumbling colonial mansions dot the wide boulevards.

Most of the businesses lining the streets are small family-run cafes and shops, with business taking place in the front and the family home in the back. At one restaurant we dined two metres away from the family living room, complete with the family photos on the wall.

Another feature in the city was the "Vertical Runway". This arch, probably the tallest structure in the city, looks similar to the Arc de Triomphe and was built between 1957 and 1968 with cement donated by the Americans to build an airport. The Patuxai Victory Gate was built as a memorial to Laotian soldiers who died in the wars and during the attempts to gain independence from France.

Our favourite part of the city, however, was the spa not far from our hotel. We couldn't resist the unbelievably cheap prices. A manicure, pedicure, and ninety-minute herbal massage was only thirty dollars. I wondered how I would ever be able to go back to real prices when I got home.

Laura had adapted well to everything and never complained about any discomforts, but as we headed towards our next stop, a home stay in the village of Ban Tabak, I was a bit worried we might be stepping way beyond our Western comfort zone. Daisy gave us fair warning of our first major culture shock. At a Hmong tribe market she told us not to take pictures or look too closely at the meat counters. Although illegal, it is common to find monkey, lizard, and other wild animals for sale. We averted our eyes, afraid of what body parts we might see.

The village of Ban Tabak has one hundred seventy houses and about two thousand people. Its proximity to a river gave us the opportunity to go for a sunset boat ride in one of the boats made, incredibly, from the fuel casings of B52 bombers left over from the Vietnam War. The village was very near the Ho Chi Minh Trail, and we learned that during the war, Laos was bombed the equivalent of one bomb every eight minutes for nine years. We were told that, per capita, Laos is the most bombed country in world history. I had no idea. Land mines remain to this day and people are still being killed by stumbling across them. We certainly didn't plan any uncharted hikes in that area. The boat ride along the river surrounded by stunning mountains was lovely, with the pinkish sky reflecting on the water, but as we had just learned all the startling statistics, my mind was a jumble of emotions.

After the boat trip we wandered through the village and found teen boys playing a variation of volleyball. The bamboo ball was transferred over the net with their head or feet only. Many kids joined our walk and followed us throughout the village. We watched very young girls packing heavy water containers, selling veggies, and cleaning up, while the boys were just playing together. Each home had a little garden and a tiny house for storing rice, and was surrounded by a bamboo fence. Chickens, roosters, and turkeys scurried everywhere. We wondered how they knew which animal belonged to which villager.

All the homes were built on stilts, which is a tribal tradition. Our home for the night was one of only a few wooden houses; the others were bamboo. Our family gave up their room for us, setting mats on the floor, covered with mosquito nets slung from the ceiling. There was a spirit house in the room and we had to make sure we did not point our feet in its direction. They had built a Western toilet for the tour groups, which was great, so we didn't have to squat, but it was out the door and around the back of the house, so it made for a long walk in the middle of the night.

We bought gifts at the market for our host family, including hair and nail accessories for the girls. While the parents were preparing dinner, we spent a few hours playing with girls and doing their hair. The girls painted our nails, as it turned out they didn't want coloured polish on their nails. In retrospect, it was probably a silly choice on our part, but they seemed to have fun playing our manicurists.

The family and our driver, Mr. Ghe, cooked our meal on the fire pit in the floor of the main part of the house, which was a large room used for cooking, eating, and living. They prepared a great feast of sticky rice and curried chicken with potatoes and carrots. It was tasty and, lucky for us, not too spicy. Mr. Ghe told us that sticky rice is the staple food here, eaten at every meal. Sometimes it is the whole meal.

Although they had electricity, they only had one bare light bulb in each room, so we were under our nets and to bed as darkness set in. Our sleep was shattered by a loud crash in the middle of the night. Most of us just went back to sleep, and only learned the source of the noise in the morning. However, Ulysses, our Swiss friend, was sleeping near the spirit house and knew what happened as it was happening. A rat, stealing the rice offerings, knocked the plate of rice onto the floor and then continued to scoot about, pushing the plate around, close to Ulysses' head. The kids caught the rat in the morning and had fun showing it off to us, the squeamish tourists. Laura and I were so happy we hadn't picked the mats by the spirit house.

As we were leaving the village, I couldn't help thinking about all the little girls we saw working so hard, and felt this was a good place to leave some of the money I'd raised. Mr. Ghe promised he would make sure my donation went to the school in the village, where girls are now attending. I have heard that in the cities equality for women is on its way, but in the countryside they have a long way to go.

The Laotians have endured many hardships over the last fifty years —civil war, the Vietnam War, Communism, and twenty years of U.S. embargoes—and still have managed to be warm, easygoing, happy people. Family and neighbours provide support for each other, proven clearly by the fact that we encountered very few beggars, despite Laos being one of the poorest countries in the world. We were humbled by their spirit and love of life, and really enjoyed our stay in this country.

Mr. Ghe had taken the time, while we were on our boat ride, to go around the village looking for a woman for me to interview. He found Chan, who joined the family for dinner, and after we finished, Mr. Ghe was happy to translate.

~

Chan – 50

Chan sits quietly on the floor, waiting for the interview to begin. She is dressed in a traditional skirt, with an elaborately embroidered band along the hem, and a light blue polo shirt, a mixture of traditional and modern, which to me defines Laos as well. Her jet-black hair is pulled back tightly in a bun, making it easy to see her face and watch it light up every time she shyly smiles. Mr. Ghe has taken this assignment seriously and found a woman who is exactly fifty.

We all sit down on the floor in the main room and Grandma, of our host family, sits down with us. She wants to be in on this and that is fine with me. Mr. Ghe asks Chan to tell us about herself. She says she was married at nineteen and had eight children. Even though I don't understand her language, I know she is telling a sad story, and when Mr. Ghe translates we are all teary-eyed. She lost two children during childbirth, another child died at fourteen from an unknown illness, and yet another died at sixteen in a car accident. She is clearly devastated while sharing this part of her life, and I ask Mr. Ghe to explain that I feel her pain, as I lost a child too. She and I have a hug and shed a few more tears as we share our mutual sorrow. We go on to talk about her family and the sadness continues. She says, "My mother died from an illness that caused swelling, when I was twelve. My father, who is seventy-three, or maybe older, remarried a much younger woman."

We manage to compose ourselves and go on with the interview. Chan was born in a village about ten kilometres away from the village we are in now. She explains that she moved here when she got married and has only travelled about forty kilometres from here in her entire life. I ask if she would like to travel or live somewhere else and she says, "No, I don't want to move. But I couldn't, because only rich people live in the cities and I am not rich." I realize she only thought as far as the city, the idea of another country didn't even enter her mind.

As we start talking about her wedding her mood changes to one of delight. She is smiling as she tells me about one of the wedding day traditions. After the ceremony, every guest ties white strings around the wrists of the bride and groom as a symbol of good luck and gives them a blessing. Then there is a party. Chan says it was a perfect day.

She proudly tells me that although her parents did not attend school, and she attended only long enough to learn to read and write, her boys have been to college and her girls went until they were fourteen. I ask her why the girls didn't go any further and she says, "They needed to help around the house."

I ask Chan to describe her typical day, and she says, "I am up at four a.m. in the summers and six a.m. in the winters. It gets cold in the winters. Sometimes the temperature drops to five degrees [Celsius]. I make the fire and prepare the sticky rice for the day. Then I look after the pig, the chicken, and the duck. Some days I do laundry, which is easier now that we have running water, because a few years ago I had to carry it down to the river. I clean the house and then take the sticky rice to the field for lunch, for my husband. After we eat lunch I work in the rice field, and then I work in my kitchen garden, where I grow vegetables for my family. I sell anything we don't need. I make dinner at around seven p.m. and we are in bed between eight and nine. We have had electricity for five years now and we have a television, but I don't watch it often. There is only one station with my language and one with another language, but I don't know what language it is. I don't like Western language."

Chan's childhood and teen years were during the Vietnam War, so I ask her what that time was like for her. She says, "I don't remember anything about it." This is when Grandma pipes up. She says she can tell me what it was like, and tells her story. "There was constant bombing. I lived in this village, and to avoid the bombings we had to spend the days in the woods, sometimes hiding in holes we dug in the ground. At night we would come out, but couldn't use lights or wear anything white. We *raised silkworms, harvested the cocoons, dyed and spun the threads, weaved it into fabrics and made clothes." As she finishes the story, she proudly shows us a skirt with a traditional patterned woven band and a vibrant blue blouse she has kept all these years. I tell her that it is hard for me to understand how she lived through all she did and created such beautiful garments. Chan does not add to the conversation.*

We get back to the interview, and as delicately as I can I explain menopause to Mr. Ghe. I don't really know if he understands, but he says, "She said she had no menopausal symptoms, but she has a bad back, and although she used to love to weave and embroider, her eyes are not as good as they used to be." I have no doubt her back is sore from all the bending she does in the fields, over the fire cooking, and over the laundry.

After hearing Grandma's story I am still curious about Chan's childhood, wondering what she must have lived through, but I don't push. While still remembering all she has endured with her children, I ask the final question, "Are you happy?" I am a little surprised when she smiles and says, "I am very happy." Does she not want to lose face by admitting to sadness, or does her Buddhist faith help her maintain such happiness?

I really enjoyed our visit. Chan was a lovely woman, and Grandma was a welcome addition who helped me learn a little more about their lives. Mr. Ghe told me later that he really enjoyed it too, because he learned more about these women than he knew before.

Perhaps travel cannot prevent bigotry, but by demonstrating that all peoples cry, laugh, eat, worry, and die, it can introduce the idea that if we try and understand each other, we may even become friends.

—Maya Angelou

Chapter 23

Vietnam

Wet. Chaos. Synchronized confusion. Ramshackle. Retrospective. Breathtaking. Loud. Delicious. Fun! These are the words my group came up with when I asked them to describe Vietnam. The contrast from quiet, peaceful Laos was astounding.

Wet: We arrived in Hanoi in a monsoon of historic proportions, the worst flooding in over twenty years. Our bus literally "inched" its way into the city, as many streets were under more than a foot of water.

When we finally arrived at our hotel, we threw our bags into the room, put on our ponchos, and headed out into the rain. As we only had a few days to see the city, we weren't going to let knee-deep water stop us.

Hanoi is famous for French-style cafes, tree-lined boulevards, and inner-city lakes, but it was hard for us to appreciate any beauty as we waded through the streets. The crazy thing was that the rain did not stop the steady traffic flow. The streets were packed with bicycles, motorcycles, and cars sloshing through the floodwaters. Within minutes we were completely drenched. We quickly found a place for lunch, and from our dry perch in the cafe watched kids scooping up fish in buckets in the middle of the road.

In the evening we added to my "stupid mistakes" list. Our decision to attend, ironically, a water puppet performance in a theatre downtown may just be at the top of that list. Not only were the streets still flooded, but it was dark when we headed out. We walked for blocks looking for cabs. We tripped and slipped and chased our flip-flops as they floated down the street. Eventually we found cabs, but not before we were soaked to the skin, again.

The art of water puppetry was started over one thousand years ago, originally performed in flooded rice paddies. (While we were there it could have been done in the flooded streets of the city.) The lacquered wood puppets are controlled on a long rod, by the puppeteers standing knee-deep in water behind a screen. The puppeteers manoeuvre the figurines to dance, swim, row boats, and walk on water. I am sure if I had not been wet and cold I might have enjoyed the performance, but instead I really just wanted it to end so I could return to the hotel and warm up.

It was the next morning when the waters had receded that we realized how stupid we really had been. When we saw the debris left over on the streets we were horrified. Drenched and rotting garbage was strewn everywhere, and the roads and sidewalks were uneven, broken, and full of holes. The fact that no one fell or broke an ankle on our outings was a miracle. Our luck ended there, however, because our tour leader, Daisy, ended up with an extremely bad infection on her foot where she already had an open cut. She was in and out of clinics and the hospital in Ho Chi Minh City, and the doctors diagnosed her with "dry gangrene". She was on oral antibiotics, then intravenous antibiotics, and was eventually admitted to the hospital.

The floodwaters rose and then receded every day, and through it all we explored the bustling city of Hanoi as best we could. We spent hours wandering the Old Quarter, where the streets are crowded with narrow shops full of artisan works, fabrics, shoes, clothing, and a vast variety of trinkets, as well as modern cafes right beside ancient temples and pagodas. Unfortunately, many shopkeepers were sweeping out the mud left behind from the flooding.

We had another wet day in Hue, which was the capital of Vietnam until 1945. Daisy convinced us it was safe to climb on the back of motorcycles and take a tour of the city. I was reluctant at first, having seen the crazy drivers, but once we took off I realized our drivers really knew what they were doing, and I enjoyed every minute of it—until the rain started! We were immediately soaked, again. Fortunately, we were close to our lunch spot, which was a tranquil monastery, where we had a chance to dry off and enjoy a delicious vegetarian meal.

As Hue was an imperial city in the Nguyen dynasty, there are many historical monuments, pagodas, temples, magnificent tombs of several emperors, and a citadel, enclosing the Purple Forbidden City. It is another UNESCO World Heritage Site, and many of the buildings are being restored to their former glory after being damaged during the war. It was an enjoyable day, despite the rain.

Retrospective: Most of our group were too young to remember the Vietnam War—or the American War, as they call it in Vietnam —but there were a few of us who did remember watching the news in 1975 and seeing the North Vietnamese tanks crash through the fence of the Independence Palace in Saigon, ending the war. Now called the Reunification Palace, it is open as a museum. That very tank sits on the grounds just inside the gate, and the interior looks like it did in the '60s, right down to the coloured rotary dial phones.

Saigon, which is now Ho Chi Minh City, is a mixed bag of old and new, with a blend of the many cultures that make up its past. We visited the modern area of the city, with its fancy high-rises, but also found many of the ornate structures the French built while they were occupying Vietnam (1883–1956), including the Opera Hall and a cathedral that is a replica of Notre Dame Cathedral in Paris.

The War Museum was where we all lost our composure. There was not a dry eye among us, whether we remembered the war or not. The photographic exhibit of the atrocities that took place during the war years, including photos of the victims of Agent Orange and napalm, was so devastating that we were all emotionally drained.

The next day we went to the Cu Chi tunnels, which was even worse than what we had seen the previous day. During the Vietnam War, these tunnels were used as hiding spots, living quarters, communication, and supply routes for the Viet Cong as they fought the Americans and South Vietnamese. We crawled through a short portion of the tunnels, which has been carved out and made bigger for larger foreigners to explore, and experienced the claustrophobic feeling inside the labyrinth of tunnels. I stumbled right into Laura, who was crawling in front of me, as it was pitch-black. I found it unimaginable that anyone could spend even a minute down there, let alone live within its narrow walls.

Above ground, the tour guide pointed out many ingenious methods the Viet Cong devised to hide the tunnels: phoney termite mounds were built with the displaced dirt, smoke was funnelled through these mounds in the early mornings to resemble morning mist, and entrances were barely big enough to squeeze through and were covered with leaves and dirt to become impossible to detect.

Our local guide showed us the gruesome ways the Viet Cong booby-trapped the tunnels and the forest to torture and kill their enemies. I was horrified and could barely look at the spikes, trapdoors, and explosive devices. I kept thinking what a devastating place for American veterans or their family members to visit. The sound of gunfire echoing through the forest from the shooting range, where tourists could fire off assault rifles, added to the already ominous feeling we had.

I imagine that those who lived in the tunnels, or the soldiers who searched for them, would never have believed that this area would one day become a tourist attraction.

Chaos: There are over eighty million people in Vietnam and thirty million motorcycles. I think we saw each and every one of them in Hanoi and Ho Chi Minh City. The floodwaters in Hanoi did nothing to stop the steady stream of motorcycles crowding the streets, and more often than not, there were at least three people riding on each. Only recently did a helmet law come into effect, a law very few seemed to follow. The twelve-dollar fine for not wearing one hasn't appeared to convince many people. Helmets were sold on the streets for two dollars, leaving me to wonder if they would have been any real protection anyway.

Chaotic, too, were the markets, as well as being extremely crowded and claustrophobic. The aisles were so narrow there was not enough space for two people to walk beside each other. The goods were squished in, piled high, and tumbling over. The salespeople were constantly pulling at us or chasing us down if we even gave the slightest look in their direction or glanced at their products. We persevered through the chaos, however, and found some amazing deals on clothes and purses.

Synchronized Confusion: Watching all the motorcycles, bicycles, cycle-rickshaws, cars, buses, trucks, and pedestrians is like watching a choreographed dance, where everyone miraculously criss-crosses, passes, and weaves around each other in pursuit of his or her destination. We were on motorcycles and cycle-rickshaws many times, and although it was extremely scary, we always made it to our destination without hitting anything or being hit, even the day my cycle-rickshaw driver was a one-eyed seventy-year-old and Laura's driver smelled conspicuously of liquor.

"Don't run!" Daisy told us over and over when we needed to cross the busy streets. I thought she was crazy, because it seemed intuitive that the faster we got across, the better. But in fact, she was right. When we walked, the drivers had more time to judge where we were so they could avoid us. Still, it was hair-raising and frightening every time.

Loud: Everyone honks, all the time. Most are not honking at anyone in particular, they just honk, honk, honk, and honk—all the time!

Ramshackle: We drove great distances throughout Vietnam and rarely found a road that wasn't lined with houses or businesses, making it impossible to know where one town ended and the next one started. The narrow three or four-storey colonial-style houses generally had lovely, brightly painted front facades, while the side walls were bare cement. The front of most houses or businesses was a ramshackle mess of supplies or piles of clutter spilling out to the road.

Ramshackle would be a polite term for many of the "washrooms" we had the unpleasant task of using. Squatters were the norm, but some didn't even provide a hole; we just splashed onto the tile. Rolling up the pant legs was a definite must. Toilet paper was non-existent, as were water and paper towels in many places. We carried wet-wipes everywhere. Laura still "hung" in there, without complaint.

Breathtaking: Despite the chaos and craziness of Vietnam there were many fantastic natural sites. Our favourite was Halong Bay in the Sea of Tonkin, in Northeastern Vietnam, where we sailed for two days on a Vietnamese junk. Over 1,900 monolithic limestone islands jut out into the bay. A low fog hung over the bay, which only added to its mystic beauty.

We sailed through the islands, explored a cave, kayaked, and swam. It was such a welcome break from the wild cities. Floating fishing villages dotted the bay, as well as floating stores and dozens of small boats, packed to overflowing with food, drinks, and souvenirs. One boat vendor tried to sell us wine—while we were swimming.

We moored in the bay for an enjoyable evening of watching the setting sun, eating a delicious seafood dinner, and playing charades. Our only disappointment was not finding the boat lady that we heard earlier in the day, yelling out, "Oreos for sale!"

Delicious: The food was fantastic, even when we didn't know what we were eating. We ate at roadside kiosks, cafes, fancy restaurants, and restaurants run with street kids as staff. And everywhere the food was tasty and cheap. We feasted on noodles, rice, rice paper, veggies, and plenty of chicken and seafood, in soups, curries, wraps, and stir-fries, with spices I have never tasted at home. We avoided dog meat, which is on many menus—or at least we think we did.

Almost every city we visited had at least one restaurant that was a training school for street kids.

In De Nang we stopped at a restaurant training deaf street kids. It was run by an American woman who had left her home in the States to open the restaurant and take in the kids. The food was great, the service was perfect, and they even gave us a tour of their immaculate kitchen. I was touched by all the hard work and felt it was a perfect place to leave some of my fund-raising money. The owner was in tears as she waved good-bye. I felt so humbled by her compassion for the kids.

Fun: Everyone agreed the motorcycling in Hue was really fun, especially when we stopped at a small village to visit a fortune-teller. The tiny seventy-four-year-old woman dressed all in purple sat on a small covered bridge, and one by one she told us our fortunes. She had a soft voice, a heavy accent, and spoke broken English, but what I heard was, "Your first husband was not good for you, but everyone loves you and you are very happy. You are going to marry a forty-three-year-old, who may or may not be Canadian, and he is going to really love you." She got the first part right. Hopefully the rest holds true!

For Laura, we think she said, "Your oldest is going to be rich and married once. Your second son will be married twice. When you get mad at your husband you get drunk and then forget. You will have a big house and money, next year." We had a great fun trying to decipher her predictions.

Another fun spot was Hoi An, one of my favourite places, not only because we actually stayed in one spot for three nights, but because it was a lovely historical town, on the river and near the ocean. We had clothes tailored for us, relaxed on a beach, and sang karaoke.

Once a trading port from the fifteenth to nineteenth centuries, it is now a "city of tailors". Every second business is a tailor shop. There were so many choices it was almost impossible to decide what to have made. I had pants, capris, and a blouse made in six hours. They fit perfectly and cost less than twenty-five dollars for all three. I was happy, but unfortunately Laura was not so lucky. She chose more expensive fabric and more difficult patterns and was unhappy with the lot. As far as the rest of the group, half liked what they had made, while the other half didn't.

Vietnam conjured up many emotions—from awe, to sadness, to wonder—and is a place I will have to return to one day.

I met my interviewee in Hoi An. Finding her was a tough chore, however, hindered by the vendors of the market. Daisy had befriended Cuc in the market the last time she was there and knew she had six sisters. We thought one of them would fall into my age category, so we went in search of her on market day. She wasn't in her regular spot, and when we asked for her the reply from several vendors was, "She no longer here, you buy from me." Eventually, when one woman realized we weren't going to buy from her, she suddenly remembered where Cuc was, just a few rows over. Cuc was very excited to see Daisy and was happy to take me to meet her sister.

~

Sach − *48*

I am more than a little reluctant to get on Cuc's motor scooter, but have no choice if I want to meet her sister. The roads in Hoi An aren't as crazy as some of the places we have been, so I hop on. She drives quite slowly and I am able to relax slightly, but she keeps leaning back to talk to me and I wish she would just drive. After twenty minutes we arrive at the beach, where her sister Sach has a restaurant.

I feel like a giant compared to these tiny women. Sach doesn't look close to fifty and I wonder if Cuc just wanted to take a foreigner for a ride, but they tell me Sach is forty-eight. She seems overjoyed to meet me and is more than happy to sit with me and tell me about herself. Their constant laughing and smiling is contagious and the three of us are best friends in minutes.

Sach's restaurant, one of several lining the beach, consists of a small kitchen area with a fire for cooking, and several plastic tables and chairs placed in the sand, covered by a tin roof. There are no customers, as this is the fifth restaurant along the beach, and it is not tourist season yet. One of her sons is here to help out and he starts preparing the "fish of the day" for me.

I ask Sach to tell me about herself, and begin to believe she is the age she reports to be. She sadly tells me that she has been divorced for the last five years. Sad, not because she misses her drunken husband, who left her after her third child was born, but because she really would like a man in her life, preferably an older man. She says, "I am happy now that he is gone, because he was very mean to me. He is just one of many men who drink too much around here."

She speaks proudly of her three boys. Her oldest is twenty-four years old and is a tailor. The next is twenty-one years old and is the one preparing the fish, and her youngest is only five years old. Both older boys finished high school.

Her smile fades when we start to talk about her childhood. She had to quit school early to help look after her five sisters. The oldest child, she was only eleven when her father, a soldier for the South Vietnamese, was killed during the war. He was only thirty-six. It was just one month after Cuc, the youngest of the six girls, was born. Both Sach and Cuc have tears in their eyes as she talks about the war years. Cuc, of course, doesn't remember anything, but Sach remembers constantly having to gather up all the girls and load them into a bomb shelter, and how hard their mother had to work to keep them all together. She said, "Our mother is seventy-five years old and still works in the market selling vegetables every day, even though she is sick with a tired heart."

I can see she has learned her work ethic from her mother, when she tells me she has had her restaurant for sixteen years and in the busy months works sixteen hours a day and has five employees, while in the winter months it is just her and her son. She sounds weary when she talks about it, but tells me she loves having her own business and working with her son.

She starts asking about my trip and can't believe where I have been. She says she has never travelled far from this area and could never afford to. I ask if she would consider living anywhere else, and she says, "I would never leave Vietnam, but would love to live in the mountains."

I get to the question about religion, and she says she has never been religious, nor are most people in Vietnam.

Considering most of the surrounding countries are Buddhist, this surprised me. (I looked up the statistics later and found that 80 percent of the people of Vietnam have no religious beliefs.)

She seems a little embarrassed when I start talking about menopause, and although they both speak fairly good English, I am not sure they really understand me. They are giggling and talking in Vietnamese and I am not in on this joke. Finally, Sach says she still doesn't have any symptoms. Neither of them has heard of HRT, and I drop the subject.

Our talk turns to happier things and Sach lights up talking about her love of karaoke. She invites me and my group to join her and her five-year-old at a local karaoke club tonight. Despite her sad past, she says, "I feel young and happy, especially since I have been single."

Here is a woman who has lived through a war, lost her father, had her husband leave her with a newborn and two other children, works sixteen hours a day, and is still happy. I told her she should be an inspirational speaker. She was a joy to meet.

Chapter 24

Cambodia

"Frogs, grasshoppers, tiny birds, shrimp, fish, eggs, and rice," I said, listing the contents in the baskets, precariously positioned on the heads of the vendors we were looking down at from our seats, high up in the bus. While we were waiting to board the ferry to cross the Mekong and enter Cambodia, we had front-row seats to view the chaos surrounding us. The border crossing was packed with buses, vans, and cars overflowing with people inside and perched on top, as well as tuk-tuks, taxis, motorcycles, bicycles, horses pulling carts, and men pulling overloaded carts. Adding to the bedlam were hawkers trying to sell their wares, cows running free, and people trying to secretly sell us U.S. dollars. (Although Cambodia has its own currency, the riel, the U.S. dollar is taken everywhere.)

When we arrived at the other side of the river we entered Cambodia. On the drive toward Phnom Pehn we noticed a difference from Vietnam immediately. Cambodian homes were similar to many in Laos, unpainted wooden structures on stilts, and there was much more wide-open space than Vietnam. Arriving in a Buddhist country was obvious as well, as we drove past more temples in the first few hours than in a whole week in Vietnam. (Approximately 90 percent of Cambodians follow Theravada Buddhism.)

We arrived in Phnom Pehn, the capital of Cambodia, to a water festival for its Independence Day celebrations. We were told the city of two million grew to four million for the events and I believe it.

The streets were so packed with vehicles that crossing the road was almost impossible. It would take a whole group of people bravely stepping out into the traffic to make the oncoming surge of vehicles have no choice but to stop. As in Vietnam, there were more motorcycles than any other form of transportation, but instead of having two or three riders, there were at least four or five passengers on most. We even saw one motorcycle carrying a family of seven, with the kids squashed in between the parents and hanging off the back. Also, motorcycles loaded to overflowing with trussed pigs, tall baskets full of chickens, huge piles of wood and straw, furniture, and towers of boxes piled on more boxes, defying all laws of balance, seemed to manoeuvre with ease through the streets.

We now had a new tour leader, Polek, as we left Daisy in the hospital in Vietnam having her foot tended to. Polek, a bright and interesting leader and a Cambodian, told us some of the horrific history of his country. The more I learned about the Khmer Rouge, the more physically ill I felt. For three and a half years—or "three years, eight months, and twenty days," as every Cambodian can quote—1.5 million people were killed directly by the Khmer Rouge, and 1.5 million went missing or died of starvation or illness due to the Khmer Rouge.

On April 17, 1975, Prime Minister Pol Pot declared that Cambodia be named Democratic Kampuchea and reset the calendar to "Year Zero". He then started forcibly evacuating the people from the cities and moved them into the countryside, to agricultural communes and into slave labour. Anyone who showed any signs of intelligence was tortured and killed. The Khmer Rouge soldiers would give people a book and if they could read it, they were targeted. They would tell them they could write a letter home and if they could write, they were targeted. Originally, the Khmer Rouge told people they were only moving them out of their homes for a few days to get them away from American bombs, but then never let them go back. Families were separated, and those who lived endured near starvation and torture. The Khmer Rouge closed schools, hospitals, and factories, and abolished banks, finance, and currency. It outlawed religion, literacy, music, and art, and confiscated all private property.

Polek told us about his own family. At one time there were seven brothers and sisters; now it is just Polek and one brother, who suffers from post-traumatic stress disorder. Polek's father gets around with only one leg, having lost the other after stepping on a land mine while trying to escape with a son in his arms. The son died. Polek was born after it was all over and his parents call him "the lucky one." He is a kind and gentle soul. Every night when we had a group dinner, he would eat less than half of what he ordered and very quietly sneak out to give the rest to the street kids.

Polek took us on a tour of the Killing Fields at Choeung Ek, as well as S-21, an interrogation camp. I had a very hard time at both sites. At Choeung Ek, the skulls of eight thousand people (only some of those that were buried there) are on display in a glass stupa. At S-21, we read about the twenty thousand people tortured and starved and then shipped off to Choeung Ek to be executed. I couldn't help but cry, and found that I couldn't go through the whole display. What happened in that country is unfathomable.

The Vietnamese took over from the Khmer Rouge in 1979 and changed the name to the People's Republic of Kampuchea. Polek explained that as he was growing up, under the Vietnamese, he was not allowed to read or write English, but had someone in his village teach him on the sly, in the fields. Then, in 1989 the Vietnamese withdrew and the country was again Cambodia.

As Cambodia is recovering from this difficult history, it is still plagued by widespread poverty (over one-third of the population lives on a dollar a day), the highest rate of HIV in Asia, and a high incidence of death and injury from land mines. One in 290 Cambodians has a land-mine-related injury, and this is evident everywhere, as we saw many maimed people begging and walking the streets. Life expectancy is only sixty-two years old. Diabetes is on the rise, with the introduction of fast food, sugars, and more motorized vehicles. (I met an American gal who was working with diabetics and left her some of my fund-raising money. Her stories of young people who couldn't afford insulin were heartbreaking.)

Despite all this, the people are warm, friendly, and have a great zest for life. We were greeted with smiles and laughter everywhere. I couldn't help but wonder how they survived to smile again. I can only hope that the future will bring a better way of life for these resilient people.

Life goes on for the Cambodians and nowhere is it more evident than in the bustle of their markets. We visited several and enjoyed soaking up the atmosphere while keeping an eye out for deals. We found the vendors less aggressive than those in many other countries, but as savvy as any when negotiating the price.

A young bookseller heard us bartering on silver and approached us, saying, "Don't buy there. I will take you to real silver." He then stuck with us for over an hour, giving us all the tips he thought we needed to negotiate the best prices. He was one of the many young kids who are recruited from countryside villages to come to the city and sell cheap photocopied books to the tourists. They are all cheerful, clever kids who would ask where we were from and then tell us who the head of our country was and the population. They all knew statistics of at least ten different countries.

Other than our walk through Khmer Rouge history, we found ourselves more involved in the water festival activities than sightseeing in Phnom Pehn. Being in the middle of the millions enjoying the lighting displays, dragon boat races involving over four hundred boats, and fireworks every night was a delightful way to spend our three days, but we realized that we didn't see the "real" Phnom Pehn. I guess I will have to return one day.

Our next stop was Siem Reap, a seven-hour drive from Phnom Pehn. We weren't looking forward to the drive, but ended up having a few fun stops which helped break up the trip. One stop involved a marketplace where tarantulas and crickets were sold by the bucketful. A few brave souls in our group actually ate them, but Laura and I chose to take photos instead of samples.

Siem Reap is smaller than Phnom Pehn, but it was just as busy with festivities. Again, we took in the ambience of the celebrations and wandered amongst the crowds of Cambodian families picnicking and enjoying the holiday.

Siem Reap is home to the Angkor Temples. There are more than one hundred temples within a fifty-five-kilometre area. These amazing architectural wonders were built between the eighth and thirteenth centuries. We had only two days to explore the area, but could have spent weeks there. The biggest and most famous of all the temples is Angkor Wat. The five-pyramid temple is even on the national flag. Another temple, with its strangling fig trees and creeping lichen, was where they filmed *Lara Croft: - Tomb Raider*. Many of the temples were surrounded by moats. I now realize the Hindu and Buddhist faiths are intertwined in the history of all Asia, as there were hundreds of statues of Hindu gods and Buddha. Bas-relief carvings of daily life, warriors, hunters, celestial nymphs, and Sanskrit inscriptions were still recognizable on the ancient buildings. Guardian lion and elephant statues protected the entrance to many of the temples. We went both at sunrise and sunset and took thousands of photos. It was truly a spectacular area.

During the filming of *Lara Croft* was when Angelina Jolie fell in love with the Cambodian children, and now I completely understand why she adopted a child from there. All of us could have taken a child home; they are all so loving and sweet.

From the magnificent temples of his ancestors, our guide then took us to visit a floating village in the middle of a flooded lake. We had to first take a boat to find the village, as it moves according to the season and the height of the flooding. We finally saw the tops of trees just peeking out of the lake and then hundreds of floating homes. Most were tiny rickety shacks, but there were also a few nicely built houses, a church, a pool hall, a school, and a basketball court—all on floats. The villagers, most of them fisherfolk, led a simple lifestyle with few creature comforts. The kids' playground was only the small decks surrounding the houses, and people's beds were hammocks hanging in tiny rooms, some not even tall enough to stand up in. Two boys tried to sell us a snake for the cheap price of three dollars, but we passed up the bargain. At the floating restaurant in the village we stopped to see the crocodile farm attached to the side. We saw many kids swimming alongside their homes; this was frightening after seeing the crocodiles, but also because we wondered where the villagers' sewage went.

Our local tour guide for the temples and the floating village was Alaan. She and Polek were very proud of their country and what they have lived through. Even though technically the horror of the

Khmer Rouge was supposed to have ended in 1979, Alaan told us that in 1993 her village was attacked. The guard was shot, and they pointed a gun at her mother while Alaan looked on. They took her mother's money and jewellery. Another time she was with a group of kids, when one picked up a piece of metal. All the girls ran, as they had been instructed to do all their lives, but the boys stayed. The boy who picked it up died when the device exploded in his hand. I couldn't fathom living with these kind of obvious threats looming everywhere, but here were two young adults, smiling, laughing, and getting on with life, and they both conveyed a loving, sweet innocence.

Alaan was in love, but was in an emotional dilemma because her father was the village fortune-teller and he didn't think Alaan and this boy were a match. In Alaan's village, when couples are going to marry, they must go to her father and he decides whether they are right for each other. According to Alaan, anyone who has gone against him has indeed split up after marrying. Her parents told her they wouldn't disown her if she married the man she loves, but she couldn't go to them if there were any problems. There was a boy in her village that would like to marry her and her father was agreeable to this one. Alaan was torn with the choices of the modern world and family tradition.

Alaan arranged for me to be picked up by a motorcycle taxi and taken to her house to interview her mother. Her home was a three-room suite consisting of a living room/kitchen with tiled floors, no indoor plumbing or cooking facilities, a counter with a bucket of water and some dishes, a bookshelf, and a few small plastic chairs. A map of the world adorned one wall. One bedroom had just enough room for a bed and a dresser, while the other had a bed with a motorcycle parked beside it. A hammock hung on the outside deck, with another bed beside it. I didn't see the bathroom, but assume it was an outside room in the back. I was not sure where they cooked and I didn't see a fridge. It was very clean, but stark! It was her home, but she shared it with a brother and a sister who were attending school in the city, and her mother, Lory, who came in from their village when she could.

~

Lory – 51

"I think I am fifty-seven, and I know I was born in the year of the rooster," says Lory, in Khmer, as Alaan translates.

"I think you are younger than fifty-seven, as I was born in the year of the rooster too, and you are definitely not twelve years younger or twelve years older than me. I think you are fifty-one, like me," I explain.

We are sitting on the tile floor in the living room, as there is no furniture. Alaan, her sister, her brother, her mother Lory, and a neighbour woman are in a circle as Alaan tells them about me and my quest. The neighbour, bald-headed and dressed in a white robe, is studying to be a Buddhist monk, but found time to join us. Alaan says they are Buddhists as well and this woman is Lory's best friend. I think she asked her to join us for support when meeting me, a complete stranger who wanted to ask her so many questions.

I ask how Lory and her husband met, and the story unfolds that she met him and married him eight days later. He had been a monk for four years, from twenty to twenty-four. He had to wait one year after leaving the monastery to marry, and when that year had passed he decided on Lory's older sister. He went, with his parents, to her parents to ask for the sister's hand. After advising him that she was already spoken for, Lory's mother said, "What about my younger daughter? She is beautiful."

When he saw her, he said, "Okay." Then Lory's family had to discuss it. Once the oldest brother approved, they had to go to the fortune-teller, who approved but said they had to marry that month. Lory was only seventeen. Shortly after their wedding, the Khmer Rouge took over the country and they were moved to a camp. With a man she barely knew, pregnant, and in a strange new communal camp, she began her married life.

I ask if she minds talking about those years of the Khmer Rouge and she starts by talking about how little food they were given. Alaan gets up and brings over a small four-inch cup and Lory says that is how much rice they were given daily to start, but eventually it went down to one cup for two people, then one bullet-size portion, and then it went to porridge. She says many people starved to death. During her pregnancy they allowed her to work inside doing milling, but once the baby was born she was out in the fields and working long hours. I show my shock and say it was a miracle her child lived. She sadly says, "My first child lived, but not my second." I am in tears, along with Lory and her friend. Her children don't seem fazed by the story.

She goes on to explain that her father was shot and killed in 1975 when it first started. Her aunt went missing the night after she refused to give up her sewing machine to the cause. Alaan says about one-third of their extended family was killed, starved, or went missing.

They went back to her husband's village after the Khmer Rouge fell to the Vietnamese, where they continued farming. She had ten children total and lost three: one at birth, one at ten months, and one at seven. Again, I am in tears, and explain that I too lost a child at ten months. I am surprised by Alaan, who says, "I don't think it bothered my mother that much, because she had so many more mouths to feed." I tell her I think she is wrong and to please ask her mother, who says, "Yes, I was sad because I carried and loved those babies." I think this surprises Alaan and her siblings.

We discuss the ages of the remaining seven children. Alaan, her sister Sievlan (who refers to herself as a mouse, not a rat), and her brother Sokky (a snake) worked out their siblings' ages by the animal under which they were born, not the month or year. There were seven girls and three boys, from thirty-three to twelve. The two oldest girls went to school until grade four, the next to grade six. Alaan has a BA in accounting, and Sievlan, at twelve, wants to be a receptionist. Sokky is in university studying English literature and wants to be a lecturer. An eighteen-year-old brother is studying to be a mechanic. They tell me Lory went to grade eleven and I am surprised, until they explain they used to count the grades backwards and that meant she went to the equivalent of our grade two. Her husband went to grade three.

Until recently Lory has not been far from her own village, her husband's village, and the camp they lived in during the Khmer Rouge time. Now that Alaan is in Siem Reap she visits often to be with the kids, and Alaan has taken her to see more of Cambodia. Despite all she has endured, she says she would never want to leave the country. This is her home and where her family is. She now baby-sits for all her children that are still in the village, having stopped working in the fields about ten years ago.

I try to ask about menopause, but Alaan is embarrassed and just says her mother still has her monthly cycle. I realize that finding out more about Asian women and menopause is not going to happen today.

I ask Alaan to ask her mother if she is happy, and Alann and her siblings start laughing. They say in unison, "She is always unhappy with us, because we stay up too late and get up too late." I insist they ask Lory to answer for herself, and she says, "I am sometimes happy and sometimes not." After all she has been through, I think I understand her answer. I have to get back to my group, and am sad to leave this pleasant family.

~

That was the end of our four-country tour and Laura was heading home. We had a fantastic time together and I am so glad she was able to join me. She was right at the beginning, when she told me she would be fine. She really had no problem with any of our hotels, and she squatted time and time again without complaint. The group got on well most of the time, and it was great for Laura to have people to go out at night with, while I went back to write and sleep. I missed a few fun nights, I am told, but I just couldn't be out every night if I was going to carry on for the full year.

I'd like to think Laura and I taught the young people on our tour that women "as old as their mothers" can still have fun and be adventurous. I know we taught them more than they wanted to know about menopause, especially when they heard us say to each other, "Don't touch me!" when we were having simultaneous hot flashes. We radiated a lot of heat!

I realize that travelling with a tour group made this an easy way to see these countries, and I don't think I would have enjoyed them as much if I actually had to make all the arrangements to get from one city to the next or look for a hotel once we arrived. The experience you get from doing it yourself can be great, but I liked having it all done for me, especially when I want to see so many places in such a short time.

Chapter 25
China

"I can't believe you just did that" I said, laughing. Marje, my new travel mate, had just used me as a battering ram to plough through a group of fellow passengers to get us off the subway. We were in Beijing (Peking), and if she hadn't tackled me and pushed, we would never have gotten out the door. The subways are so full that the doors are blocked with a wall of people, and no one willingly moves when they open. The lack of personal space was something we had to get used to very quickly. The interesting thing was, we were told that most Chinese people don't like to be touched or hugged, but we found no one seemed to have a problem "snuggling up" in the subways.

We had to learn and adjust to several things in order to enjoy our stay in China. We had to accept that if we were in a line for anything, the locals would jump in front of us. We also had to get used to being stared at—everyone stared, and not discreetly. They would stop and stare, and quite often try to sneak a picture of us, although some came right out and asked to be in pictures with us. This was a reversal for those of us who were always trying to sneak pictures. Another habit we adjusted to was at restaurants, where the servers would hand us a menu and then stand as close as possible, hovering, until we'd order. We would try to ask them to give us a minute, but they never understood our request and would wait until we made our choice. The one thing I never got used to was the dramatic, loud horking up and subsequent spitting done by many people. Leading up to the Olympics, which were a month before our visit, there was a campaign to try to persuade people to abandon this age-old custom, but apparently many people didn't comply.

I arrived at my hotel in Beijing at the exact minute the group meeting for my next tour began. To get in my fifty countries in fifty weeks I had really booked this journey tight, but this was probably the tightest. Eleven people were on the tour—five Aussies, four New Zealanders, and a girl from Lithuania, who was my roommate. Unfortunately, one of the Aussies was a "half-empty" gal and I was ready to throttle her many times. It is amazing how one bad travel partner can affect the whole group. I explained Laura's and my "half-full" motto to Marje and she kindly whispered it to me anytime our Aussie mate was driving me crazy.

Our tour leader was Marcia (her "English" name). She was from a small village and now lives in Beijing. Surprisingly, she was from a family of three children. Her parents defied the one-child policy and, in doing so, lost their jobs as government workers in the city and had to move back to the country to farm. The one-child policy is no longer in effect, but parents pay higher taxes for each child they have. Marcia's family has no religious beliefs, which is in line with the vast majority of Chinese, who are atheist. She was a sweet girl who tried very hard not to "lose face" by getting mad at our less-than-sweet Aussie girl.

Marcia started out by saying, "China is like the toilets. It looks nice on the outside, but underneath, nothing actually works." She went on to explain that, "Despite the modern facade there remain many political, environmental, and social welfare problems." China is the third-largest country in the world, with over 19 percent of the world's population, more than 1.3 billion people, consisting of fifty-six different ethnic groups. The one-child policy has produced ten million more boys than girls, which has started to cause some obvious social problems. As we were in China for only ten days, we barely broke the surface of this fast-changing country.

Beijing has a population of about seventeen million, but is still only the second-largest city in China. Peking is the English version of the city name. There are so many cars in the city that on the weekdays, people can only drive on odd or even days, depending on their license number. The city had been cleaned up for the Olympics, so on our visit we experienced very little air pollution. At Tiananmen Square they even had city workers with little polishers cleaning up when people spat.

Of course, standing in Tiananmen Square brought back memories of June 4, 1989, when, according to the Chinese government, 241 died and seven thousand were wounded during student protests. (Most other reports indicate many more people were killed.) According to our local tour guide, Tiananmen Square is the largest public square in the world, and people now come to see the thirty-seven-metre-high monument to the People's Heroes, erected in memory of "the martyrs who laid down their lives for the revolutionary struggles during the nineteenth and twentieth centuries." Also in the square is Chairman Mao's mausoleum, where you can rent flowers and see his crystalline sarcophagus lying in state. Many people lined up for hours for a view, but we passed up the opportunity.

Next to the square, in the very centre of Beijing, is the Forbidden City, which is the beautifully preserved Imperial Palace. It was home to twenty-four emperors of the Ming and Qing dynasties. The first construction started in 1406, although most of the current buildings were built in the eighteenth century. "Ordinary people" were not permitted to enter, which explained why it was named the Forbidden City. Not surprisingly, it is a UNESCO World Cultural Heritage building. We spent the better part of the day exploring all the magnificent buildings, the historical relics, and the many precious works of art.

Marje and I wanted to find the "real" Beijing, so we searched out a neighbourhood of narrow alleys lined with thousands of drab grey traditional courtyard homes, known as *hutongs*. We were definitely out of place walking the cramped streets, but we ignored the stares and carried on. We hung over the shoulders of men gathered to play mah-jongg, and unwittingly scared a few children who were unused to seeing foreigners walking in their hood. We didn't recognize many of the foods being sold from the bicycle carts and small stalls, and I was too timid to try anything, but Marje tried the deep-fried scorpions that were alive, wiggling on the stick, until she ordered them. I was glad I didn't try them when she said they had an indescribable meaty taste. We peeked into some of the cluttered courtyards to get a glimpse of the ordinary life: women doing laundry in cement wash basins, clothes hanging on lines, bicycles parked up against the grey walls, kids playing, and close neighbours chatting. Currently, a quarter of Beijing's population lives in *hutongs*, but many are being demolished for newer roads or developments, which is changing the lives of many.

While on our outings we also found several markets. At first, we felt bad ignoring the many, many people vying for our money, as the vendors would send out their workers who spoke English and had the best sales pitch. Eventually we learned to just smile and keep walking, but when we found what we wanted, we figured out we could get most items for about a tenth of the starting price. I was able to pick up a ski jacket and gloves for less than thirty dollars, which was great because I only needed them for the week in China, where the weather was cooler than I had expected. If I was visiting only China I could have picked up many great bargains, but there were still several more countries to go.

We benefited from the Olympics having just finished, as there were many signs and menus in English. We had a good chuckle at many of the translations, which were usually lovely soft word choices. Instead of "Attention", the sign would read "Warm Notice", and instead of "Watch your valuables", the signs read "Take care of your treasures." In an elevator the sign asked that we "Choose the pressed key reasonably." One hotel's outside banner had "We are less dirty."

Getting out of the city and travelling two hours to find one of the Seven Wonders of the World, the Great Wall of China, was one of my favourite excursions. The Mitianyu section of the Great Wall, built in 555 and renovated during the Ming Dynasty (1300 to 1600), and again about one hundred years ago, is in exceptional condition. We were told one of the key ingredients holding the wall together is sticky rice. As far as we could see in either direction, the wall twisted its way up and down the mountains, with watchtowers, platforms, and garrisons placed strategically on every hilltop. They were very serious about keeping the Mongols out.

To get up to the wall we could have taken a chairlift or a gondola, but we chose to hike up one thousand stairs. Our hike along a small portion of the six-thousand-kilometre wall was one of those surreal moments in life where I again realized how lucky I am. To be fortunate enough to see one of the most magnificent structures ever built and hike for hours up and down the wall was magnificent. To top it all off, we took a wild ride back down on wheeled bobsleds. What a great day!

From Beijing we took an overnight train to Xi'an (pronounced She-ann). It's a city of ten million, but it didn't seem that big to me. Xi'an is one of six ancient capitals of China and the city wall from the Ming Dynasty still surrounds it. I rode a bike the fourteen kilometres around the top of the wall, getting great views of the new and old sections of the city. It was the only place I would ride a bike in China because it was exclusively for walking and riding, free of the crazy traffic in the city streets.

Xi'an has many interesting things to see, but the main reason we stopped there was to see the Terra Cotta Warriors, about an hour out of town. These amazing statues were only discovered in 1974 by a couple of farmers digging a well. Now there are three large buildings covering three pits where statues have been found. It is believed that there are at least thirty pits of statues in total, but a complete excavation had not been done. Two of the pits have been opened for display, one displaying two thousand statues and one with around seventy. When first discovered, many of the statues still showed signs of colourful paint, but the paint faded when exposed to the air, so now they are leaving the rest covered until they can work out a way to keep the paint intact. When the statues were discovered, the farmers had to turn over the land to the government. I am told the farmers were paid, but not very much. One of these farmers was at the site, signing books about the area, but his salesmanship needed work, as he was continually horking and spitting, so I didn't get close enough to buy a book.

The statues were commissioned by the first Chinese emperor, Qin Shi Huangdi, around 200 BC, to stand guard over his vast necropolis and protect him throughout eternity. It is believed that in the first pit alone there are over six thousand statues. Uncovering these statues was a surprising archaeological discovery, as there was no historical record of them.

Of the statues they have uncovered, there are infantry, charioteers, and cavalry dressed in armour holding crossbows, swords, spears, and other ancient weapons. All the faces are different. There were also two half-size bronze chariots. It is a phenomenal sight, and it's hard to imagine the egos, or the superstitions, of these rulers that needed to build such enormous tombs for their afterlife.

Our next city, Suzhou, was small in comparison to the others: only five million. The city is known for its beautiful Chinese gardens and the interlocking canals that feed them. A classical Chinese garden consists of many rock structures, bamboo, water, trees, plants, chimes, incense burners, inscriptions, and buildings of lovely architectural design. Created to produce a setting for the contemplation of balance, harmony, proportion, and variety in life, they were a welcome, peaceful respite from the bustle of the big cities.

We also took a canal cruise in a man-powered boat, which was rather like going down the back alleys of the city. We sailed closely past people's homes, peeking in their windows, as the buildings are built right into the canal, like in Venice. We floated under willow trees and small arched bridges that were perfectly reflected in the smooth waterway. Our oarsman even sang for us. It was another quiet, peaceful, enjoyable experience—until we passed the man peeing into the water. He did not care at all that we were sailing past. If that was an indication of their sewer system, I am glad I didn't fall in!

From Suzhou it was only two hours by bus to Shanghai, the mother of all cities: twenty-two million, according to our guide, and eighteen million according to several Web sites. There were more high-rises than I have ever seen in my life. It is considered a young city compared to the others, only started in 1846. Since the 1990s it has been built into a huge, thriving metropolis, with a few of the older buildings scattered amongst the massive, glittery new buildings.

Despite its population, there were no restricted days for driving, so of course traffic was always in an unbelievable gridlock. Along with the cars there were thousands (maybe millions) of motorcycles and scooters, which I was told are all supposed to change over to electric soon. Not surprising, then, was the pollution. It was so thick most days that the gigantic high-rises on the other side of the narrow Yangtze River were blocked from view. Many people wore face masks to protect them from the filthy air.

It was obvious from the start that this is a business city, crowded with well-dressed locals and business people. We spent most of our time just wandering the city, taking in all the glitz, with every known European and American franchise you can name. We were constantly approached by hawkers trying to peddle their wares, from silly plastic toys to jewellery and clothes. They were more persistent in Shanghai than in the other cities. One of the lines we heard often was whispered clandestinely in our ears, "Watches, bags." The first time I heard it I thought someone was trying to tell me to watch my bag. How nice, I thought, believing he was only trying to warn me of pickpockets. It took a few more of these people sidling up to me before I realized they were trying to get me to follow them to their store where they sold watches and bags.

My "stupid mistake" list got bigger in Shanghai. In most places we had stayed, having our laundry done through the hotel had cost less than six dollars. So when we arrived in Shanghai I didn't even look at the price list before sending out my laundry. It arrived back with a sixty-dollar bill. Another lesson learned. Had I read the laundry list provided—which, although challenged in its translation, with "shocks, stocks, and plorts weater"—did have a price list with prices clearly written.

While in China I had to try a Chinese massage, of course. Despite the language barrier, I managed to show in sign language that I wanted a massage and not a manicure or pedicure, and a lovely young girl took me to a quiet room, said something in Chinese, and then left. Shortly after, a young man came in, said something in Chinese, handed me a silk top and pants, and then left. I was hoping the girl would be coming back, but in walked the young man. He pointed to the chair that looked more like a lounge chair than a massage table and I sat down. The chair did stretch out to a bed and that is when the young man climbed on too. I just had to laugh and see how it all played out. I was glad for the silk outfit. As in a Thai massage, he had me in several different twisted positions, stretching me beyond what I thought possible, and eventually he was off the chair and starting a more traditional Swedish-style massage. Even though I had been having massages for the last month, he did an incredible job of finding more kinks that needed work, caused by the many months of sleeping in so many different beds and lugging around my suitcase, which was heavier by the day. I can't say no to all the hawkers!

During our trip we visited a school for the mentally disabled, where we were entertained with song and dance, and they even had us all doing the chicken dance. The students were well cared for and appeared very happy. We bought some of their jewellery and I left them some of my fund-raising money.

To see as much as we did, in the short time we had, we took two overnight trains. Whether I was finally getting used to overnight trains or just plain exhausted, and despite having open rooms with people staring at us constantly, I managed to sleep both nights. I did not, however, get used to squatting in a dirty toilet on a moving train.

The food was great, because we had Marcia order for us in most places. Even though many menus were in English, it was better that she order and we just eat. She promised that she didn't order us anything too weird, but at many restaurants there were live turtles and frogs on display, so I don't really know what we ate. It was great eating out as a group because we had so many different dishes to choose from. It wasn't as inexpensive as Southeast Asia, but it was never too expensive.

One of the great meals we had was served at a local's home near the site of the Terra Cotta Warriors. They served up a delicious lunch with many dishes, including sweet potatoes, persimmons, veggies, noodles, rice, and tea, of course. The wife cut up the food, the granddad cooked, the husband served, and the grandma looked after the children. The kitchen had one hot plate, a rice cooker, and a tiny fridge, which explained why they served only one dish at a time.

The grandma, who was fifty-six, agreed to be my interviewee.

~

Chen – 56

Chen speaks no English, so Marcia will be translating. We are standing outside her son's townhouse in the courtyard after lunch, and the kids in the neighbourhood are encouraging my group to play jump rope with them. Chen, Marcia, and I are in the middle of the chaos, so I am not sure how much of the interview we will get done.

I ask Marcia to ask Chen about herself, and after they talk for a bit she tells me that Chen was married at twenty-one, after knowing her husband for five years. They have two children, a boy and a girl, and this is her son's house. I ask Marcia to ask what happened when they chose to have two children, but Marcia says, "I can't ask that." I now realize this interview will be accomplished only by respect of their culture and not allowing anyone to "lose face".

Chen appears quite shy and a bit embarrassed that she does not understand what we are saying, so I try to ask short questions so Marcia and I are not talking too much in English. I ask about where she has lived. Marcia explains that Chen grew up on a farm; then her husband was in the army, and they moved quite a bit for several years, but for most of their married life they lived on a wheat farm, until recently moving to live with her son and his wife in the suburbs of Xi'an. Chen says that although she has never been outside of China she is not interested in leaving, because she wouldn't understand anyone. I guess my instincts were right about the language barrier.

Again, the issue of "losing face" comes up when I ask Marcia to ask Chen about her education. "No, I can't," Marcia says. "I don't think she went to school, so it would not be right to ask."

"Okay," I say delicately, "what about menopause? Can you ask her about that?"

Now I have embarrassed even Marcia. She looks shocked and says, "I wouldn't even ask my own mother about that!" This isn't going well; I am stomping on everyone here.

Okay, back to maybe less-invasive questions. "Are your parents still on the farm?" I ask, only to find out that both her parents are dead, one at fifty years old and one at sixty years old. She doesn't say how, and I now know not to ask, but suspect hard farm work, pollution, and smoking may have contributed to their early demise. I have seen that smoking is a very common habit in China, and Chen is herself an obvious smoker, with heavily stained yellow teeth that she tries to hide by putting her hand in front of her mouth when she smiles.

Let's try again with easier questions. I can't get in too much trouble asking about hobbies. Chen says that when she isn't looking after her grandchildren, she loves to sew. Finally, a question that doesn't seem to embarrass anyone or bring up painful memories.

Chen has been smiling, and covering her mouth, through most of the interview, but I am not sure if it is a nervous smile or sincere. My final question is, "Are you happy?" With a huge smile, not covered up, she says in English, "Yes." I still don't know if it is a real yes or a saving-face yes, but they seem like a happy family and I think it was real.

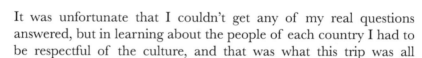

It was unfortunate that I couldn't get any of my real questions answered, but in learning about the people of each country I had to be respectful of the culture, and that was what this trip was all about.

Although we saw many fascinating things, ate well, and had some fun moments, I left with a bad cold (probably due to the pollution), almost lost my "half-full" attitude by being around the Aussie gal, and didn't get a satisfying interview, so China won't be on my "favourite tour" list.

Chapter 26

Nepal

"If you don't give me some fruit, I am going to tell the goats on you," said Ankit. He was the three-year-old grandson of my Nepalese interviewee. I am going to start my story of Nepal with the day of my interview and how it all happened, because this really goes down as one of the best experiences of my trip up to that time. On my first day in Kathmandu, I met a cycle-rickshaw driver, Arjun, and he told me his wife was fifty-one. I asked if I could meet her and he said she lived in their village about one and a half hours away on a very bad road. Keen to meet her, I blurted out, "I don't mind bad roads," not having any idea what I was getting myself into. When he saw I had no problem with that, he said he and his twenty-seven-year-old son, Ram, a cab driver, would come and get me at my hotel the next morning.

I was very excited about taking this excursion, and then started wondering if I was crazy to hop into a car with two strangers and head out to a village of which I knew nothing. Arjun had told me earlier that he had been working outside my hotel for thirty-five years, so I made sure the guard at the hotel gate knew I was with him, and I had the guard take down the license number of Ram's cab when they arrived to pick me up early the next day. The guard knew both father and son, so I felt safe and happy to be on my next adventure.

We had to stop for petrol, and lucky for us there was some available at the second station we tried. There was a shortage of petrol in Nepal, and Ram told me that a few months ago he lined up for six days to get five litres of petrol at two dollars a litre. The day we bought it, it was one dollar and twenty-five cents a litre, which was still a lot of money, considering I was told the average daily wage is less than two dollars.

On the way to their village I asked Ram to stop at a market so I could buy some fruit as a gift for his family. I told him to pick out what he thought they might like and he only picked up a few oranges. I said, "No, pick out many things." He couldn't believe I was letting him just pick and pick. We ended up with three large bags of oranges, apples, pineapple, mangos, bananas, and pomegranates. Then he saw some juice boxes and told me his son loved them, so we got some of those as well. He was beaming with joy and it only cost me about fifteen dollars.

We also picked up a chicken to bring home for lunch. I chose not to go in the butcher shop because I have peeked into those places before and I knew I probably wouldn't be able to eat the meat if I saw the conditions under which it was butchered. (Out of sight, out of mind—that's my way of coping with these things—and to just hope I don't get sick.)

The drive was as promised, on a very jagged, rocky, narrow road, but it was fantastic getting out of the crazy city and heading into the mountains. We drove through small mountain passes, not the tall peaks you imagine of Nepal. However, from the top we could see far off in the distance, where the beautiful snow-capped Himalayas glistened in the sun. The views of the terraced valleys below were equally stunning. Some of the passes we went over were so steep, and the car so weak, we had to push it up to the summit. And because the roads were really just ragged narrow trails, only wide enough for one car, we had to back up more than once to let cars and buses pass. I was shocked to see the size of the buses that took this road daily to the villages in the area.

We drove through several small villages with houses of unpainted bricks or mud and rock, passing farmers busy in their fields of rice, potatoes, and cauliflower, and haystacks piled higher than the houses. We were stopped in one village to pay a "road tax" in order to get through. It was just a group of young boys collecting money and we paid it gladly. I think it was about thirty-two cents. The little boy they had tagging along was a bit afraid of me until I gave him an apple, and then we were instant friends.

Arjun was very proud to show me his country and his region, and getting closer to his village, he mentioned we would go a different way back so I could see even more. And then we got a flat tire. We had a spare, but it was the small emergency kind, not fit for these road conditions. Then he began to worry about us getting back at all. Ram kept telling him not to worry, but Arjun was obviously embarrassed. I kept trying to make him feel better, saying I wasn't worried, but of course I was a little.

We finally arrived in their village and stopped at the local teahouse for tea before hiking to their house, which wasn't accessible by car. The teahouse was a tiny shack barely big enough to stand up in. It had dirt floors, smoke-stained walls, and sacks of food and staples piled high. The tea was sweet and delicious and a much-needed refreshment before we started our hike to their house. Even though Arjun was about sixty-five, he had to wait for me to catch up to him more than once. Ram had gone on without us. Their home was on the top of a hill overlooking a picturesque, lush green valley. I stopped to take many pictures, but really that was just an excuse so I could catch my breath.

When we finally made it to their home, Kancsi, Arjun's wife, was sweeping out the cow barn, which was the room next to the kitchen. She said a quick hello and kept working. I was not sure she was even aware we were coming, and I think she may have been a little put out that we arrived unannounced, just like any of us would be if our husband came home with a complete stranger.

There were two homes on the property. In one lived Arjun and Kancsi, Ram and his wife and son, and their widowed daughter and her three children. In the other house lived their oldest son, his wife, and their three children. The second house had just been rebuilt with the help of the whole village because the original house had burned to the ground. Arjun and Ram spend the majority of their time in Kathmandu, working, but that still left twelve family members living in one house for months while the other was being rebuilt.

The main house had two floors, constructed with a wood frame and mud-packed walls. Its windows had wooden shutters but no glass. On the main floor there was one room for the goats, a dirt-floored room for cooking and eating, complete with an open fire in the floor, a small storage area, and the room for the cow and buffalo. There was no indoor plumbing or running water and only a few light bulbs. The upper floor, reached by a ladder, had bare wood floors, faded painted walls, and two bedrooms, one with a bed and the others with mats on the floor. A picture of the last king and queen was displayed proudly on the wall. There is no longer a monarchy, but the Nepalese love them anyway. The second house was about half the size of the main house, but still had a room for the cow.

On the front, a corrugated tin canopy ran the length of the house between the floors. Vegetables were stored on top of the canopy and corn was hanging from the rafters. The goats were eating straw and branches that hung from the rafters, and the cow and buffalo roamed free.

Ankit, Ram's young son, was very excited to have this surprise visit from his dad and grandpa, and when he saw the fruit he could hardly be contained. He was running around showing everyone, "Look what my dad brought." And of course the juice boxes were a real hit. It was when Ram put all the food away that Ankit said, "If you don't give me some fruit I am going to tell the goats on you."

The women, Kansci and her daughter and two daughters-in-law, were all barefoot and dressed in colourful working saris. They kept at their chores: feeding the goats, cleaning out the stalls, sweeping up, and making lunch. They were making so many dishes that they had food cooking in the house and on a fire outside. I think they felt a bit uncomfortable in my presence, as none of them spoke English.

Ram kept me busy by showing me his wedding pictures. He was married at twenty-three, in his wife's village, just three weeks after his father told him he was going to get married and two short weeks after he saw his future wife of only fourteen years old. He readily agreed to marry her, explaining to me that he will always obey his parents and do whatever they ask of him. His wife was then moved to his village to live with his mother and siblings, and he and his dad went back to Kathmandu, coming home for a day or two every few weeks. Their son was born within the first year. I asked him how she felt about moving to this village, moving in with strangers, and then having him be away most of the time. He said, "What do you mean? This is the way it is." He did not consider for a minute that it would be hard for her to just leave her family, because their culture and the tradition go unquestioned. His wife was very quiet, kept busy with chores, and had little to do with me.

When lunch was ready everyone crowded into the main room and sat on the ground, except me. They gave me the only chair. I would have rather sat on the floor with them than loom over, but thought it would be rude not to accept their gift of a chair. Kancsi piled my plate high with rice and then, with the little room left, piled on a portion of the chicken, tomato, and spinach in a spicy curry sauce, and finally naan bread. I hadn't realized that 80 percent of Nepalese were Hindu, so I was surprised to eat food I would have associated with Indian cuisine. It was delicious. I used my skills learned in Syria to eat the meal without utensils. I tried as hard as I could to eat all the rice because I didn't want to be rude, but there really was way too much. I hoped I didn't offend them by not finishing it all, and I am sure they were surprised I didn't, because they all had seconds of rice.

After lunch we did the interview.

~

Kancsi – 58ish

Ram will answer most of the questions and ask his mother or father the ones he doesn't know the answers to. We sit outside overlooking the beautiful valley. The cow, goats, and buffalo wander around, and the women are now cleaning up. Little Ankit is sitting on his dad's lap, trying to peel an orange. He can't get enough of the fruit. Kancsi has barely sat still, except for a brief moment to eat, but even then she was constantly getting up to fill people's plates. Before she started cooking lunch, she had a quick wash with water from a hose that brings water from a spring up the hill, and she is now dressed in an orange and yellow sari skirt and a red, black, and white silk blouse. She is still barefoot. She looks much older than the fifty-one that Arjun told me. She is a tiny, thin woman with a proud but worn face. Ram tells me that his parents also had an arranged marriage and Kancsi was twenty-five years old when she wed. As his oldest sister is thirty-three, I realize she is probably around fifty-eight or fifty-nine. I don't bother to correct Arjun on his wife's age.

As in China, I realize I am walking on thin ice here when it comes to culture and tradition, so I don't even bother to ask Ram about menopause, and ask him to tell me about the children and education. The two sons are twenty-nine and twenty-seven and the two daughters are thirty-three and thirty-one years old. Kancsi and Arjun cannot read or write and did not attend school. The boys attended school until they were seventeen. The oldest daughter did not go to school and lives with her husband's family. (We passed her on the road carrying a stack of wood bigger than she was.) The other daughter, who is a recent widow, went to school until grade five and now teaches at the school. Ram works as a cab driver, and the other son works on their family farm.

Both Kancsi's parents passed away in their late sixties, which is slightly above the life expectancy of sixty-five years old, but Ram does not know what caused their deaths.

Ram said that his mom and dad have travelled to visit relatives in India, but other than the village she grew up in, she has not travelled anywhere else and very rarely even goes into Kathmandu. When I have him ask her if she would move to another country, she shakes her head vehemently and says she would never consider moving anywhere else.

I ask if they follow the Hindu faith and it seems an odd question to him. "We don't follow it, we live it," he says. Kancsi has the red bindi dot on her forehead, which Ram says is not only a religious symbol, but also shows she is married.

She is now back in the house with most of the family and we follow her in to ask the last question. "Are you happy?" She puts her arms out to point around at her family, and with a broad smile she says, "Yes, very *happy." I see her life as one of hard work, extremely busy and tiring. They have no modern conveniences and everything is done by hand, including fetching the water from a nearby creek, and yet she would never move away and is truly happy.*

I leave sadly, wishing I could have communicated more with the women, but happy I had such a great opportunity to see how they really live in their little village miles from the city.

It was such a peaceful area, so far removed from the hustle and bustle of Kathmandu. I felt bad for Arjun and Ram, having to leave their families and village to make a living in the city. We made it back on the spare tire and only had a slight worry when the car made a loud noise for about a minute. We stopped, looked under the hood, didn't fix anything, closed it up and started it again. The noise stopped and we carried on. (I figured my guardian angels were watching again.)

I really felt privileged to have been able to spend the day with lovely people in a village where likely very few tourists have visited. I was touched by the story of how the village helped the family rebuild their house, and I knew they were still struggling to finish it, so I contributed some of my fund-raising money towards their efforts.

Back in Kathmandu, my first impressions dashed my expectations of a Himalayan heaven. Having done absolutely no research, I was shocked at the condition of the city. It was very polluted, with more rubbish laying about than anywhere I had been, and ranked up there with the worst traffic and road conditions I had yet encountered. I expected to be in the mountains, silly me, and while you can apparently see them in the distance on a good, not-so-polluted day, those days are few and far between.

However, I was willing to give the city a chance, as my first impressions of a lot of cities, especially big ones, often give way to a more favourable opinion once I get used to them. Arjun took me on a cycle-rickshaw tour of the city. As soon as we got to the main road, I remembered how crazy the traffic had been on my trip in from the airport. There were four-lane roads with seven lanes of traffic and I was in it with no metal doors to protect me, but I couldn't jump out, so off we went to see the sites in this messy, dirty, crazy city. Arjun pedalled us over five kilometres to Patan amidst bikes, motorcycles, cars, horse-carts, trucks, buses, and cows. On a few of the hills I had to get out and help Arjun push the rickshaw. He was sixty-five and I was not a light load!

Patan was worth the ride, as it is one of the three royal cities in the Kathmandu Valley. Durbar Square, in the heart of Patan, is another UNESCO World Heritage Site. It was packed with temples, shrines, stupas, statues, carvings, and ornate architecture, as well as a marketplace of food and handicrafts. Hindu and Buddhist relics blended once more with prayer wheels, bells, deities, and gods dating back to the eleventh century. It was a photographer's paradise. Incense burned throughout the square, and a band of drummers with elaborately decorated drums wandered through the crowds. Between the artifacts, the women dressed in colourful saris, the market, and the kids playing, I could have spent hours exploring and snapping photos. The best part of this place: no cars.

We then travelled back to the city, passing hundreds and hundreds of tiny, tiny stores that lined the busy streets. The roadsides are cluttered with billboards, signs, and electrical wires that radiated out of every pole, making intricate patterns resembling spider webs.

I had Arjun drop me in Thamel, the backpackers' area of Kathmandu, where narrow alleys are lined with tiny stores and stalls, restaurants, Internet cafes, and tour companies, and packed with every vehicle known to man. Touts, as they call the harassing vendors, soliciting business at every second step made this a mind-boggling place that didn't encourage me to hang around. I escaped to my hotel and met up with my new tour group, with whom I would be travelling south into India.

The next day the tour began with a visit to Pashupatinath, where we watched a Hindu cremation ceremony. As part of the ritual, the body was placed on the funeral pyre and the family circled around three times. The son prepared the body by taking off all the clothes, and then they set the fire. A narrow river separated us from the family and I was glad to be far enough away not to see this up close. We were told that they throw the remains of the fire into the river, which is considered to be holy. Several temples surrounded the area and monkeys pranced in and out of windows and on the rooftops. Colourfully dressed shamans (holy men) wandered the site, but our guide told us most of them were not shamans, but men who just dressed up to make money by allowing their pictures to be taken. I fell for the sham, and they made for great photos.

Next up, we went to Swayambhunath, which is also known as the monkey temple. It was great fun watching the monkeys play and scramble over the stupas, shrines, and temples. Although we were close to the hotel, it took over an hour to get back in the crazy, busy streets. We even saw two men carrying full-size sofas on their backs. I could only think this had to be part of *The Amazing Race*, but perhaps this was just the fastest way to get through the streets with a sofa.

As we left Kathmandu, we drove south towards India along cliff sides that followed a winding river. We passed many ramshackle houses perched on the very edge of the cliffs, with no fences. We watched kids playing and I had to wonder how many people have fallen off. Then we drove along the Terai, which is a marshy belt of grasslands and forests that led us into Chitwan National Park.

The park has some of the best wildlife viewing in Nepal. Our first day, we rode bikes into the park and rode elephants through the forest to see crocodiles, rhinos, and monkeys. The quiet of the lodge we stayed in, within the park, was so nice that I decided to stay back while the rest of the group went on a two-day hike. Going from one tour to the next, with little time to rest, had caught up with me and I needed some downtime. I spent the days reflecting on my time in Nepal, and while I won't be putting Kathmandu on my favourites list (which is getting too big anyway), I will put the day in the village on the list of "favourite days".

I travel not to go anywhere, but to go. I travel for travel's sake. The great affair is to move.

—Robert Louis Stevenson

Chapter 27
Bhutan

"Gross National Happiness is more important than Gross National Product," the king of Bhutan declared in 1972. I read that years ago, and have always wanted to visit Bhutan to see if the country embraced his idea. When I started planning this trip, it was one of the countries at the top of my list. I found out the only way to get into the country is by private invitation or with a tour group. As I knew no one in Bhutan, I went with option two. I discovered you must spend at least two hundred dollars a day, and that was getting over my budget, but I decided to go anyway, and am glad I did. It was worth every penny.

I arrived with my tour group just weeks after the coronation of the fifth king of Bhutan. In his inaugural speech, he said, "…we must always remember that as our country, in these changing times, finds immense new challenges and opportunities, whatever work we do, whatever goals we have—and no matter how these may change in this changing world—ultimately without peace, security and happiness we have nothing. That is the essence of the philosophy of Gross National Happiness. Our most important goal is the peace and happiness of our people and the security and sovereignty of the nation."

During the recent election campaign both parties pledged to follow the king's guidelines of pursuing Gross National Happiness. All government ministries must apply to the Gross National Happiness

Commission for approval of all new projects. Need I say more? They are serious about this.

Does it work? Are they happy? Of course I can't answer that. The local newspaper had articles about gambling and domestic abuse, so all is not perfect, but I loved the country, and the people we met were lovely and gracious, and most seemed very happy.

Bhutan is "the last Shangri-La", according to the tourist ads. I tend to agree. After a fifty-minute flight over the majestic Himalayas, including a view of Everest rising above all else, we arrived to the peace and tranquility of Paro, a city of fewer than five thousand. I can barely explain the sense of calm we all felt after leaving the insane streets of Kathmandu. Flying into the Paro Valley, seeing the traditional wooden homes and monasteries sporadically dotting the forested hillsides, seeing the prayer flags fluttering in the wind, and noting the absence of billboards and traffic lights was pure joy.

My group was the perfect size, only six of us. We knew the moment we stepped off the plane and were greeted with a white prayer scarf by men in dresses that Bhutan was a magical place. The dresses were *ghos*, knee-length robes worn by men only. Women wear a *kira*, which is ankle-length and always made of bright-coloured woven fabric. In the city most people wear this traditional clothing during the working hours and in the rural areas they wear it all the time.

It became evident immediately that the Bhutanese love their kings. Not only had they just had the coronation, but they had also celebrated one hundred years of the monarchy. Displayed prominently in the airport were huge posters of the five kings, as well as posters all over the country, and there is also a museum dedicated only to the kings. The Wangchuk Dynasty has ruled peacefully for the last one hundred years (with the exception of a 1993 incident where they expelled about one hundred thousand ethnic Nepalese; this lasted a few days and resulted in some casualties).

Even though Bhutan recently became a democratic country, the king is still very much a part of this country's leadership. It was the fourth king's idea to change from a monarchy to a democracy. The Bhutanese people were against it at first, but they loved and trusted him so much that they went along with it. It is one of the only countries to change forms of government without a battle.

Bhutan, around the size of Switzerland, has fewer than seven hundred thousand people. It only opened its doors to the world in 1961 and then started the process of planned modernization, building roads, bridges, schools, and hospitals, all with aid from India. There are, however, still villages that do not have roads, and some areas that do not have electricity. Agriculture provides the main livelihood for more than 80 percent of the population.

Although some of the laws in Bhutan would be considered "lack of freedoms" in some countries, they seem to work in Bhutan. This has made the country a very unique place to visit. Bhutan is in the Eastern Himalayas; however, mountaineering is not permitted, leaving Gangkhar Puensum, at 22,623 feet (around seven thousand metres), the highest unclimbed peak in the world. The Bhutanese say this is designed not to "disturb the spirits", and it also leaves the mountains pristine and not cluttered with rubbish, as has happened in Nepal.

Smoking is not prohibited, but they do not sell cigarettes in Bhutan. You can bring them in but must pay a 200 percent tax to do so. Plastic bags are prohibited, and if you don't bring your own bag while shopping the merchants will provide a cloth bag.

Television has been legal only since 1999 and signs of its influence are just starting to show. The younger generation wears non-traditional clothing, visits nightclubs, and plays video games in Internet cafes. Most people we met spoke English, as it is taught in school, and most signs were in English.

Chickens and dogs run wild throughout the country. As Buddhists, they do not like to kill anything. The dogs are becoming a problem because there are so many. In the daytime the dogs seem safe, but at night they can be dangerous, and the constant symphony of barking can be quite annoying. The puppies were sure cute, however.

The king has committed to keeping 60 percent of the country forested, which has left beautiful, lush landscapes of rolling hills and profuse green mountainsides. Although mountaineering is prohibited, hiking is encouraged, and there are many amazing hikes for both overnight and day trips, where almost every path leads to an impressive temple, shrine, or monastery.

Tourism is controlled by a strict quota—every tourist must take a tour with a local company and the tour company must apply to the government with the tourist's information and itinerary. Then the tour company must pay the government sixty-five dollars per person plus 20 percent of their profit. The tourist must pay at least two hundred dollars a day to the tour company. However, once you are in the country the only money you spend is on alcohol (which isn't always available) and souvenirs. Everything else is covered—food, accommodations, tours, and transportation. In my seven days I was hard-pressed to spend the 150 dollars I had changed into ngultrum, the Bhutanese currency.

The food was good, as long as we stayed away from the chilies. Red rice and chilies are the mainstay of the diet in Bhutan and those chilies were hot, hot, hot. All the places we stayed at had smorgasbord-style dinners with choices of chicken, pork, and occasionally yak, which was a little chewy for me. Pumpkin, cauliflower, potatoes, eggplant, beans, and cheese filled out the meal.

Our accommodations were always good, as most tourist places are relatively new. One area we stayed in was still without electricity, and that hotel was our favourite in Bhutan. They used a generator between six and nine a.m., and five thirty and nine p.m. Additionally, our rooms were equipped with candles and fireplaces, and when we went to bed the hotel staff had our fire roaring and placed hot water bottles in our beds. It was delightful.

Our tour guide, Pema, and our driver, Jigme, were informative, kind, and helpful. They made sure we had everything we could possibly need. Pema also bent over backwards when our tour mate Craig got lost one day while we were hiking. Craig had gone back to find his hat he had dropped, while the rest of us carried on. Pema probably should have told him to forget about his hat, but he wanted to please everyone, so he led the rest of us to a spot where we could see our final destination and then went back for Craig. Pema searched for nearly three hours, and had finally enlisted the help of locals, who were just about to get out their horses to search in the dark, when Craig called from the local monastery. Craig had taken the wrong path back to find us and found the monastery as darkness was falling. The monk who greeted Craig wouldn't let him leave until he fed him.

Pema had taken this loss of a passenger very hard and was visibly shaken by the ordeal. His caring, and that of all the locals who were willing to help, demonstrated how kind the Bhutanese people are. What could have been a horrible night turned out just fine and we had lots of jokes at Craig's expense. (I had spoken to my guardian angels while he was missing and asked for some help—I think they heard me.)

There are twenty districts in Bhutan, and as you enter each one your tour company must register the visitors. As this is a small country, we went through two or three districts in one day, so it did delay our journey. I never minded the delay because there was barely a spot that wasn't picturesque. I don't think you could stand anywhere and not see prayer flags waving in the wind, a beautiful terraced valley, lovely traditional Bhutanese architecture, and friendly people who didn't mind having their picture taken. The traditional clothing, the unique faces, the loads they haul on their backs, and the children laughing and playing always provided something to watch or photo.

With their tapered roofs and intricately designed wooden shutters, ornately painted *dzongs* are found throughout Bhutan, on hilltops or at the convergence of two rivers. These dzongs, dating back to the 1600s, were fortresses, usually enclosing a monastery and a temple. Many have been recently restored to their previous beauty and are truly magnificent. Most of the houses in Bhutan are built with the same unique design. The paintings around the wooden windows and door frames are works of art, with specialized painters dedicated to creating patterns. We visited a school where young men were learning this very art.

The most famous of the dzongs is the "Tiger's Nest", or Taktshang Monastery. It sits clinging to the cliffside of a mountain near Paro. We could barely see it from the ground and the only way to get to it is to hike, which we did. Even though we only had to climb nine hundred metres, the Tiger's Nest sits at 3,120 metres (10,300 feet), making it a hard hike, especially for me, preferring sea-level air. But I made it, and it was worth every step. Up top were seven temples with incredible artwork and Buddhist artifacts. It was originally built in the 1600s, but a devastating fire in 1998 destroyed most of the original building. We were fortunate enough to come just after it had been rebuilt. It was hard to believe they could build it now, let alone in the 1600s. The legend is that Padmasambhava (Guru Rinpoche) flew there on the back of a tiger and built the original temples. Personally, I think that's the only way he could have gotten there; it sure would have been easier than the hike.

We visited the prayer hall where a statue of Guru Rinpoche is displayed. People bring a variety of odd offerings to him; a wine bottle, a box of biscuits, and juice boxes. During the fire, this statue fell through the floor to a cave below and was saved. The monk who watches over the statue tied a "string of luck" on our wrists and said a blessing. This is often done in monasteries and we were encouraged to leave them on until they fell off on their own to maintain the luck.

During our time in Bhutan we visited many of the dzongs, *chortans* (stupas), and temples, and found them all beautiful, with courtyards, colourful mandalas, prayer wheels, and burgundy-clad monks and mini monks walking about. (It is encouraged in every family that at least one son becomes a monk.)

The other dzong that must be mentioned is that of the Divine Madman. Imagine hiking for forty-five minutes through a small village, then tromping through a rice field, and finally climbing a hill to arrive at a dzong, where a monk greets you with a very large phallic symbol, and inside others pray to a statue while raising a phallus towards their head and lowering it. (We managed to stifle our laughter until we were outside.)

The story of the Divine Madman is a crazy one for this conservative country. According to legend, the Divine Madman travelled through Tibet and into Bhutan in the 1400s. He had a reputation of leading a very unusual lifestyle, apparently drinking and having sex with many young women, while performing blessings, exorcising evil spirits, and mysteriously transporting himself to far-off locations. Now people protect their homes from evil spirits and promote fertility by painting phallic symbols on their houses. (We passed many that had done this.) Women travel to his dzong to pray for good fertility.

Not surprising in a Buddhist country, hunting is prohibited. So Bhutan has many tigers and bears, but we didn't see any of them. We did see yaks, monkeys, takins, and black-neck cranes. The cranes fly in from Tibet every year. We were very lucky to see them, as there are only eight hundred left in the world. The takin is the national animal of Bhutan. It is a strange beast with what appears to have the head a goat and the body of a cow. Legend has it that the Divine Madman was asked to demonstrate his magical powers. He demanded a whole cow and a goat for lunch. He devoured both, put the head of the goat on the bones of the cow, and then snapped his fingers, causing the creature to rise up and run off to graze. The takin continues to befuddle taxonomists, who cannot quite relate it to any other animal. They have put it into a class by itself—maybe the legend is true!

The national sport is archery and I happened upon a match while walking around Paro. What a great performance! The team members, dressed in their traditional garb, line up on opposite sides of a field and shoot the arrows 140 metres to the opponents' side of the field. The target is so far away that the men at the target must do different dances and wave ribbons around to show the archers where the arrow hit. The shooters then do their own dance (not unlike the "chicken dance") if they have a good shot. While the match was going on, there was more activity on the sidelines as well. A group of women were performing a traditional dance with music provided by a band of musicians playing Bhutanese music. This was a local event and I was the only tourist watching the game. I really enjoyed being part of the festivities.

We all enjoyed the week in this beautiful, almost undisturbed country. We hiked most days and took in the quiet ambience of the people and countryside. I know for sure the Bhutanese cherish their kings, their culture, and their traditions. I can only hope that by letting the rest of the world in they don't lose their beauty and innocence. I feel privileged to have visited this country while it is still relatively undisturbed and only hope they can hold fast to all they believe in and maintain the beauty within.

I did get an interview before leaving the country, but not with the help of Pema. He explained that the respect of parents and elders is one of the virtues still maintained faithfully by all. Consequently, I think he didn't want to ask any woman if she was fifty. So on my last day I just wandered through Paro going in and out of shops looking for a woman I thought might be the right age.

In one of the last shops I found her. Her shop sold books and was one of the busiest I ventured into.

~

Thrimi – 49

The woman selling books looks to be the right age, but she is busy with a customer. In perfect English, the other salesclerk in the store asks if he can help me. I explain my quest and he immediately tells me he is Dorji, this is his mother's store, and she is indeed forty-nine and will be fifty soon. I ask him to ask her if she would be interested in answering some questions and he turns to speak to her. She looks at me, smiles, and speaks to Dorji. I assume she says it is okay, but she keeps working. He says, "Just ask me, and I will ask her anything I don't know." I was hoping she would be more involved, but I only have an hour until we leave for the airport, so I will have to settle for this.

Dorji tells me his mom's name is Thrimi. His parents were married when Thrimi was eighteen years old, after she had known her husband for five years. Dorji explains it was an arranged marriage and his father was fourteen years older than his mom. I can tell he doesn't really like his dad very much, which surprises me in this country where respect of elders is so important, but I'm more surprised when he tells me that his father was a big drinker! "I didn't think Buddhists drank," I tell him. Dorji says, "Well, my dad drank a lot. My mom was his second wife. In our country men can have more than one wife at the same time. He had two children with his first wife and then three with my mom. We didn't all live together. He went back and forth. My dad passed away three years ago and we don't really miss him, as he was always in and out of our lives." He knows that this is not a normal situation in other countries, and tells me, "Even our fourth king has four wives, and they are all sisters." I tell him I had seen all their pictures at the museum and found that a very strange situation.

Thrimi is still busy with customers and Dorji is speaking in a low tone, but I don't think she understands much English, so she doesn't know what we are talking about. I would have liked to get her reaction to this discussion, but I guess that isn't going to happen. I keep looking up at her, but she doesn't seem willing to interact. I wonder what he told her about this interview.

Dorji tells me about himself and his full siblings. Dorji is thirty and has just returned from six years of studying Buddhism; he is not married. His twenty-seven-year-old sister is a teacher who has a four-year-old and is "on a break" from her marriage. His other sister is twenty-five years old and owns the shop around the corner. She has a one-year-old and is married. Thrimi did not attend school, but she owns this shop and has run it herself for the last sixteen years.

The customers are leaving now and Thrimi walks out with them. This isn't the interview I had hoped for. "Where is she going?" I ask.

Nonchalantly, Dorji says, "I don't know, maybe the market." I am now sure that he didn't really explain my quest to her at all, but we carry on without her.

Thrimi has lived in Paro all her life. She has travelled to India and a bit around Bhutan. She is not here to ask if she would consider moving to another country, but Dorji certainly doesn't think she would.

I don't think I would have been able to ask about menopause, but now I can't anyway because she is gone. So I guess we are done. I am disappointed that Thrimi left, because I really wanted her picture. I have to leave in about ten minutes, so Dorji suggests, "Maybe my sister knows where she is." As we walk around the corner to his sister's shop, we find Thrimi, sitting and chatting with her daughter, chewing betel leaves. The betel leaf and areca nut chewing is a tradition we saw many Bhutanese people take part in. Red-stained teeth and lips are a common sight.

Dorji has to explain a little more to Thrimi now, as I would like a picture of her and me together, and of course I want to ask her the last question. She seems fine with the idea of the photo, and as Dorji takes the picture he also asks her, "Are you happy?" A bright smile forms on her red-stained lips and she says, "Yes!" But what else could I expect in the land of Gross National Happiness?

Chapter 28

India

"I met my husband on the second day of our four-day wedding ceremony and I was fourteen years old," said Ansuya, my Indian interviewee. Believe it or not, that wasn't the most surprising part of the interview. I will start my India story with the story of Ansuya. While we were in Orchha we took a cooking class, and I asked Vandana, the teacher, if she knew anyone I could interview. She told me her landlord's wife would be the perfect candidate. So the following day I hired a cab, we picked up Vandana and her three-year-old daughter, and we went over to Ansuya's house.

~

Ansuya – 48

We arrive at Ansuya's house and the door is answered by a teenage girl. "Come in. I am Deecha. Mom is in the bedroom," she says as she leads us into a bedroom, where Ansuya is lying in bed, breastfeeding one child while another sleeps beside her. Oh no, she can't be close to fifty if she is breastfeeding, I think to myself. Vandana must not have understood my age criteria. But I don't say anything out loud. It will be fun to speak to these ladies anyway, and I still have a few days left to find someone around fifty before I leave India.

"How old are the babies?" I ask.

"They are twenty-two-month-old twins," Vandana answers. She goes on to explain, "Ansuya conceived them through in vitro fertilization. She was forty-six, had lost a child at birth many years ago, and was very sad and depressed because she had no boys and no child of her own. I convinced her to have IVF and she conceived on the first try."

I look over at Deesha and say, "I thought Deesha just called her 'Mom'."

"Oh, she is adopted. She's not her real child. It is just not the same," Vandana says with no hesitation, even though Deesha understands English. I look at Deesha and she doesn't seem to mind the inference of not being a "real" child. At the same time I am clearing up that question, I am quickly doing math in my head, to come to the conclusion that Ansuya must be close to forty-nine years old. Vandana did understand me. Okay, back to plan A, and on with the interview.

As Ansuya sits up and untangles herself from the sheets on the bed, I see her more clearly and she looks tired and every day her age. Her long black hair is streaked with grey, and the lack of sleep shows in her eyes. She smiles weakly and sends Deesha off to make us chai. She straightens out her colourful saris and pulls one up to cover her head. The jangle of her many bracelets seems to awaken her spirit and she welcomes us to her house.

Deesha brings in the chai with the help of Ansuya's nephew, who is around twelve years old. After they serve us, they join her on the bed. The twins, a boy and a girl, and Vandana's daughter are running around, climbing on all of us, and I feel like one of the family. I almost forget that I am here to do an interview, but after some chai and playtime with the kids I get back on track.

"Tell me how you met your husband, and about your wedding," I say. Ansuya replies, "My grandparents arranged my marriage. I met my husband on the second day of our four-day wedding ceremony. I was fourteen years old. He was eighteen. The first day is with your own family and the second day I met him. Two more days of ceremonies and parties happened after that."

"I can't even imagine getting married at fourteen, let alone to a stranger," I say. Both Vandana and Ansuya say that is just how it is done here and they can't imagine it being any other way. They are shocked that I am

divorced and travelling on my own. I am not sure if they think I am scandalous or brave. They say being divorced is not an option for them.

"Some women in the big cities are now doing that, but we would never consider divorce."

After China, I am a little worried about asking about education, for fear of embarrassing anyone, but I ask anyway. "Did you attend school?" I ask.

"I went for two years, but I wasn't interested, so my parents didn't make me continue. It was not important for a girl to go to school. Deesha is in grade ten and will go to university, though. I think it is important now. The twins will also go to school and on to university, I hope," Ansuya answers.

"Do you think your life is better than your parents' life?" I ask.

"Oh yes, definitely. My husband is a lawyer and a good husband," she says proudly. "My parents are both dead now, but my father never had a good job, and bringing up four children with little money was very hard on them both."

"I read that eighty percent of Indian people are Hindu. It seems to be a big part of your life. Can you tell me more about that?" I ask. The ladies explain that being Hindu is who they are and it is very important to them. They tell me about some of the traditions of a married woman: they put red dye in the part of their hair, and draw a bindi (red dot) on their forehead. They must wear a sari, toe rings on both feet, bangles on their wrists, and the necklace their husband gave them on their wedding day. Then they admit that they have put away the good necklace they received and wear a less expensive one for everyday wear. Vandana explained that an unmarried woman may do some of these, but not the red dye on the part or the necklace from the wedding day.

I would love to know more, but Vandana has to get back soon, so we carry on. "Have you travelled much?" I ask. Ansuya tells me she grew up in a farming village, moved to her husband's farming village, and fifteen years ago moved here to Orchha. She has not travelled around the country at all.

"Would you like to travel, or live anywhere else if you had the opportunity?" I ask.

"Only if my husband wanted to," she answers sincerely.

Not believing she would have time for them, I ask hesitantly, "Do you have any hobbies?"

Deesha answers for her mother. "Sleeping," she blurts out. We all laugh, but I know it is something she longs for, but doesn't get much of. Deesha speaks up first again when I ask Ansuya how she would describe herself.

Deesha says, "She makes good dahl." Ansuya seems happy with that and does not contribute her own answer.

Finally, I ask, "Are you happy?" Her answer comes quickly. "Yes. When I did not have my own child, I was very depressed, stayed in bed almost all the time, and did not want to do anything. Now that I do, I am very happy."

And with that we have to leave, as Vandana has a cooking lesson. We hug good-bye, I kiss the kids, and we hop in the cab that has waited for us. I really had a great time with the ladies and am sad our visit is over so quickly.

My impressions of India are based on only a very small area in what is the seventh-largest country in the world, with the second highest population at over 1.1 billion. I visited only a few cities in two of the twenty-eight states: Orchha in Madhya Pradesh province, and Varanasi, Agra, and Delhi in Uttar Pradesh province. I have often said India was not on my list of places I wanted to visit. After seeing movies and pictures of the overcrowding, the poverty, and the filth, I really didn't think I would like it.

Indeed, the cities were crowded, it was filthy in many places, and the signs of poverty were everywhere. I won't say I loved it, because it was a test of patience, tolerance, and compassion, but I did really like it. It grabbed me and pulled me in.

My tour group for the India tour was young and fun and, luckily, very patient. I don't think we ever got a meal in less than an hour, and generally there was something missing or wrong, or something forgotten at every meal. Many times they would not bring the drinks until the meal was served. Many restaurants did not serve liquor or meat. However, when the food arrived it was always delicious. I definitely ate things I never thought I would, and loved it all. Nothing seemed too spicy, but I think they may use less spice for the tourists.

Tour guides, salespeople, market vendors, cab drivers, and beggars were relentless in their quest for our money. I tried to ignore them when possible, and when I had the time I would try talking to them and asking them questions. And, of course, I did get talked into a few small trinkets.

The poverty is widespread. Seeing the children begging and people dressed in rags and sleeping on the streets or in hovels at the side of the road was heart-wrenching. I don't know how these people will ever overcome their situations, but we definitely saw lots of entrepreneurial spirit in the adults and kids we met. It is apparent that the family unit is very important and they take care of each other.

We visited a few businesses that sought to help the poor, including a paper-making factory that supported and hired local women. Over eighty women were working there. They would be given leftover fabric pieces from various garment manufacturers and then turn those scraps into paper to make paper bags, various decorations, books, and wrapping paper, which we all bought.

The dirt roads, lack of sanitation, and rubbish everywhere is shocking. One day we watched a rat and a monkey fighting over an orange peel in front of our hotel. This state of chaos and mess was something we had to get used to. Wet-wipes and hand sanitizers helped with our confidence and cleanliness as we toured through the country.

The first city we stopped in was Varanasi, also known as Benares, Kashi, the City of Light, the City of Temples, and the City of Shiva. It is another city that claims to be the oldest city in the world. It is known as one of the holiest places in India. Mark Twain wrote: "Benaras is older than history, older than tradition, older even than legend and looks twice as old as all of them put together."

I loved this city! Varanasi sits on the banks of the Ganges, the Holy River. We arrived in the dark, packed ourselves into a rowboat with all our luggage, and were rowed slowly down the river to our hotel. I gasped when I first laid eyes on the backdrop of ancient temples lining the shore and the series of continuous steps, the ghats, leading down to the water. It is a sight I will never forget.

We learned as we sailed along that there are over one hundred of these cleansing ghats on the river's edge. Pilgrims come from all over to bathe in the Ganges, expecting spiritual rebirth.

In the morning on our way to the riverbank we saw many people perform *puja* (prayer) while dipping their heads under the water, as mantras by the *sadhus* (wandering mystics) filled the air. From the banks, we launched off for a mesmerizing, misty sunrise boat ride along the river.

During the day, as we wandered along the huge steps we watched many more people come to dip, to pray, and to wash in the Ganges. People, including the hotel staff, were doing laundry while children happily swam in the filthy water. Clothes and hotel laundry lay on the steps to dry as cows and dogs casually wandered over them.

Not far from our hotel, which overlooked the ghats, were the cremation ghats for devout Hindus, who believe that souls can better reach the afterlife if their remains are deposited in the Ganges. The smoke billows up and infuses the air and the debris from the cremations floats along the river. The daily life along the ghats is busy with vendors, beggars, women in colourful saris, sadhus in orange cloth, and children playing and flying kites, while tourists, cows, and monkeys wander along. I had a fascinating day hanging out, talking with some of the kids and being shown around by a fifteen-year-old street hustler.

The first kids I met, a brother and sister around six and eight, whose mother was doing her laundry in the river, were trying to sell me coloured powders. I just wanted to talk to them, so I let the girl draw some flowers on my hand while we talked. They both spoke English fairly well and told me they went to school but, "Today is a holiday." I didn't really believe them. We had a lot of fun talking, and I found it interesting to hear them try their sales pitch on me.

Not long after the children joined me, Durgesh, a young man of about fifteen, joined us and told me, "I took today off school because I slept in." I didn't buy that either, but he was fluent in English and a wealth of knowledge, so we hung out for the rest of the day. When I told him I was from Canada, he asked, "Vancouver or Toronto?" When I told him near Vancouver, he said he knew it well because, "That is where Goldie Hawn lives, and my uncle is a friend of Goldie's."

He took me to meet his uncle, a roly-poly little man with an orange band painted on his bald head and an odd-shaped bindi pasted on his forehead. He was very proud to show off his photo album of pictures of him with Goldie, as well as a framed letter from her. The two of them then took me to a small back room of wall-to-wall shelves lined with fabrics. I sat on the floor while the two of them pulled piece after piece out, draping them over themselves and me. "A good price just for you," they smiled eagerly. After much negotiation, we reached a price I was happy with, and I bought a lovely scarf and a piece of fabric for the quilt I hope to make with fabric from all the countries I visit. It was great fun.

Durgesh then took me to see a famous "baba" (a so-called holy man) who did readings and was "only in town for a week." He explained, "How lucky you are to meet me because I can arrange a reading, while others have to wait days." I knew he was playing me but I went along with him, to see how it played out. We went into another tiny room and there sat the baba, a large figure with long shaggy hair, a dishevelled beard and moustache, a dhoti wrapped around his waist covering his legs to his knees, and a sleeveless white T-shirt that didn't quite cover his round belly. What had I gotten myself into this time? Chai was served immediately and we agreed on a price for a reading. He wouldn't just do a palm reading. I would have a reading with my numbers as well. But the combo was only twenty dollars, so I agreed.

Here we were in this tiny room and he pulled out a cigarette. He asked me if I minded if he smoked, but lit up at the same time, not really waiting for a response. I thought the whole thing was something out of a spoof movie, so I just let it all happen as it happened. I gave him my birth date and time of birth, and he consulted his books and worked out my reading. We were interrupted twice. People just walked in, and once in the door, chai was served. The first group consisted of three travellers who had met on the train; a girl from Slovakia and two men from Russia and Israel. They were there for the girl, who wanted a palm reading only. Baba would not agree to this, but we had to finish our chai first, so we all talked. The man from Israel showed his scepticism clearly and said he didn't want to know his future. That didn't stop baba from telling him, "You will live to be at least seventy-eight."

Next in were a man and his daughter from Norway, wanting baba to arrange puja for them. The man wrote down his name and those of his three kids and paid sixty dollars. Baba was then to arrange for a Brahmin to perform puja for them. Coincidentally it was the father's fiftieth birthday. (My theme was following me.) In between all this going on, he gave me my reading. He did well with my past, picking up on things about my marriage and my upbringing, and his reading of my future was intriguing. He said some very similar things to the little lady in Vietnam, concerning the younger age of Mr. Right, who is apparently just around the corner. (Look out, all you forty-three-year-old single men out there!) He told me February and November are my lucky months, Tuesdays and Thursdays my lucky days, and seven and nine my lucky numbers. I resolved to look on a calendar and see if all three coincide one day in the future. (Maybe that will be the day I round that corner.) He gave me a few other suggestions, saying that on certain days I should wear certain colours and eat certain foods. His funniest advice was "Do not accept challenges while drunk." Good advice! Lastly, he declared I will live until at least eighty-three.

Durgesh took me to a local restaurant, where I was the only tourist. He helped me order, but would not let me buy him lunch. He waited outside and then showed me the way out of the winding alleys back to the ghats and my hotel. It was a day of surprises and mystic charm.

The evenings are a whole other experience on the ghats and the river. My tour group went out for a sunset row and a flower ceremony, where we set banyan tree leaves, shaped into a bowl and adorned with flowers, adrift on the river. Each bowl held a small lit candle. We made a wish, and if our bowl made it to the shore with the candle still lit our wish would come true. The river was alight with thousands of these earthen lamps floating to shore. It was spectacular. (Imagine the mess in the morning!)

Further down the river, in front of one of the temples, a musical ceremony took place nightly. With dozens of holy men lined up on stage, chanting began, slow and mesmerizing, and the men performed a dance. First incense sticks were waved about, filling the air with smoke and a sweet smell. The men then performed synchronized moves with elaborately lit candelabras, swinging them around their bodies and over their heads. Finally, there was a dance with beautiful feather plumes. Bells were rung, and the audience joined in the chanting to a fevered pitch. Then all of a sudden, a conch shell sounded and it was over. The masses of people in boats crammed up to the shore dispersed in a muddle of oars. We didn't have to be Hindu to feel the spirituality and magic of the moment.

If the ghats were my favourite part of Varanasi, the rest was another story. We had arrived by way of the river because otherwise we would have had to carry our bags through many tiny alleys to get to our hotel on the river. When we finally ventured through these alleys of tiny shops, markets, and food stalls, we found the main streets. Take everything I have said about every other crazy city with its traffic, people, and dogs, and then add hundreds of cows to the madness. I know I keep saying it and I should have been used to the chaos, but the wandering cows took it to a whole new level. The evening we were in town, amidst all the chaos a wedding party paraded down the middle of the street, ignoring the traffic. The groom was dressed in his finest, astride a horse, following the guests. There were hundreds of beautifully dressed women in bright-coloured saris, and small boys carrying candelabras and music boxes (plugged in with extension cords to a generator in the back of a truck). We didn't see the bride, so I don't know if this was before or after the actual ceremony. It just added to the bizarre cacophony of the streets.

When we did eventually have to get into the cycle-rickshaws to catch the train to our next destination, I screamed and squealed the whole way, as we avoided cars, bikes, dogs, goats, and oh so many cows. The streets were mostly dirt or uneven pavement and were absolutely strewn with rubbish. There were garbage heaps, shanties, and street people everywhere.

My tour in India was an equal mix of crazy and quiet, and our next few days were quiet, as we were slowly rowed along the Ganges. Our canopied boats were comfy, with padded cushions so we could lounge as we sailed past villages, watching kids playing, women doing washing, and fishermen in their boats. The serenity of the two days was such a welcome respite from the city.

A cook boat rowed alongside us, supplying us with delicious meals, and at night we camped on a sandy island in the middle of the river. We had thick, thick fog on our second day, and it was a little worrisome when we watched our oarsmen scratching their heads and looking lost, but eventually the fog cleared enough to find our way back into Varanasi. One of my tour mates had a guitar and a songbook, so we sang our way along the Ganges. It was very enjoyable. This was really a lovely way to see some of India's landscape.

Next up was Orchha, in the state of Madhya Pradesh on the Betwa River. In the sixteenth century, Orchha was the capital of one of the largest and most powerful kingdoms of central India. What remains are weathered temples, palaces, and cenotaphs housing parakeets, vultures, and black-faced langur monkeys. This small city of less than ten thousand also has a lively market, many small stores, and enough history to keep a visitor busy for a day or two. While there, we also rafted down the river to get an unobstructed view of all the medieval buildings.

There were not many tourists, so we were very conspicuous and the locals were extremely friendly. The kids grabbed our hands and wanted to play. The men stopped and literally stared and then wanted to talk to us. Many people wanted pictures, which we gladly posed for.

This is where we took our cooking class. Vandana was a great teacher and we enjoyed drinking marsala chai, tasting *aloo palak* (potatoes and spinach), *baignan* (eggplant), and *shahi paneer* (cottage cheese/peppers/curd), curry, and chapati. The class took place in her small home with her kids and the neighbour kids running in and out. When we finished eating she painted hennas on all her female students, placed flower garlands around our necks, and painted bindis on our foreheads. We left looking like a group of goofy tourists, with our stomachs full and our spirits high.

Next up was the city in India everyone wants to visit, Agra, the home of the Taj Mahal. We stayed about a minute's walk from this spectacular Wonder of the World. I was afraid it wouldn't live up to all the hype, but I need not have worried. The magnificent building surpassed expectations. When I first laid eyes on it, it just looked like all the pictures and I was a little disappointed. But when I got closer, I realized what a tremendous feat of architecture it is. The inlaid jewels and sculptured walls are amazing. As I wandered around the grounds the sun caught the walls in such a way it actually glistened in the sunlight.

The "Dream in Marble", as it is called, took twenty thousand men, one thousand elephants, and twenty-two years to build. It was completed in 1648. It is made of translucent white marble from Rajasthan (another state in India) inlaid with jade and crystal from China, turquoise from Tibet, lapis from Afghanistan, sapphire from Sri Lanka, and over twenty other semiprecious and precious stones.

The fact that it was built to be the tomb of only one woman is either incredibly romantic or just crazy. Shah Jahan was the ruler of the Mughal Empire from 1628 until 1658. He met Arjumand Banu when she was fourteen and he was fifteen. They married five years later. She was his constant companion and the love of his life. She died shortly after giving birth to their fourteenth child. (That would certainly kill me.) He then had the Taj built as her tomb. However, even though he meant it for his wife alone, his daughter had him entombed there as well.

In Agra we also visited the Red Fort, which was started by Shah Jahan's grandfather, Akbar the Great, in 1565, and was added to over the years. It was not in as good shape as the Taj but was also impressive, with seventy-foot-high double walls surrounding the mosque and palace. The most interesting part of the fort was the story of Shah Jahan's son, Aurangzeb. In 1658, Shah Jahan fell ill and that sparked a power struggle between his four sons.

Aurangzeb, who was the third son, came out the victor, after having his oldest brother killed. Then he imprisoned his "dear old dad" in one of the chambers in a palace at the fort. He wasn't all bad, though. He gave Shah Jahan one of the nicest rooms, with delicate marble lattices and gilded decorations and, most importantly, a view of the Taj Majal. So for the last eight years of his life, Shah Jahan remained in that room with one of his daughters, who volunteered to stay with him.

One afternoon in Agra I wandered around the streets and alleys in an area where most tourists don't usually go, and I started following a group of monkeys playing in all the crazy wiring along the tin eaves of the shops. What I will do for a picture! I found myself in a slum that was only minutes from the Taj Mahal. The contrast was striking. The narrow dirt streets were cluttered with garbage and open water drains. There were monkeys, dogs, cats, pigs, goats, cows, and kids running all over and women sitting outside their dilapidated houses. I could see inside some of their homes, which had only blankets on the dirt floors, as well as small fire pits for cooking.

I had to ask a group of teenagers (everywhere I went the teenagers knew English) if I was better to go back or keep going forward to reach the street to my hotel. They all had a good laugh at my expense, but one of them pointed forward and off I went. I wasn't sure he was telling me the truth, but I had no choice, really, so I followed his directions. I guess getting that far into this dodgy area has to go down on my "stupid things I did" list. Fortunately, the boy was being kind, and after another few minutes I could see the Taj in the distance and found my way to a main road.

Once there, I was approached by two young boys with a cycle-rickshaw. They were desperate to take me for a ride. I tried to explain that I really wanted to walk, but they were not taking no for an answer. So first I had them let me cycle and pull them. They got a real kick out of that, and then I let them take me on a tour. Again, they both told me they had the day off from school. One was about sixteen and the other twelve, and both spoke English fairly well. We had a great afternoon touring around Agra. We went to the riverbank behind the Taj, which was not a regular tourist spot. The beach was filthy, but the view was spectacular. Then I let them take me to a carpet shop. They got a commission whether I bought or not, so I thought, why not?

I did something there I never thought I would do—I bought a carpet. I had no thought of doing it, but I found a lovely narrow carpet at a price that was considerably less than I had seen in Turkey, where I had been to many carpet shops. I enjoyed watching the weavers, drinking chai with my salesman and discussing religion, of all things. He was a Muslim, as are most of the citizens of Agra, knew a lot about other religions, and was studying to be a healer.

The boys then took me to "an uncle's" jewellery store. I bought a small pair of earrings there and spent fifteen minutes fending off the uncle, who apparently fell in love with me the moment I appeared in the door. He was quite amusing, but I declined the invitation to dinner. The boys did all right by me, with commissions and my payment for the tour, so I think they had a good day. I sure did.

A good night's sleep in Agra can only be enjoyed if you have good earplugs. As it is a Muslim area, the call to prayer is broadcast five times a day. The hundreds of stray dogs of the city either love the almost haunting sound or hate it, I am not sure which, but they howl throughout the call and then continue when it is over. As the first call is at sunrise, unless you are hoping to see the early morning light, those ear plugs are a necessity.

New Delhi was the last city on our tour. It is a modern city, with "real" roads and no cows I could see. I didn't have much time there, but did a short tour of one area. In the space of a few blocks we visited a Sihk temple, a Hindu temple, and a Catholic church. We also wandered through the colourful, crowded flower market that opens at five a.m. daily.

The people of India seem to live and breathe their culture in their clothing, their rituals, their temples, and their family values. There is a mystical, spiritual feel to this country that left me wanting more.

The next day I would be off to Bali. I looked forward to a week of sleeping in and reading by the pool. This back-to-back touring had left me exhausted. I needed time as well to continue planning the next portion of my trip. I touched base with my sister, who was doing so well after her heart attack that she declared she wanted to join me somewhere. We decided she would join me in the Caribbean on a cruise.

So, thirty countries down and it was all going well, other than getting a little tired. I felt that it would have been nice to spend more time with my interviewees, but considering most were arranged on the fly it was working out quite amazingly.

Chapter 29
Indonesia - Bali

"Would you like to come to a cremation tomorrow?" asked Made, my room cleaner. "Sure," I answered, even when I realized tomorrow was Christmas Day.

My original plan for Bali was to have two weeks of rest, but who was I kidding? I can't rest for two weeks. The word *relax* has not found its way into my vocabulary. So the week before I arrived, I booked a hotel for one week in Ubud and then a tour for the second week. The hotel I stayed in was wonderful, with traditional Balinese bungalows and all the amenities. The grounds had beautifully maintained flowering shrubs and tropical plants around the pool with stone carvings everywhere. Blooms plucked from the trees were left on the beds and decorating the walkways. The staff made a point of knowing everyone's name and they all vied for the chance to be every customer's personal guide. Made, (pronounced Ma-dee) took me under his wing and arranged to show me around Ubud when he was off shift.

Bali is one of the six thousand inhabited islands of Indonesia's 17,508 islands. (I wonder who counted them all.) It is not a very big island, only about ninety kilometres from north to south and 140 kilometres from east to west. Just over three million of Indonesia's 237 million people live in Bali. I was surprised to learn that Indonesia is the world's fourth most populous country and has the world's largest population of Muslims. Bali, however, is mostly

Hindu. The traditional clothes are not saris, as in India, but rather sarongs worn as skirts for men and women and a shirt tied with a sash.

This island is a true tropical paradise. The trees, plants, rivers, lakes, waterfalls, ocean, beaches, volcanoes, rice paddies, and monkeys make it absolutely stunning. I decided to spend my week resting in Ubud, after hearing the beaches of the south can be crowded and crazy.

Ubud is a great little town of about eight thousand. It is the cultural and arts centre of the island. Artisans' shops, galleries, temples, markets, cafes, restaurants, and spas line the streets. Every business, house, statue, and temple has an offering of flowers and rice placed at the doorstep daily. The remnants of the offerings are the only litter on the otherwise clean streets. While there is no litter, the sidewalks are uneven and constantly under construction. One of the girls in my group fell into a hole in the sidewalk, right in front of me. I think I screamed louder than she did. Lucky for her, only one leg went down, and she came out with only a skinned shin. It was hard to believe I navigated the streets without hurting myself. I guess I'd had lots of practice watching my footing from the last few countries.

My first few days were truly a rest, as I was sick. I think it may have been airline food, as this was the second time I was sick the day I arrived somewhere. It was good timing, though. I would rather have been sick in that nice clean room, alone, than the one with a roommate in India.

When I was feeling better Made whisked me off on his motorcycle —I was getting good at this motorcycle touring—and off we went to attend the cremation and see some of his countryside. Having a local guide to myself to answer all my questions was great. He was married, had two children, and lived about thirty minutes outside of Ubud. Having the name Made meant he was the second-born in his family. All Balinese are named by their birth order. The first child is Wayan, the second is Made, the third is Nyoman, the fourth is Ketut, and the fifth is Second Wayan, etc. They use the names for men or women. So there is never a worry for parents about what they should name their baby, but it sure must be confusing at school.

Even at the hotel, when I asked, "Where is Made?" the response was always, "Which one?"

During my visit they were preparing for an upcoming election and campaign posters decorated the whole island. It was interesting to me that the vast majority of candidates were either Wayans or Ketuts. Someone should do a research paper on politicians—are they always the oldest or the youngest in the birth order?

Made shared some of the Balinese rituals with me, starting with *metatah*. One of the first things I noticed about Made was his great smile. His teeth looked perfect. He explained they have a ritual called *metatah*. Most Balinese Hindus at the age of seventeen or eighteen will have their upper front six teeth filed down to make them even. It is not done by a dentist, but by someone of the Brahmana caste called a *sangging*. They believe this will rid the youth of lust, greed, anger, insobriety, confusion, and jealousy. Apparently, only demons have crooked fangs. What does that say about all of us Westerners?

One of the most important rituals in Bali is cremation. Balinese believe the soul cannot be freed as long as there is a body. The cremation returns the body's five elements of air, earth, fire, water, and space to the cosmos. Because Balinese believe death is not the end, but a new beginning, cremation is a time of celebration.

Made first took me to his home, and on the ride there I thought all the streets were lined with temples. There are rock or cement walls with decorative gates, Hindu carvings, and statues everywhere, and I assumed that meant there were temples behind the walls. However, when we stopped at Made's house, I learned that there are family compounds behind the walls. Most have several buildings surrounding a courtyard, allowing extended family members to live close together while having their own space. Every compound has a family shrine in the courtyard. Made and his wife (also Made) stopped to give a small offering and a prayer at the shrine before we walked out to the street to join the other villagers to parade to the cremation site.

The woman who died was eighty and lived in Made's complex. I think she was a sister-in-law's mother. Everyone was dressed in his or her finest colourful traditional clothes. The whole village seemed to be involved in the ceremony. Women carried offerings on their head and led the procession, followed by an elaborately built chariot carrying the body. Behind the chariot came a band playing Balinese music. The rest of the villagers and I followed. We passed the village temple, where they turned the chariot around three times, and then went into a field a little further on. The women then sat down and the men took the chariot apart and added it to the pyre. Then the body was added, the offerings placed around the body, and finally it was set alight. I tried not to think about what was actually happening, and take in the culture and tradition of those surrounding me. It was a privilege to be a part of this glorious ceremony and a Christmas Day I won't soon forget.

Once the cremation was over Made and I hopped back on the motorcycle and visited a botanical garden, but to be honest I think the whole island was a beautiful botanical garden, so it really wasn't necessary to stop there. What was spectacular was our visit to the village of Petulu. Made didn't tell me where we were going. I was just enjoying riding through small villages, past beautiful terraced rice paddies and through tropical forests, and then I heard it: the chirping of thousands of birds. Nesting in the trees along the road were over seven thousand white herons. Made explained that the herons showed up during a ceremony after a massacre of suspected Communists in Indonesia in 1965. Villagers believe that the white herons are the souls of those who were killed.

We sat at a local *warung* (cafe) to watch and listen. There were three different types of herons and they shared the same trees, although they don't intermingle. The herons spend most of the day flying around and finding food, but in the late afternoon they return to the trees. The otherwise green trees look completely white. It is an amazing sight.

We also passed many men sitting on the stoop outside their gates, with roosters at their side. This is because cockfighting is a big pastime in Bali. They have legal cockfights before ceremonies and festivals and illegal cockfights for gambling. The men we saw all seemed very proud of their birds.

Another day Made took me to visit Ketut Leyer, the medicine man and fortune-teller written about in the book *Eat, Pray, Love*. This eighty-nine-year-old man was sitting cross-legged on the porch of his home, blessing a basket of medicine for a local couple, when we arrived. When they left he had me sit with him. He had the biggest, almost toothless, grin. He asked how I found him. I said, "I read about you in the book." He brought it out and said, "What she say about me? I don't speak English." I grinned and said, "Oh, she said all bad things about you." He said, "You joking," and we both laughed. Then, as if he didn't know, I said, "She respects you very much."

Before he began to tell my fortune, he said, "I will only tell you what I see, good or bad, as lying is not my cup of tea." I laughed, because I remembered he used that expression many times in the book. He started by telling me that from my ears, he could tell I was good; from my nose, I was healthy; from my mouth, I was happy; from my eyes, I was smart; and from my hand, I have a long life line and would live to 105. Yikes! He said he knew I'd had one child, a short marriage, and was divorced. He also said I would get married two more times before I was fifty. "Oh no, sixty," he said, when I reminded him I was already fifty-one. In his defence, he said he thought I was thirty-five. He was quite a charmer!

He declared that I have good kidneys, heart, lungs, and knees, and no arthritis. "Good all over," he said. He also said I will be rich—that's good. Baba said something like that too. He said I would be back in Bali for my honeymoon and I should come to see him. I wondered if that will be my next marriage or the one after? He allowed me to take his picture, but not before he put on his best clothes, a headscarf, and jewellery. Another fortune done. They all think Mr. Right was somewhere out there. Even two of them, according to Ketut.

While in Ubud I also fed my spa addiction with four massages, a pedicure, and a manicure. One of the massages was at a spa built into the side of a cliff overlooking a river and a tropical forest. Instead of having a canned recording of birds singing and water lapping on a shore, I had a body scrub, massage, and lotus flower soak while listening to the real sounds of the forest and river below. It was wonderful.

If I had to be away from my family and friends at Christmas, Ubud surely was a nice place to do it. I rested, swam, relaxed, read, caught up on e-mails, and still managed to see many things in the area.

My second week in Bali was action packed. It was another great group of people: six Aussies, a couple from the States, and Andy, an Aussie tour leader who had lived in Bali for eight years. It is hard to believe we had fun, considering one girl was bitten by a monkey, one fellow had a very bad stomach ailment, our tour guide was so sick with dengue fever he couldn't get out of bed, three of us had eye infections, including me, and several people had sore throats and running noses. Visits to the medical clinic became a daily event.

Despite all the ailments we went white-water rafting, hiked through beautiful rice fields, biked through several villages, snorkelled along a stunning coral reef with an incredible array of tropical fish, hiked to the top of a volcano and walked around its rim while warming ourselves on the steaming rock, boated out to see dolphins, visited a coffee plantation, and hiked to a waterfall. I am sure I lost a few pounds with all the hiking. It was a good thing I had the relaxing week first, because in the second week we barely sat still.

On one of the hikes we stopped at a shop for a drink and a local man came by and asked where we were from. When he heard most were from Australia he said he had been there with a Balinese choir. Then he just started singing "Amazing Grace" and we all joined in. This song is very special to me. One of my brothers died when he was twenty-one (I was fifteen). My mother heard "Amazing Grace" that day, and ever since it seems the song would be played on the radio or TV on his birthday or the anniversary of the day he died. Now when I hear it I think of all the people I have lost. As this was Christmastime, it seemed just right to hear it and sing it out loud in such a beautiful setting.

It really was a great two weeks, on a fabulous island. I loved Bali. The weather was hot but manageable, the prices were quite cheap —my lovely hotel was only thirty-five dollars a night—the food was very tasty, and the people were warm and friendly. Towards the end of the tour our replacement guide, Jasmen (Andy was still sick with dengue fever), found me an interviewee.

~

Ayu – 48

Jasmen picks me up on her scooter and I squeeze on the back. We ride over to Ayu's warung. Ayu and her husband run this tiny roadside cafe. She and her daughter, Wayan, are sitting at one of the two tables in front of the take-out window. Ayu's husband is in the back of the cafe grinding grain. There are no customers to tend to.

Wayan is eleven years old and sits protectively on her mom's knee. Her face is decorated with rice glued to her forehead in the shape of a flower. They tell me they are on their way to a celebration when we are finished here. Jasmen explains my quest and Ayu is happy to answer my questions.

Jasmen told me on the way over that she wasn't really sure how old Ayu was, but thought she may be around fifty. I ask and Ayu says, "I don't keep track, but I was married at thirty-four and that was 1995, so I guess I am close to forty-eight"

"That will work," I say. I ask her about her husband. "I met him when I was thirty-four and we were married a month later."

"Why so quickly?" I ask.

She says, "I come from a family of eight and I really wanted children. I was getting old, so I prayed for a husband. When my friends set us up we liked each other, so we saw no reason to wait." She says he was from the same caste as her, and that was important. I told her I had not noticed the differences in castes, and she said that although the caste system is not obvious to an outsider, it definitely exists in Bali.

She and her husband have had this warung for two years and prior to that they both worked in various other restaurants. She said they don't make much money, but enjoy having their own business. I ask if she has any hobbies and she says, "Cooking."

"Did you go to school?" I ask.

"My father had a low-paying job, so most of my siblings and I only went to elementary school. We needed to help make money for the family. My daughter is only in grade six now, but she will go all the way to university. She is my only child, and I want her to be able to do whatever she wants."

I hope I am not pushing too far and ask about menopause. Ayu says she has no symptoms, but her older sister has started menopause and is getting constant headaches. I ask if her sister or any of her friends take HRT or any kind of medication, and she responds quickly by saying, "I don't know what HRT is. We don't talk about these things with our friends." Again, I realize I have gone as far as I can with that subject.

Ayu says she has lived in Bali and Lombok (another island of Indonesia), but would love to move to the United States, if she had the opportunity. She has friends there and thinks life would be easier.

She has to get to the celebration, so we finish up with the last question. "Are you happy?" I ask.

"I am not very happy, but I have to be happy because if you are not happy you can get sick and I can't afford a doctor," she answers sadly.

I feel bad that I have to leave on this sad note. Here I am, in one of my favourite places, and this woman, who is as hardworking and ambitious as all the other women I have interviewed, is not happy. But she is off to a ceremony and Jasmen has other places to go, so we hop back on her scooter and she takes me back to my hotel.

$\sim$

Since I left Bali, I have read that there is now free medical available to both the rich and the poor, provided they are prepared to accept treatment in third-class medical wards.

Chapter 30

Australia

"If you lie on your immigration and customs forms you will be severely fined" stated many big signs posted at the Sydney airport. The list of things you can't bring in seemed endless: food, wood, souvenirs filled with straw, lacquered items, handicrafts made from plant material, bamboo, seeds, and on and on. I had several of those items and was worried I was going to have to give up half my treasures. I wasn't going to lie, not after all those warnings, so I let them go through my bag. They picked up the wooden things, asked where they were from, put them back in my messy pack and let me take them. Between the customs staff, dogs, x-ray machines, and cameras, you would have thought we were in a country full of terrorists, and yet after all that I was able to walk in with all my contraband. It took longer to get through Australian customs than any other border I had been through.

After I left Bali, I spent two days in Bangkok and then flew into Australia. Having been in Australia twenty-five years earlier, for six months, I have always called it "Canada with warmer weather and an accent." Both countries are part of the Commonwealth, both have very little political upheaval, both have among the smallest population densities in the world (Canada is 3.4 people per square kilometre, Australia is 2.84), and both have beautiful oceans, coastlines, and beaches.

Although I had met many Australians on my tours, none were from Sydney, so I had to find a hotel and the area of Glebe was recommended. It is just three kilometres from the city, making it less expensive than city centre. Glebe is a trendy area full of art galleries, bookstores, music shops, bakeries, and funky cafes. There is also a great market on Saturdays. I really enjoyed staying there instead of in the middle of the city.

Australia is a huge country with lots to see, but I had only six days and didn't want to spend it travelling, so I decided to stay in Sydney and get reacquainted with the city I fell in love with so many years ago. Not surprising, however, after twenty-five years the only places that I found familiar were the famous Harbour Bridge and the Opera House, and even those were in the wrong place, according to my memory. Funny how that works. I am guessing they changed the configuration of the waterfront since my last visit.

Sydney is ranked in the top ten of the world's "most liveable cities", and I must agree. Even though it is a city of over four million, it seemed safe and had great transit, many parks, and an abundance of cultural events and festivals. There was fabulous shopping and a huge variety of great restaurants with many different ethnic cuisines.

It is often called the "Harbour City", which is appropriate, as the harbour, crowded with kayaks, sailboats, ferries, and cruise ships, is the focal point of the city. The last time I was here, I was in a sailing regatta. I have to say that was one of the scariest things I have ever done. We had to race around the ferries and I was constantly worried we were going to sail right into one. I couldn't imagine kayaking in that busy harbour, but saw many people doing it.

I spent my days visiting other travelling friends who happened to be in Sydney. First I hooked up with Alex, the eighteen-year-old daughter of a friend from home. I have known her since the day she was born. She was in Sydney after months in Thailand as part of her Gap Year. She is an amazing young woman, very confident and self-assured. She had her friend Jen visiting as well, and gave us a tour of her adopted city. We started at Darling Harbour, which was developed for the Australian Bicentenary in 1988. It has an exhibition space, a convention centre, the National Maritime

Museum and aquarium, waterside restaurants, and pedestrian boardwalks. We had a great visit, plus dinner and a movie. It was almost like being at home.

On another day I explored more of the city with Kelly, the German girl from my Southeast Asia tour. She had spent the time since the tour in Australia and was on her way to New Zealand. We had a good day catching up on each other's trip and wandering around Circular Quay and The Rocks. They are in the main tourist area near the Opera House and the Bridge. The Rocks is close to where Sydney was first settled in 1788. Now it is all shops, bars, restaurants, and a great weekend market.

The Opera House can now be added to my list of UNESCO World Heritage Sites. The design competition was won in 1957 by a Danish architect. Construction started in 1959, but it wasn't completed until 1973. There is not only an opera hall, but also a concert hall, a drama theatre, a playhouse, a studio, and a multipurpose venue. The acoustics are purported to be the best there are. It is an amazing building with a rooftop of over one million ceramic tiles that glisten in the sun.

The Australians have worked out a way to make money from the Harbour Bridge: you can now climb to the top. I didn't try it, but I saw the people hiking over the top. They would have had a great view, but after my busy week in Bali it looked like a bit too much work for me.

One afternoon Jen and I spent a few hours at Bondi Beach, which is a beautiful golden sand beach full of sun worshippers and surfers, not far from the centre of the city. I loved watching the surfers riding the waves, and we had a great walk from one end to the other. Across from the beach, trendy shops, and restaurants lined the main street. Knowing the prices would be beyond our budgets, we had an ice cream and headed back to the city.

My last visit was with Angela, an Australian I met on my Syrian tour. She lives in Wollongong, just outside Sydney, and came into the city for the Sydney Festival. It is a three-week event held every January and I was lucky enough to arrive for First Night, when all events are free. The streets are cleared of cars and people wander around freely while over six hundred musicians, dancers, and artists from around the world perform on open-air stages across the city.

We visited several venues and enjoyed some great music. The theme of the event that year was "Sydney Dances" and they taught all the spectators "the Sydney", a new dance. Then at eight thirty the whole city became one massive dance floor. At every venue the same song was played and everyone danced "the Sydney". I could have benefited from a few more lessons, but it was fun watching everyone trying all the same moves.

Although I enjoyed my visits and seeing this great city again, it was an odd week for me. After being in Asia for two and a half months, I think I was going through culture shock, homesickness, and definite wallet shock. Sydney is a very expensive city.

Maybe in New Zealand I would mellow out.

~

Angela – 53

Angela and I were so busy at the music festival we didn't have time to do an actual interview, so she answered the questions I didn't know the answers to by e-mail. When I met her in Syria she had just come from two weeks in Iran. She is an adventurous traveller and has been to many places I am still yearning to see. I am not sure about Iran, although she really enjoyed it and highly recommends it. She had many helpful hints for countries I have yet to visit.

She is fifty-three, but says she feels thirty-five. Having travelled with her, I tend to agree; she has a great vibe and energy level. She used every moment of our trip in Syria to explore and shop in each place we visited. She would return from our free time with stories of places and items she had found that no one else did. She had already sent a few boxes home from Iran and had overfilled her bags in Syria. She had a good eye for unique items and bought some really beautiful jewellery and artwork.

Although not married, Angela and her boyfriend have been together for thirty-five years. They don't have any children. She does a lot of her travelling alone, but they have also travelled together.

She still has some menopausal symptoms, but is not taking any medications for them. Her daily routine starts with exercise every morning before leaving for work and she feels that helps to alleviate many problems.

Her parents finished high school and were married for fifty-five years. Her father passed away at seventy-six. Her mother is still alive at eighty-seven. She feels her life is better than her parents'. Angela is a lawyer and has worked at her current job for thirteen years. Religion is not part of her life.

She would move to another country, but only for part of the year. She said almost anywhere, but Spain and Italy are at the top of her list. And yes, she is happy!

We may run, walk, stumble, drive or fly, but let us
never lose sight of the reason for the journey, or
miss a chance to see a rainbow on the way.

—Gloria Gaither

Chapter 31

New Zealand

"Sorry, we didn't hear back from you sooner and now we are having others staying with us," wrote the people I thought I was going to stay with in Auckland. Relatives of a friend of mine had said I could stay at their house while in Auckland, but because I was thinking of skipping New Zealand I didn't let them know the exact date until two weeks before I was arriving. That meant another hotel for five nights. It's official: I really don't like travelling alone and staying in hotels alone, a strange confession for a gal who set out to travel around the world by herself. It's a good thing I have so many friends that were able to join me, and that I found such great tours to take.

The good thing, however, about having no set plans for Auckland was that it gave me a chance to work on the next part of the journey. I had fifteen countries left. I had places to stay in Kenya, Uganda, and Costa Rica, and my sister and I had agreed on a Caribbean cruise, so I had to piece it all together.

After a few days of inquiries and e-mails to a multitude of tour companies, cruise companies, and airlines, my plan came together: five countries in Africa, five in the Caribbean on a cruise, and five in Central America. With that done, I spent a few days exploring Auckland.

Having visited New Zealand twenty-five years previously, it has always been on my favourite country list. It too reminds me of home, even more than Australia. The weather is closer to our weather and the countryside more evergreen than tropical.

When I was last in New Zealand everything seemed to be a few years behind in terms of fashion and culture. Not so on this visit. Auckland has tied with Vancouver as the "fourth highest city for quality of living" and is an easy, safe, modern city to explore. There is great shopping and restaurants, but its best feature is the location. The city is surrounded by breathtaking scenery, beautiful beaches, great walking trails, and small islands. It is situated on a narrow isthmus, giving it harbours on both the Tasman Sea and the Pacific Ocean.

New Zealand is an outdoor enthusiast's paradise. Hiking, kayaking, sailing, beach holidays, and scenic road trips can be found on both the North and South Island, but I felt the need to stay in one place for more than two days and just enjoyed my days in and around Auckland. I tried to be more relaxed than in Sydney—I slept in, watched TV, read, walked for miles, and only did a few sightseeing trips.

On one trip I took a thirty-five-kilometre ferry ride to the island of Waiheke. This picturesque island is twenty-five kilometres long and I joined a bus tour to see the vineyards, olive groves, forests, farmland, and beautiful beaches that make up the island. I would have loved to have had my own vehicle to visit a few of the twenty or more wineries. After the tour I had a delicious lunch of local seafood and wine while enjoying an impressive ocean view. (It would have been so much better, however, to have had someone to join me.)

Another day I took a tour to the Bay of Islands. It was a four-hour drive north of Auckland through beautiful countryside of rolling hills and farmland. I was surprised to see more cows than sheep, as there are apparently twelve times more sheep than people in New Zealand. From the town of Paihia, we departed on a boat tour to "swim with the dolphins". I was excited in Sea World in San Diego to merely touch captured dolphins, so this promised to be much more exciting. Not long into our journey we spotted about thirty blue nose dolphins jumping in front of our boat, swimming at our bow, and frolicking alongside us. Unfortunately we couldn't swim along, as there were babies with them and the tour companies don't allow you to swim with young ones. It was a spectacular show watching them in their own habitat. I was in awe and not at all disappointed that we couldn't get in the water. Frankly, I think I would have been quite scared to be that close. We saw many more groups of the sleek beauties as the day went on. It was a fabulous tour in a lovely bay of almost 150 islands.

The day of the dolphin tour would have been my mom's ninetieth birthday, so I had her on my mind. Incredibly, on the way back to Auckland, the driver put on his favourite CD, and the third song was "Amazing Grace".

To top that day off, I later went into the local casino and had a hoot playing in a poker tournament. I was the only woman amongst fifty-three men. I came in fourth and walked away with five hundred dollars! It sure was a great way to end a super day.

The strange thing about my stay in New Zealand is that I didn't get an interview. I just never met anyone in the right age category. I had a taxi driver who told me his wife was the right age, but we didn't make any arrangements to meet again. Here I was, in a country where they spoke the same language, and I failed to find someone. I was weary and a little discouraged. I failed to see the rainbow. I realized I was in serious need of some downtime, so I was happy that after my next stop, Hong Kong, I would be going home for a few weeks to recharge before finishing off my last fifteen countries.

Travelling is like flirting with life. It's like saying, I would stay and love you, but I have to go: this is my station.

—Lisa St. Aubin de Teran

Chapter 32

Hong Kong

"I love this city!" I declared, after only a short time in Hong Kong. For a gal from a city with not one skyscraper and a country density of 3.4 people per square kilometre, it is hard to believe I would like, let alone love, a city with over 7,500 skyscrapers and a density of over 6,300 people per square kilometre. There was just something about Hong Kong that drew me in. It didn't hurt that the temperature was twenty-three degrees, which is my favourite temperature. I found it easy to work out the transit system, and walking around the markets and shopping areas was pleasant. The city was clean and orderly considering the amount of people and traffic, and there were very few motorcycles or bicycles trying to zip in and out of the flow of cars. Vehicles and pedestrians actually obeyed the traffic lights! There were vendors trying to get me into their shops, but they weren't too aggressive, and lots were happy just to talk about Canada. I found that many people spoke English.

Hong Kong has been a special administrative region of the People's Republic of China since the handover from British rule in 1997. However, little has changed in terms of the way it carries on; it is now "one country, two systems". Hong Kong still maintains a capitalist system and operates within its own rights and freedoms until 2047. I think there are many theories about what will happen then.

My expectation for Hong Kong was that it would be just a big crowded city of seven million with good shopping. Instead, I found a beautiful city where the ocean is never far away and there is actual green space. I read that 40 percent of Hong Kong is dedicated for parks and nature reserves. Hong Kong is made up of Hong Kong Island, Lantau, Kowloon Peninsula, and the New Territories, as well as 260 other islands. I stayed on the Kowloon side.

I had received several suggestions for places to see and things to do from friends who know Hong Kong well. Even though I was travel-weary, I was excited to see as much as I could in the two days I had. I stayed in the nicest, and of course the most expensive, hotel I had stayed in on this journey, so I was happy to see the breakfast I ordered was only twelve dollars. Sadly, I then found out the tea was nine dollars!

Although many things were expensive in Hong Kong, not everything was. The Star Ferry across Victoria Harbour between Hong Kong Island and Kowloon was only fifty cents, and the buses and subway were reasonably priced. There were many different markets in Mongkok, the area in which I stayed. I had a great time exploring the ladies market, the electronics market, the jade market, and the sports market. I missed the bird and goldfish market. The shopping opportunities were endless, from high-fashion malls, trendy boutiques and antiques to traditional Chinese product stores, but they would have to wait until next time. I still had much more to see, so I took a bus tour around Kowloon and part of Hong Kong Island, which gave me a fantastic overview of the city.

I also took the Peak Tram up to the Peak Tower Sky Terrace to get a spectacular view of the city skyline and harbour and a good prospective of the size of the city. All that, and I still found time to take a city bus out to Stanley, a small town on the southeastern part of Hong Kong Island. The ride itself was a treat, travelling along the coast to this cute seaside village. Once there I found another busy market and restaurants lining the promenade along a lovely little beach.

My first day was not over. I still had time for the Symphony of Lights. During this event, which takes place every night, over forty buildings on both sides of the Victoria Harbour are decked out with lights that twinkle, flash, and dance to the beat of music. That was my nightlife experience in this city, but of course in this world-class city there is also world-class dining, entertainment, and nightlife.

On my second day I took the train and then a cable car ride to Ngong Ping Village on Lantau Island. The cable car ride offered a breathtaking view of Lantau Island and the South China Sea. In the village is the "biggest sitting Buddha", the Tian Tuan Buddha. I thought it was an ancient Buddha, but have since learned it was built in 1993. The village was just full of expensive souvenirs shops and cafes, but the ride out was a great way to see more of Hong Kong.

On the cable car and train ride back, I thought I might have met Mr. Right. He was from Scotland, good-looking, loved travelling, and seemed interesting. We talked about travel, our favourite books, and music. My mind whirled, first trying to understand his accent, and then wondering if he was forty-three (as predicted). Then all of a sudden, he realized we were at his stop. He jumped up and off he went. I laughed at myself when he left. One little conversation and I was planning our future together. I am not usually prone to falling for someone so quickly, but all those fortune-tellers had me looking at every forty-three-year-old man as the next love of my life. I laughed out loud and the people around me must have thought I was nuts.

Busy as I was in Hong Kong, I still managed to squeeze in an interview. My friend Bob used to live in Hong Kong, so he set me up to meet a friend of his, who in turn set me up with his business administrator, Daisy.

～

Daisy – 49

I manage to find Daisy's office amongst the thousands of high-rises and am waiting for her to finish some work. She has given me tea and set me up in the boardroom to wait for her. I am not dressed to be sitting in a fancy business office, so I think she is really just hiding me from their clients.

After about twenty minutes she joins me and we begin. She is happy to meet a friend of Bob's and to help me with my questions. She tells me she is forty-nine. She has two brothers. I ask about the one-child rule and she explains that Hong Kong did not have that rule. In her parents' generation they were encouraged to have two children. Now the government is encouraging couples to have three children, to tackle the declining birthrate. Hong Kong has the lowest birthrate in the world. In the country with the highest density in the world it is really not hard to imagine why women do not want to add more kids.

I ask her about her marriage and kids, and she says she lived at home with her parents until she was married at twenty-seven. They dated for a year before they were married. Arranged marriages are not common in Hong Kong. They have two children, a boy thirteen years old and a girl ten years old. They live in a three-bedroom flat in a twenty-seven-storey building. It is about thirty minutes by bus to her office.

I am a bit off topic, but I have to ask her about the thousands of women sitting in groups all over the city that I saw the day before, which was a Sunday. Daisy explains that these were the Philippine domestic workers, who all have Sundays off. They meet at every open space they can, bring lunch and visit. She explained that many Hong Kong households have domestic help. Her current helper has been with her for eight years and does everything from child care to cooking and cleaning. Daisy's helper goes home every two years to see her husband and sends most of her money back to the Philippines. Daisy tells me that many of these women stay until they make enough money to go home, buy a house, and have domestic help themselves.

She has worked at her present job since she was twenty and couldn't have done it without her helper. She calls herself the "girl Friday" of this insurance brokerage.

Asking about university opens up an interesting conversation. Neither Daisy nor her parents went to university. She says the education system in Hong Kong has been called "stuffed duck". There is no creativity to the system, students are force-fed the information and told to memorize. The instructors stand in front of the class and read the textbooks, barely looking up from the page. "People that can afford it send their children out of the country for higher education," she says.

She says she is Christian, but doesn't attend church often. (I read that about 10 percent of the population in Hong Kong are Christian.)

Daisy's face lights up when she talks about her hobbies: shopping and travelling. "Well, you live in the perfect place for both," I say. She has been to Canada, the U.S.A., Europe, Southeast Asia, Australia, and China.

"Would you live anywhere else?" I ask.

"No, I love Hong Kong. The only thing I don't like is the pollution, but it has gotten better in the last few years since many factories have moved to China because of cheaper rents and wages," she says.

She has no problem talking about menopause and says she has started having hot flashes. She takes traditional Chinese medications, as do all her friends. None of them use HRT.

"How would you describe yourself?" I ask.

"I love movies and singing along to music. I am a very basic, normal Hong Kong female with a job and a family," she answers.

And finally, "Are you happy?"

"Absolutely!" she proclaims with a big smile. She has to go back to work, and I need to find my way back to my hotel to get my luggage and head out to the airport. I am on my way home!

Our happiest moments as tourists always seem to
come when we stumble upon one thing while in
pursuit of something else.

—Lawrence Block

Chapter 33

Kenya

"You put the blue in my sky," said Nelson, the Kenyan leader of a group of Canadians and Kenyans I met while I was home in October. They were at a friend's farm to do volunteer work as part of a Canada World Youth Program. The program advocates learning by doing. Young volunteers learn by getting involved in communities in Canada and abroad.

Nelson was very excited when I told him about my journey, and I asked if he could help with my visit in Kenya. He was thrilled that I asked for his help and suggested I stay with someone in his village. He felt it was important that I stay with someone other than him because he wanted the people in his village to have the experience of meeting people from other countries. He said his goal in life was to help people, so I was helping fulfill his goal. That is why I "put the blue in his sky." What a great expression! And now it was time to take him up on his offer.

I spent two weeks at home after Hong Kong, just long enough to unpack, visit with friends and family, finish arrangements for my last three months, and repack. It wasn't until I was on the third plane on my way to Kenya, country thirty-six, that I started wondering, What have I got myself into this time? A village in Kenya? I really had no idea what to expect.

Thirty-six hours after leaving Victoria I arrived in Kenya. It is fortunate that I was able to go to Kenya at all, considering that, when I started planning this trip in late 2007 and early 2008, Kenya was in crisis. After the December 2007 presidential election, troubles started. The opposition supporters alleged electoral manipulation. A violent rampage took place in several parts of the country, resulting in over one thousand people being killed and over two hundred thousand people being displaced. After a few months the president agreed to make the opposition leader the prime minister, a position they did not have previously, and they created a coalition government.

I heard on the TV while I was there that the government had pledged "to deal with those who started the violence," but numerous attempts to begin the process had failed. During my visit a bill to set up a special court to prosecute the main perpetrators was defeated in parliament. So the whole process was turned over to an international criminal tribunal at The Hague. There was worry that this bill's defeat might cause some troubles, but while I was there things were fine. (Let's hope it stays that way.)

The airport is only sixteen kilometres from the city of Nairobi, but the drive took over an hour due to the gridlocked traffic. I had time to read some local news, which was probably not a good idea. The headlines read: "Shooting in Broad Daylight in Front of the Hospital" and "Fire Kills 27 in Downtown Market." This was not very comforting news for a gal spending a couple days alone in the city. As we got closer to the city the smog thickened. It was not a promising welcome.

I checked into my hotel, had a much-needed shower and a short nap, and then went on a city tour. I was the only passenger, so I had the undivided attention of my driver, Ben. He put the blinkers on, I assume because he was driving slowly, but I had to laugh because the traffic was still gridlocked, so the blinkers were unnecessary. The city is a cluttered mix of modern high-rises (the highest is thirty-six floors) and ramshackle older buildings. The sidewalks were as crowded with people walking as the roads were with cars, but I saw very few tourists among the crowds.

There were hundreds of billboards lining the streets, and the interesting thing about that is that the ads were in English and most of the people in the pictures were white. Coke was the biggest advertiser I had seen the world over and Nairobi was no different.

We passed the hospital where the shooting was, the market where the fire was, and the place the American embassy "used to be" (it was bombed in 1998). Ben told me of some great restaurants and cafes, but with all these violent events in mind, I didn't plan to go too far from my hotel.

I did, however, go to the city market, which I remembered from 1986 when I first came to Africa, and I was shocked to find it looked exactly as I remembered. The majority of the market is for the locals, but there are also handicraft stalls geared for tourists. Being the only tourist for miles around certainly got me plenty of attention. Everyone tried to get me into his or her stall, with all the same lines used the world over: "One little sale for me." "Special for you today." "Beautiful lady, best prices here." "Almost free!" I have to wonder if there is a book, *English for Market Vendors*, they all have read. I did get lured into one shop where two women, Anna and Theresa, were not afraid to just come out and ask for money; they didn't even try to sell me anything. Both explained they had husbands who didn't work and between them they had twelve children. I imagine they see every tourist as a possible donor, and if I hadn't planned to donate my fund-raising dollars in Nelson's village, I would have considered helping them out. I spent about an hour talking with them, so they were very disappointed when their pleas were left unfulfilled, and I found it hard to walk away.

Nelson and Ruth (my hostess for the week) came to my hotel to meet me the next day. Ruth spoke English well, and within minutes she told me she was a born-again Christian. She decided her mission this week was to have me take Jesus as my personal saviour. I, ever the polite guest, agreed to listen, but hoped I could avoid too many heavy discussions about my religious beliefs, or lack thereof.

They had come to Nairobi in a *matatu* (a minivan used as a taxi/bus service), so that is how we got back to their village. Nelson helped take my luggage to the matatu stop, helped us find the right matatu, and left us to get back to the village on our own. He had some errands to tend to in the city. Instead of signs with their destinations on the front, the matatu drivers rush around shouting out their destinations. Once their van is full, they leave, but the definition of "full" is up to the driver. Most vans that have signs reading "14 seats" generally squeeze in at least eighteen people. I wanted to meet the locals, but this was a little too up-close and personal. In our case, the lack of space was made worse by my luggage, which was underfoot, on my lap, and on the lap of the lady sitting beside me. Ruth was perched half on someone else's lap. The door was left open and the helper hung halfway out trying to get more riders as we drove along. I kept thinking they couldn't squeeze more people in. But squeeze they did. There were police checks for overcrowding and licenses, so sometimes people ducked or sat on the floor. I really just had to laugh and go with the flow.

After an hour, we stopped on the main road just outside Ruth's village, Magina. The cost for the ride was about one dollar and thirty cents, but I would have been charged more if I wasn't with locals. Magina has about 1,500 people and the homes are scattered amongst the rolling hills of the village. There is a very small main street with a few stores and a petrol station. Beyond the main street there is no driving. All the roads are dirt and many are simply walking trails. The houses are mainly unpainted wood buildings with rusty corrugated tin roofs.

It was not easy pulling my bag along the dirt road to Ruth's house, but within a minute a neighbour boy came and helped us out. It was hot, the roads were hilly, and my mind raced, questioning my bright ideas of "staying with locals." The old saying, "be careful what you wish for," sprang to mind, but there I was and I would just have to adjust. Five days; I can do anything for five days, I thought to myself.

I was the only white person in the village, making me an instant celebrity. I loved the kids running out from far and wide, shouting, "How are you, how are you?" For some, it was all the English they knew, and when I would reply, "I am fine, how are you?" they would just giggle and say again, "How are you?"

Ruth was in her late thirties, living with her mother, who was seventy-nine, and her sister, who was in her forties. Their home consisted of three wooden slat buildings. The building used for cooking was unpainted, had dirt floors, and a fire for cooking in the middle of the room. Another building, with painted walls and cement floors, housed the living room, which doubled as the dining room, and two tiny bedrooms on either end. The last building was Ruth's bedroom. It had cement floors and the walls were wallpapered with old newspapers, magazines, and sewing pattern pieces. There was one light bulb in each room, but the power was off more than it was on while I was there. It was windy most of the time, so I don't know if that caused the outages or if it goes off on a regular basis. Water was fetched from the stream down the hill from the house. They had no appliances and no refrigeration.

You can imagine how surprised I was after seeing what they "didn't have" to see the grand lunch they prepared: lentil soup, carrots, tea, and a cake decorated beautifully with "Welcome to Kenya." How do you bake a cake on an open fire? No one explained it to me, but I know they not only baked it but decorated it with three different colours of icing flowers on top. It was tasty too. Ruth had also knit a little ornament for me and made me a hot mat from bottle caps covered with wool. The mat was in the shape of Kenya with the colours of its flag. She explained, "Black represents the people of Kenya, red is for the struggle for freedom, green represents Kenya's agriculture and natural resources, and the white is for unity and peace."

The rest of the day was busy, with every relative and friend from the village coming to see the *mzungu* (white person in Swahili). Ruth's twenty-one-year-old son Joseph, his nineteen-year-old wife, and their children, two-year-old Namji and two-month-old Johnson, arrived in time for dinner. When Namji came in the door, she stopped in her tracks, looked at me, and shrieked in her native language of Kikuyu, "There's a white person in the house!" Everyone had a great laugh when they explained to me what she said. It took her awhile but she eventually warmed up to me and would sit on my lap and stroke my white face. She was very cute, and every day after she would run in and ask for me.

I heard that after I left she was very upset I was gone, but that might have had something to do with the fact I brought gifts. Chocolate was everyone's favourite and I watched them savour small nibbles and save pieces for later. I guess the toothbrushes and toothpaste I brought were a good idea after the chocolate. I also brought calendars with pictures of Canada and they were fascinated by the pictures of the snow and the mountains. Ruth's first comment was, "There is no dust." One of the kids asked, "Do you have the same fires for cooking as we do?" In retrospect, I should have brought only pictures of our wilderness, as the pictures of Victoria's Inner Harbour and the luxurious yachts and the grand Empress Hotel were so far out of reality for them, they just skipped those pages and went on to scenery photos.

It was a busy day of visiting, with many adults and kids in and out. The kids (Ruth's nephews and nieces, who numbered about twelve) loved playing with my hair and singing and dancing for me, especially when I showed them their picture or video afterwards. Many of them spoke Swahili, Kikuyu, and a good bit of English. Mama Mary, Ruth's mother, didn't speak English, but somehow she and I connected, and I fell in love with her. She had such a gentle spirit, always singing and smiling. Her days consisted of starting the fire, watching the fire, and constantly cooking food. She did all the food preparation, right down to plucking the chicken. The chicken was a gift to me from one of Ruth's brothers and they took quite a bit of joy teasing me about how I would have to pluck it myself. But in the end they took pity on me and Mama Mary did the plucking. A few of the traditional dishes Mama made were *njahi* (black beans, potatoes, and green bananas) and *ugali* (maize, flour, and water). Both are mixed to a doughy consistency and they always served big portions. They were very "heavy" to me and I had a little trouble cleaning my plate every meal, but tried my best.

Bedtime comes early when there are few lights. Being only about one hundred kilometres south of the equator, the days and nights are equal so it gets dark at around six p.m. I don't carry a watch and they had no clocks, but I think we went to bed around eight thirty every night. I shared Ruth's tiny bedroom, which had just enough room for two single beds. The village is in the central highlands and I found the first night I was quite cold, sleeping on a very thin mattress with not enough blankets. Added to my discomfort was my dreaded nightly adventure to the outhouse, which was out the door, around the back of the building, past the sheep and chicken hut and up a little dirt hill. The door didn't close properly, it was very dark, and I had to squat. It is hard to hold a flashlight while squatting and there was nowhere I wanted to put it down, so I just went by the light of the moon. Lucky for me there was a full moon while I was there.

The mornings started early. Ruth was up at the crack of dawn. She walked up to the main street to get fresh milk, and then down to the stream to get water. Mama Mary would get the fire started and boil the water for the tea. Ruth's son would come and join us for breakfast, which was two slices of plain white bread and a banana or an egg and tea. I don't like bananas but I ate whatever was offered. Ruth would bring everything into the living room and then they would sit down. Then Ruth would ask me to serve them. I am not sure why she chose breakfast for me to serve, but that became the morning routine. Then Joseph would leave to take the sheep to the grazing grounds about three kilometres away, and Ruth and I would clean up for the day. Every second day we would have a "bath", which meant we would take a pail of warm water about two inches deep to wash up with. There was a little closet room behind the house for privacy. I had to ask for an extra cup to wash my hair. Ruth didn't think about that, as they don't wash their hair as often. Men and children are usually shaved bald and women keep their hair in braids.

One day Ruth and I did the laundry, in two basins of water. We scrubbed, rinsed, and rescrubbed. Ruth made sure I did my share. I was surprised to see the iron (a very old iron—no steam), but not surprised when Ruth asked me to iron her clothes. She really wanted me to be part of the family and I was truly glad to participate.

My days were busy with Ruth and her pastor friend Martha. Martha, who was thirty-two, was a laugh a minute. By day two we were calling ourselves "sisters from different mothers." Martha's home was a tiny room that had just enough space for a bed, a small couch, and a counter for her dishes and books. There was no plumbing in the room. I think her complex was once a storage locker. There were about eight "suites", with one shared latrine and water tap. Her next door neighbours' room was about twice the size but still tiny, and in it lived a couple with their three grandchildren. The kids were part of a family that had been displaced during the troubles the previous year. Martha said, "We were not 'affected' by the conflict in our area, but we were 'infected', because we are having to help all those who were displaced."

Martha and Ruth showed me around their area, told me more about their lives, and tried to help me find Jesus. We had some heavy discussions about religion and faith, and in the end they were at least happy to know that I live by the golden rule of "treating others the way I would want to be treated," and have a good heart. They were still worried that I wouldn't go to heaven because I hadn't declared Jesus as my personal saviour. They didn't know I was counting on my mother to pull me through.

Everywhere we went we had to take a matatu, so I got very good at contouring myself into small spaces. We went to Kimende, a bigger village down the road, for shopping, and while there Ruth took me to visit the local finance office. At this office, when they put money in monthly for a minimum of six months, they can then borrow three times what they deposited. Their original money stays in, and borrowers pay one percent interest while paying the loan back. Once it is paid in full they get the original money back. Ruth has joined so she can get enough money to start a grain store. She says there isn't enough grain available in their village.

One day we were on an errand with a neighbour who had a car, and not too far from the village we stopped to gaze down on the Rift Valley. Looking down the 2,400 metres I realize how high up the village was, which explained why I was breathless when I arrived and tried pulling my luggage on the dirt road.

Another day Ruth took me to Jambo Sana College, to meet her cousin Steven. Steven was a teacher, and realizing how many children were coming to school hungry, he started a program that fed forty children lunch each day. Then, in order to help the parents, he started a computer, hairdressing, and dressmaking program. The students were all squeezed into tiny, tiny rooms, with nine girls and one boy in the dressmaking program, eight in the computer class, and eight girls working on one wig in the hairdressing course. In the dressmaking room a few small children were playing under the tables. Steven explained, "Many young women have children as a result of being hijacked." I took that to mean *raped*. Steven had plans to include a carpentry course as soon as he found a volunteer teacher and more funds. I had already made too many plans for my donation money to give him any, but made a note to send some in the future.

On Valentine's Day, Martha promised Ruth and me a surprise trip. Two hot and squashed matatu rides later we arrived at Lake Nairvasha Country Club. It was the last place I expected to go to, considering the humble surroundings we had been in up to this point. The club had a lovely colonial hotel, situated on fifty-five acres of beautifully manicured green lawns. We found lounge chairs and tables shaded by acacia and fever trees, with lovely gardens and a path leading down to the lake.

Martha had been there before but Ruth hadn't, and I think she was a little overwhelmed. Martha hadn't explained what we were there to see, but when we walked to the lake we found boats available for hire to cruise the lake. Martha and Ruth were extremely happy when I said I would pay for us all to have a tour. Just before we got on the boat, a fisherman approached us with a bucket of crayfish, which neither lady had ever seen, and a large black bass. The ladies wanted to buy them, but I reminded them we couldn't carry them around all day, so we had to pass. Then, fitted out in our lifejackets, we hopped aboard for Ruth's first-ever boat ride.

Lake Naivasha is the highest lake in the Rift Valley at 1,884 metres. It is home to a wide variety of birdlife and we saw many species, but for us the best feature was the hippos. We squealed and whooped while sailing around the huge creatures. They were a little scary, because we were told that in Africa, more people are killed by hippos than any other animal. We didn't get too close to the railing of the boat. We sailed around for about an hour enjoying the peace and spotting many beautiful birds. The boat captain dropped us off on Crescent Island.

Crescent Island is a private game sanctuary on the other side of the lake from the country club. He told us it was a one-hour walk around the reserve, walking with the wildlife. Because there are no predators on the island, we were free to walk safely amongst the zebras, wildebeests, gazelles, monkeys, hares, waterbucks, and giraffes. What an amazing opportunity to be this close to such beautiful animals! Well, you can't actually call a wildebeest beautiful, but it certainly is unique. The legend is that God made the wildebeest from bits and pieces that were left over after He had finished creating all the other animals. He gave it the face of a mule, the beard of a goat, the horns of a cow, and the body of a horse. Our guide told us they brought these animals there for the movie *Out of Africa* and then just left them there, where they continued to breed. I tried to find out if this story was true, but could not find any reference to it on the Internet.

As interesting as the walk was, it was unfortunately not one hour long, but closer to two and a half. I hadn't come prepared with sunscreen or a hat and by the end we were all exhausted. We rested at the country club, where we had a delicious lunch in the shade. It was so decadent and strange to think of the humble abode we were going back to in a few hours.

The thought of two more matatu rides back was not very encouraging. The ladies wanted to stop in the town of Naivasha to pick up fish at the market. They took quite a while to decide on which ones they wanted. I hoped they would decide not to get any because they looked like they had been sitting in the sun all day, but eventually they picked some and off we went back home. As we were waiting for the last matatu, Ruth said, "I will never forget this day, and I will never forget you." I was so pleased I could be part of this day with her that I forgot how tired I was as we squished into the last matatu back to the village.

Another day we visited Nelson in Kimende, where the World Youth Program was wrapping up its three-month stint in Kenya. I had a short visit with some of the participants I had met back in Canada and they said they had had a great time, but I think it was a huge adjustment for the Canadians having to live in the conditions they did for three months. Some lived in homes without electricity or indoor plumbing. They were all looking forward to going home.

In Kenya their program works with Kenvo, which is a community-based conservation group with the mission "to conserve natural habitats in Kikuyu Escarpment". Ruth and I took a tour of their tree farm and planted a tree to offset some of our carbon footprint.

One of the Kenyan participants was Sam, who had billeted at my friend's home in Canada. They had sent some gifts for him and I wanted to learn more about a project he had started, so he arranged some time off from the program to take us to his village, Rironi, and to his Ray of Hope Resource Center. Seeing a need for his villagers to have access to resource materials, he had collected books, magazines, and newspapers from Canada and Kenya and started a library, something his village did not have. In his "free time" Sam was also promoting an environmental program in the primary schools. I was inspired by this amazing twenty-four-year-old, with his vision for his community.

My week in Kenya went by much faster than I expected, and despite my original trepidation I had an incredible time getting to know these lovely people who work so hard every day—fetching water, growing much of their own food, tending to their animals, cooking on fires—and who seem so happy. I know for all those I met, family and God are what keeps them going.

I found so many places to leave some of my fund-raising money, but in the end spread it out between Sam for his library, Nelson for his new house, Ruth for her grain store, and my interviewee Rose for her kids.

My interviewee was a friend of Ruth's. I met her several times during the week.

~

Rose – 49

Our walk to Rose's house takes us about twenty minutes from Ruth's house. The road gets worse the farther we go and eventually we are heading uphill on a dirt track, washed out by the rain, and I am huffing and puffing again. Ruth and Martha don't seem to be having any problem. We arrive to find Rose standing in front of her tiny, dilapidated wooden house, with the broadest, brightest smile. She has put on her nicest blouse, skirt, and headscarf, and I realize how beautiful she is. Her skin and teeth are perfect and her smile lights up her face. She welcomes us into her living room, which is very similar to Ruth's, with a couple broken-down couches and a newspaper-covered wall.

Rose insists on making us tea and something to eat, so off she goes into her cooking area in another building. She comes back with tea and finally sits down. Martha says a blessing and we start the interview. Ruth and Martha translate for Rose, as her English is minimal.

I ask first about marriage, and they tell me that Rose and her spouse were never officially married. Although she is very devoted to the Africa Inland Church now, when they got together she wasn't. Often, in their culture men and women just move in together and that constitutes marriage. Rose was nineteen years old when she met her husband, and they moved in together one month later. She is forty-nine years old and their eight children range from nine to twenty-nine years old. Sadly, her husband passed away a few years ago.

Rose gets up again to prepare food for us, even though we said there was no need. While she is gone, five of her children come home from school. They are barefoot and their uniforms are dirty and close to rags, but they all have a smile on their face until they see the mzungu in their midst. Martha introduces us, but they are all shy and leave as fast as they can. Rose returns with a piece of white bread and a fried egg for each of us. As we eat, she tells me that she and her three oldest only finished grade seven, but she says proudly, "I will make sure that all the rest finish high school." I know this will be a challenge, as she must pay for uniforms and books, but I can see she is determined to make it happen.

I ask about her parents, and she says her mother and one of her grandmothers, who is over one hundred, are still alive. Her father has been dead for many years. "I can see the women in your family must be strong and I see how strong you are and how hard you work with your garden, your cows and chickens, and raising eight children, all without the help of a husband," I commend her. She is reluctant to take the compliment, but admits she works very hard. As if on cue, a rooster wanders into the room, looks around and walks out.

I really have no idea whether I can talk about menopause, but throw it out there. The ladies all talk amongst themselves in Kikuyu, and then

Martha says quietly, "She says she has no menopausal symptoms at this time." I think I stepped out of bounds again, so I carry on, asking about her hobbies, although I think she is probably way too busy for any. But her eyes light up again and she says she loves singing and is in her church choir.

"Would you move out of your village if the opportunity arose?" I ask.

"I think I would like to move to Canada after I saw the pictures on the calendar you brought," she answers with a laugh.

The kids are coming in and out now and Rose says she has to start dinner, so I ask the last question, is she happy? "Yes, I am happy, because of my love of God," she answers, with her now familiar smile.

I leave with Martha and Ruth and know I am going to miss these ladies!

Don't tell me how educated you are, tell me how much you have travelled.

—Mohammed

Chapter 34

Tanzania

"Oh yes, very close," the tour operator answered, when I asked her if the toilets were close to the tents. The only week of my last three months that wasn't organized was the week between Kenya and Uganda. I decided on a safari in Tanzania, since it didn't involve another flight, as I got picked up right from my hotel in Nairobi. Once I made that decision I had to work out if I would do a camping or lodge trip. Finances decided for me, as the lodge option cost too much at this juncture of my journey.

Camping is really the last thing I thought I would be doing. First, because after doing a ten-week safari in Africa years ago I swore I would never get in a tent again; and second, because the thought of tramping through the campsite on the way to the toilets in the middle of the night, watching out for wild animals, was not my idea of fun. However, I chose to believe the tour operator and booked the safari.

From the beginning of the tour things started to go wrong. The bus from Nairobi to Arusha, in Tanzania, was supposed to take about six or seven hours, depending on the border crossing. We started out making good time, but about an hour before we reached the border we stopped and sat on the side of the highway for over two hours, waiting for a group whose plane had been late.

When we finally got to the border we had to get off the bus and walk between the border gates. While walking in no-man's-land between countries, a group of men, without uniforms or badges, approached everyone who was walking through. They first asked for our passports, and then said we needed to exchange our U.S. dollars for Tanzanian currency. They said they were with the bus company and that we had to use Tanzanian shillings to pay for our visas at the customs office. Where I found the guts to defy the rather large men I don't know, but I said, "I'm not giving you my passport. I will take my chances at the booth." Nobody handed over their passport, but several did exchange money (at a very bad rate). When we got to customs we found out you can only pay for the visa with U.S. cash. By the time those who had fallen for the ruse went out to find the con men, they were gone. One couple had no U.S. currency left, so I loaned them some. Several of us tried to give the bus driver a bad time for not warning us, but I think he was in on the scheme. Interesting, that these guys could get away with their scam right in front of both countries' border guards.

Because of the delays we arrived in Arusha very late at night. The fellow from the tour company who picked me up at the bus station was obviously mad that he had to wait so long, and so he was not very friendly. Our meeting went from bad to worse when he said he noticed I didn't have a sleeping bag and that he could rent me one for sixty dollars a day. I said, "I wasn't told I needed one and there is no way I will pay you that much money." Twice in a day people were trying to rip me off. Not a good sign for this country. By the time we arrived at the hotel, he made a few phone calls and his fee for the sleeping bag had come down to ten dollars a day. I don't know if they were real calls that he placed, as he was speaking Kiswahili, but I was happy with the results.

To end this already bad day, my late arrival meant I could not buy food anywhere and my hotel room was about as big as a closet. The bathroom door couldn't even be opened fully because it hit the bed, and if I put the luggage on the floor I couldn't open the door to get out of the room. I guess it was better than having to hop in a tent the first night, but I was disappointed that I had to go to bed hungry.

After much-needed sleep and a good breakfast I met up with my tour mates the next morning. There were only four of us, plus a driver and a cook. My tour mates were a couple from Poland and a guy from the Czech Republic. All of them spoke perfect English and had travelled extensively so we had lots to talk about. The Czech was too young for me, so this wasn't the corner where Mr. Right was hiding.

This tour, although not luxurious, was a step up from my last tour in Africa. Back then we had to set up our own tents and cook our own food. This time those chores were done for us. I may have caved in and decided to sleep in a tent again, but I am sure glad I didn't have to do all the work as well.

As for the toilets, that tour operator lied. At the first campsite, in order to get to the squat toilets, I had to travel an obstacle course around other tents and lines, around a fence and over a rock path. In the second campsite the toilets weren't as far, but we weren't allowed out of our tents in the night because of the dangers of wild animals. I am generally up at least once a night, so this wasn't good for me. I guess my decision to believe the tour guide will go down on my ever growing list of "stupid things I have done." I was conned!

I can honestly say, however, that despite my nighttime issues and the first day misadventures it was a great trip. Our driver and cook were loads of fun, willing to drive through the game parks for as long as we wanted and serving up great food. My tour mates were kindred spirits who had many great travel stories to swap and were extremely interesting and pleasant, a blessing when you are in such close quarters for days on end. We spent each day in the jeep, either travelling from one park to the next or exploring the parks. Evenings were spent dining under the stars, chatting, and listening to the sounds of the wild.

We visited Lake Manyara, Serengeti National Park, and the Ngorongoro Conservation Area. All were incredible.

Lake Manyara is the smallest of the parks, and even before we were in the gates we were surrounded by baboons. I now know where the term "nit-picking" comes from. These entertaining animals were playing and picking to their heart's content. Only minutes into the park we were as close to a herd of elephants as I would ever want to be, and the ride continued that way, spotting zebras, impalas, velvet monkeys, blue monkeys, giraffes, wildebeests, buffalo, warthogs, more elephants, hippos, and several different kinds of birds. It was a breathtaking introduction to our wildlife adventure.

We spent two days in the Serengeti National Park. The name in the Maasai language means "endless plains", and that is very appropriate because it covers over twelve thousand square kilometres. The landscape varies, but the areas we explored were open grass plains and vast savannahs with huge acacia trees and scattered *kopies*, which are rock outcrops that just seem to pop out of the flat lands. The kopies provide shelter and they also capture water in the crevasses, helping the lions and other large animals in the dry season.

We drove for hours enjoying the surroundings and seeking out wildlife. We saw lots of impalas, dik-diks, topis, hartebeests, zebras, giraffes, and hundreds of wildebeests, and learned to tell the difference between Thomson's gazelles and Grant's gazelles. We thought we were stumped the first day when looking for lions, but just before we were going to turn around we came upon a pride with two lazy males sunning themselves and two females prowling about. We sat for over an hour just watching these magnificent animals.

On our second day in Serengeti, we were up early enough to view the sunrise over the plains. It was as beautiful as anticipated and as we watched, off in the distance, hot air balloons floated into the sky above. That would have been a fun way to see the park!

The park was busy with other groups, but it is so big that we went for hours without seeing anyone else. When we did pass another vehicle the drivers always exchanged information about where to find which animal. The busiest crowd we encountered was while watching a leopard. There he was, with his belly resting on a branch and his legs hanging down, and he didn't seem bothered by all the attention.

Not only did we experience the sights and the sounds of wild Africa, but we also took in some unique smells as well. The hippo pool was fascinating, but the smell was disgusting. We managed to put up with it, however, to watch about fifty of them wallow in the mud, pop in and out, belch and roar. As an added bonus there were several crocodiles slithering around amongst the hippos.

Our first view of Ngorongoro Crater was from the rim, which is nineteen kilometres around. Looking down to the crater floor 610 metres below it was hard to believe there were animals down there, but in fact there are over twenty-five thousand animals within the three-hundred-square-kilometre crater.

Once we drove the winding steep road down into the crater we witnessed hyenas hunting, lions feasting on a buffalo while jackals waited for the leftovers, a cheetah on the prowl, and we even found the elusive black rhino. We saw all the other expected animals, but learned that there are no giraffes in the crater. Their long legs make it too difficult to negotiate the hike to the bottom.

Our driver was extremely happy when we found the black rhino because this meant he had accomplished his task of helping us see the "big five": lion, leopard, rhino, elephant, and buffalo. This term was originally coined by the big game hunters due to their ferocity when they are cornered, but now it is the goal while on safari.

I haven't even mentioned the birds we saw: flocks of beautiful pink flamingos, ugly buzzards and vultures, gangly ostriches, egrets resting on the backs of hippos, and so many more. The safari definitely improved my feelings towards Tanzania and made me forget that first day. What an amazing opportunity to watch these incredible animals in their natural habitat. The lions were my favourite!

I didn't plan for an interview in Tanzania, knowing there wouldn't be an opportunity on the safari. I was pleased and surprised, however, when we were able to stop at a Maasai village and learn a bit about their culture. When I was in Africa years ago it was illegal to take photos of the Maasai. We were told they believed photos took away their soul. Now, this doesn't seem to be the case. Not only can you take their photo, they encourage it, by opening their villages to tourists.

There are more than 120 different tribes in Africa. I don't know how many have kept their tribal traditions, but the Maasai certainly have. They are nomadic herdsmen and warriors found mainly in southern Kenya and northern Tanzania. As we travelled throughout the area it was easy to spot the tall Maasai walking in their tire-soled sandals, dressed in their bright-coloured *kangas*, carrying their long walking sticks and herding their cows, sheep, or goats.

A kanga is sheet of fabric tied at the shoulder. You can imagine my surprise when I was in Kenya and a Maasai walked into the Internet cafe I was in, sat down to use a computer and his phone rang. He reached under his kanga and brought out the phone to answer it. How did he have it secured under there? This was before I knew they were now allowing pictures. I really wanted to take a picture of this traditional warrior at a computer with a cell phone.

At the village we were welcomed by most of the tribe dancing towards us in all their finery of beautiful red, blue, and purple kangas, and adorned with incredible handcrafted beaded jewellery.

The village was enclosed in a circular fence of thorned acacia, built by the men. Inside were thirty huts of mud and cow dung, built by the women. The villagers performed a traditional dance, which included the men jumping as high as they could. The Maasai are tall people and they jump very high. It was cute watching the little children trying to jump along with them. Once the dance was completed most of the villagers went back to their daily routine, and a young man, who told us he had a university education, took us on a tour of his village. He told us 150 people lived in this village. He invited us into one of the tiny huts. The huts are only one and a half metres high and three metres wide, so we couldn't even stand up straight. A family cooks, eats, sleeps, and stores all their possessions in this tiny space and our guide told us that some families can be up to eight people. It was dark, cramped and reeked of smoke. I couldn't stay in for more than a minute.

In the Maasai culture, the measure of a man's wealth is the number of cattle and children he has. Our guide and two of his friends, who followed us on our tour of the village, said their fathers had eight wives each. Most of those wives have at least five children. The boys explained when a man marries another wife, she builds a hut next door and they move in. The youngest of the wives (and they can be as young as twelve or thirteen) is left with the most menial of chores for the extended family. Consequently, wives sometimes encourage their husbands to marry again so they can move up in the hierarchy.

We also visited the village kindergarten, where the children recited the alphabet in English for us. Education is becoming more widespread among the Maasai, and although in the past it has been geared more for boys, female attendance is apparently improving slightly.

Another tradition that is still carried out for some of the young women is female genital excision (female circumcision), a rite of passage ritual to "get them ready" for marriage. The tradition has been replaced in some areas by a "cutting with words" ceremony; however, some Maasai men may reject a woman who has not had this done.

This tribe we visited made the decision to make money from tourism, but they obviously still live a very traditional life. Some of the women were offering to sell us their beadwork, while most were sitting on the ground, leaning against their huts. Dozens of small children were playing in the dirt and crawling all over their mothers, while flies were swarming them all. I tried to speak to the women, but didn't find any who spoke English, and I got the sense that they weren't very happy to have us there.

My travels in Tanzania turned out much better than they started, but I left the Maasai village sad instead of thrilled to have finally seen a traditional culture still intact. I wanted to see "real tradition", but couldn't handle hearing about and seeing how the women are treated.

A long and uneventful bus ride back to Nairobi, a good night's sleep, and an early morning flight to Kampala, Uganda, came next on the agenda.

Only he that has travelled the road knows where
the holes are deep.

—Chinese proverb

Chapter 35

Uganda

"The potholes have pieces of road in them," Sally laughed, as we bumped our way along the streets of Kampala. Sally, my new Ugandan friend, was not exaggerating. Kampala, the capital of Uganda, is now top on my list for the city with the "worst road conditions". It is a wonder there is any suspension left in the cars, and no wonder that those who can afford it drive four-wheel-drives. The city also holds a spot on my list of cities with the "craziest traffic". I only saw two stop signs, and I never saw anyone stop at them. One corner had traffic police, so people stopped there, but that was the only time I saw a vehicle not moving. It is survival of the bravest. You must drive and not hesitate. To add to the chaos are the hundreds of *bodas* (motorcycle taxis) that continually weave and bob around everyone. This scene is scary enough in a car, but being a pedestrian is even worse. Trying to cross a road takes a lot of patience and fearlessness. I thought I would have been used to wild traffic by now, but this truly seemed worse than everywhere else I had been so far.

The city is dirty, dusty, and crowded with ramshackle buildings and stalls, congested alleys, and people living on the streets. Garment workers at sewing machines line the alleys and various goods are placed on blankets and cars crowding out the sidewalks. I saw children who looked younger than three sitting on the sidewalk, begging. Many times I could not see a parent anywhere nearby.

"Can you imagine?" This was Sally's most used expression and it was said repeatedly while I was there. Imagine leaving a child of less than three alone on a sidewalk and not have him or her running into the traffic. Those wee children have obviously been trained to stay still.

In a country where over 80 percent of its people are Christian and only 12 percent are Muslim, it was odd that the biggest building, which looms high on a hill over the city, is the Gaddafi National Mosque. It was paid for and is maintained by Libya's Muammar Gaddafi. An imposing presence, it is one of the city's few clean and modern buildings, and is surrounded by a mishmash of dilapidated buildings.

Sightseeing was not the reason I went to Uganda, however; meeting Sally and her girls at the King's Daughters Ministry was. Sally is thirty-one, and since she was twenty-two, this amazing woman has been helping vulnerable girls who have been exposed to abuse or who have just needed help. My friend Linda, from Victoria, met Sally, who is Ugandan, several years earlier when Linda was with her husband, Jeremy, who was volunteering his help at the Mengo Dental Clinic in Kampala. At the time, Sally had fourteen girls under her care. Linda and Sally became fast friends and Linda found her calling. She decided immediately to help Sally and the girls, and went back to Victoria to fund-raise.

Between Linda, Jeremy, their fellow church members, and friends, they have helped the King's Daughters Ministry to become a home for thirty-two girls and women. In Sally's last report, she said, "More than ever before, I realize the goal to reach these vulnerable girls of our nation is a race, and it is not for those who run fast but rather for those who keep running even when the finish line is not in sight."

In a country of thirty-two million people, where more than half the population lives below the international poverty line of US$1.25 a day, and people have a life expectancy of only fifty-three years, Sally's goal seems almost impossible. However, she is one of the hardest-working, kindest women I have ever met, and she is racing on.

I spent the week getting to know Sally and the girls, who ranged from six to twenty-eight years old, with the majority being teenagers. Most of their stories brought me to tears. In answer to Sally's constant question: No, I can't imagine. Many of the girls had been physically and sexually abused by fathers, brothers, uncles, or strangers. (I am told that this abuse isn't illegal in some villages.) Some were married off at thirteen or fourteen to abusive and much older men. A few had lost one or both parents to HIV, while others had never known their fathers. Several of them had lived on the streets for at least part of their lives, while the two youngest have lived on the streets their entire lives, until they came to King's Daughters. One girl ended up in the women's prison because, after her father was jailed for sexually abusing her for most of her life, the authorities had nowhere to put her. Sally heard about her and brought her to the house. One girl told me that her father had been married seven times, and that she was one of sixty-eight children.

I have mentioned several times that I haven't really kept up my religious upbringing and can't claim Jesus as my personal saviour, but I have to say that I saw God in that house. Those girls had endured more than I could ever believe possible and were the loveliest girls and young women I had ever met. Their faith in God, and their love of Sally, Linda, Jeremy, their Auntie Grace, Paul, and George (the men on the board of KDM), and each other was awe inspiring.

Each night they had an "hour of power" where they read and discussed a passage from the Bible, shared challenges, praised God, and gave thanks for what they had. I was brought to tears every night listening to them thank God for what they had—including me! Their thought-provoking ideas of what the daily Bible passage meant to them were articulated beyond what I thought girls their age capable of, not to mention the fact that they were speaking English, which isn't their first language.

Uganda has several different ethnic groups, with many different tribes amongst them. English is the official language, but there are over forty different languages spoken. Some of the girls come into the house speaking no English and not understanding the other girls. A few of the younger ones had only been in the house for six months when I met them and they still had trouble speaking English, but could sing every English word of all the songs they sang to praise God. I really enjoyed the evenings that they sang, danced, and drummed gospel songs. By the week's end I too was singing along.

Sally helps the girls discover and develop their talents, and nurtures them by teaching life skills that include tailoring, beadwork, baking, cooking, and computing. They take turns with the meals and have a little store attached to their house to sell all their handiwork. When one of the girls learns a skill, she helps teach the others. I now have several beautiful beaded necklaces and a hand-sewn bag.

All the girls are enrolled in school. When I visited only one girl was in public school. Her class size was around 120 students and she was "lucky", as some class sizes can be over two hundred. The rest of the girls were in private schools, thanks to sponsors that Linda and Sally have found. Even in the private schools class sizes can be close to sixty students. The literacy rate for girls in Uganda is less than 60 percent. The girls of KDM are working hard to up that rate. Several of the girls have finished high school and are now enrolled in programs such as nursery teaching, cosmetology, catering, and social work, and one girl is even in dental school.

The vision of the King's Daughters Ministry is: to see the vulnerable young women equipped with skill, empowered by faith, with a purpose to transform a generation.

I think they are definitely accomplishing this goal. I saw these girls full of self-confidence, love, and the ability to trust, that I am sure most lacked before coming into the house. By having men on the board that come to the house and council and help the girls, they have come to trust men, which in itself is a miracle after what most of them have endured at the hands of men.

My week with the girls was incredible. Several of them had fun doing "fashion shoots" and they are all so beautiful they could be models. I helped some girls with their homework and went with a couple others to register for their new school. We had fun playing with my camera. The littlest girl, Rose, loved to get my camera and take everyone's picture. I had some of the pictures developed and bought a cork board to display them. The next day several pictures were missing. Some of the girls had never owned pictures of themselves and wanted them for their rooms.

Just enjoying their laughter and spirit was inspirational. I couldn't help but think about some of the teens at home who complain if they don't have a cell phone or a new outfit. Many have no idea how lucky they are to have all that they do have, to live in a country where they are safe, and where they have so many advantages and privileges available to them.

During the week I also visited Lynn, another friend of Linda's. Lynn and her husband are Americans who came to Kampala several years ago. Lynn's husband is a dentist working at the Mengo Hospital. Lynn introduced me to Fausta.

~

Fausta – 53

Fausta and I sit down for the interview after a lovely afternoon tea party with Lynn, Grace, and Sally. Fausta speaks perfect English, so the ladies leave us alone to talk.

Fausta tells me she is fifty-three. She came from a family of eight children and they lived in a village with no plumbing or electricity. She knew her husband for four years before they married. They had a big wedding, with over two hundred people. They moved to Kampala a few years after they were married. Her husband died several years ago.

I want to ask how her husband died, but she didn't offer it, so I carry on. "Did you attend school in your village?" I ask. "Yes, I have a high school education and went on to take courses through the bank I worked at. My parents never went to school, but they learned to read and write through the church."

"Are you parents still alive?" I ask.

"No, but they both lived until they were eighty-seven. My dad had a coffee plantation, raised goats, and made ropes."

"What about your children's education?" I follow up.

"I have four children; two finished high school and two have been to university," she says proudly. "One son has followed me into banking." I know from our earlier conversation that she retired from the bank a few years ago.

"I know you attend church, because that is where you met Lynn, but have you always been religious?" I ask.

"I always attended church, but it wasn't until 2000, when I went to see my son commit himself to the Baptist church, that I really became devout. I didn't know God was looking for me, but he used my son to get to me. My life was changed when I accepted the Lord into my life," she says happily.

"Can I ask you about menopause? Do you have any symptoms and do you take HRT?" I ask hesitantly.

"I think I am through with it, and I didn't have any problems. I don't know what HRT is," she says, sounding a little put out. Oh no, I have stepped out of bounds again.

"Why are these questions important?" Fausta asks. I explain that I am asking all the women the same questions and using them to get to know a little about women around the world. "Aren't you going to ask me about my health?" she finally blurts out.

I explain that I didn't know if women would want to tell me about their health, but if she wants to, please go ahead. "I am HIV-positive," she says. I am stunned, and feel bad that something so important to her was almost left out of the interview. She looks healthy and I would have never thought to ask. Being HIV-positive is something she really wanted to share, "I was diagnosed in 1997, but probably had it since 1988. My husband died in 1997 with complication from AIDS," she explains, without sounding bitter.

"I was lucky to find a donor who helped pay for antiretroviral drugs from 2002 until 2004, when they became free. I am doing very well on them," she says. I am at a loss for words now, because this is what she really wanted to talk about and I was asking her what she felt were very trivial questions. Lynn comes back in the room and asks Fausta, "Did you tell her what you do with the women?"

Now she brightens and tells me, "It was very hard in the beginning because of the stigma and discrimination towards those of us who are diagnosed. I am not ashamed, but there are still ignorant people who think women who are HIV-positive have asked for it or deserve it. I couldn't believe when I met Lynn at a Bible study group and told her, that she did not treat me differently. Now I am the treasurer of Mulago Positive Women Network. We have 120 women members who meet once a month and we are currently fund-raising to get electricity and water for a house we will use for meetings and teaching programs. There are currently over nine hundred thousand people living with HIV and over one million children who have been orphaned by AIDS in Uganda. We also go out to the villages to help educate women."

One of the girls from King's Daughters has come to walk me back to the house, so I have to go. "I have one final question, if you don't mind." I say. "Are you happy?"

"I am really happy with myself. I have a good life because of His calling. Thank you for God," she answers with a big smile.

I give her a huge hug, and give her a bit of my fund-raising money for her women's group. She is very happy, and asks me to remember her and her group when I return home.

I left Uganda feeling both sad and hopeful. Sally, Fausta, and all the girls are people who have overcome insurmountable odds with amazing determination, and I have no doubt will continue to do so. I am again humbled by their spirit!

The journey, not the arrival matters.

—T. S. Eliot

Chapter 36

South Africa

"This is the only street in the world that was home to two Nobel Peace Prize recipients: Nelson Mandela and Desmond Tutu," said my tour guide as we drove through Soweto, originally a black township under South Africa's apartheid government, but now a suburb of Johannesburg. Those two men certainly demonstrated that out of adversity great things can be accomplished.

I felt the safest way to see the Johannesburg was on a tour, and as it turned out I was the only one on the tour, with two tour guides. They were very informative and happy to answer all my questions. Our first stop in Soweto was an eye-opener. I was in Soweto in the '80s during the time of apartheid, when there was forced segregation. But although apartheid has been abolished since the early '90s, it didn't seem that much had changed. It was still predominately a black suburb of over three million people. There was street after street of brick matchbox houses, and while there were a few areas with nicer homes, there were also huge slums. I took a walking tour through one slum called Kliptown. The people there were living without electricity or plumbing, in homes built out of scrap metal or other discarded materials. Only recently were they given chemical toilets. I was told there are fifteen thousand to twenty thousand people living in Kliptown. The hopeful part was that I saw many children returning to their shanty houses in school uniforms. Hopefully, education will get them out of that hovel.

My guides, both black, did not think much had really changed for them since the end of apartheid. One said, "We may be able to live wherever we want, but we couldn't afford to move even if we wanted to." Although the current government, the ANC, is predominantly black, my guides didn't have any faith that things were going to change any time soon.

During my visit there was an election coming up. The man who was expected to win was Jacob Zuma, who was charged with rape in 2005, was acquitted, and was currently in a long legal battle over allegations of racketeering and corruption. During the rape trial he denied rape, but admitted to consensual sex and knowing the woman was HIV-positive. He also admitted to not using a condom, but said in his defence that he did "shower afterwards". This is a country with the highest number of HIV cases in the world. When most countries were distributing antiretroviral drugs, South Africa held back due to the AIDS denialist policies of the current government's administration. (They believed HIV did not cause AIDS and that the antiretroviral drugs were poisonous.) They were over a year behind Uganda in the distribution of the drugs. Considering this is the richest country in Africa it is hard to see the hardships so many still endure.

NOTE: Zuma did win the election. The charges against him were dropped. In the *Africa World News*, a report on October 29, 2009, by Nkululeko Ncana, said: "Almost ten years to the day since Thabo Mbeki set the HIV/denialist tone for his government by telling the National Council of Provinces that it would be 'irresponsible for the state to roll out antiretroviral drugs,' President Jacob Zuma told the same house of his administration's determination to lead the fight against the pandemic. 'We must come to terms with this reality. If we do not respond with urgency and resolve, we may well find our vision of a thriving nation slipping from our grasp.'" Maybe things are looking up!

After seeing Soweto, we drove through the Jewish area and a few other beautiful suburbs, including the one where Nelson Mandela now lives. The opinion of one of my guides was, "These areas are for the cream of the crime." I am not sure he would have been as candid if there were more people on the tour, but I think he wanted to tell me how he really felt.

Before we ventured into Johannesburg, we drove to a lookout on a hill above it. We were being serenaded by several church groups praying and singing in a field nearby. This high spot brought them "closer to God." We stood on an abandoned building to look at the cityscape of high-rises as you would see in most big cities. However, my guide told me that several of them were empty. Huge buildings totally empty. He said due to the high crime rate in the city many people and businesses have moved out, leaving the buildings vacant.

Once in the city, we saw a lot of construction and revitalization going on as South Africa prepared for the 2010 FIFA World Cup. Since South Africa was not allowed to play international sports during the last of the apartheid era due to sanctions, the World Cup was a highly anticipated event. I was told that the Johannesburg government had asked former New York Mayor Rudolph Giuliani to help bring down the crime rate before the event.

In the city, my tour guides took me to the Traditional Medicine Shop, which was crammed full of bones, pelts, feathers, plants, traditional walking sticks, and hundreds of jars of mysterious ingredients. There was a consultation room identical to an African hut and the shop gave you the feeling you were in the middle of the bush. I would have loved to spend more time in the store watching what people were buying, but we had to keep moving.

The shop was in what once was the "Coloured Area". During apartheid, every person was required to register and be classified as white, black, or coloured; the coloured category included Indians, Asians, and anyone of mixed descent. Still today, most of the shopkeepers in this area were Indian or Asian.

I had only one day and night in Johannesburg, but I managed to get together with an old friend I had lived with in London in 1980. I only reached her the day before, so she was very surprised to hear from me and I was lucky she had time to visit. Sharon is one of the 9 percent of white people in Johannesburg (79 percent black, 9 percent coloured, and 2.5 percent Indian or Asian). She and I are the same age.

~

Sharon – 51

I open the hotel room door and there she is. It has been over twenty-four years since I have seen her and at least twenty years since we last wrote Christmas cards, but I would have recognized her anywhere. Always bright and bubbly, with an infectious laugh, she rushes in to hug me. We assess each other, top to bottom, and hug again. It feels like we have never lost touch, and we are laughing together and both trying to talk at the same time.

We raid the minibar and find a nice little bottle of South African wine. It is way overpriced, but this is a special occasion. We have a lot of catching up to do. We both do a brief synopsis of our lives in the last twenty years, and sadly she tells me that her husband, Ralph, passed away in 2001, from colon cancer.

I finally explain about my journey and my quest to interview women, and she is more than happy to help out. I start with her marriage. She knew Ralph through the shoe business (they were the middle-people between the factories and the shoe stores) for six years before they got together. They were together for five years before they married, when she was thirty. Ralph had two daughters from a previous marriage and they had a son together, who has just turned twenty. Sharon says now that he is out of school and working, she will consider dating. Until now she has not had any interest in dating.

I see she is sad talking about the years after Ralph died, so I go on to the next group of questions about education. She finished high school, as did her mother, but her father only went to grade nine and then joined the South African air force. I have made her sad again, because now she tells me that both her parents have passed away as well. They were both seventy-nine. It's a good thing we had some laughs before I started interviewing her or this would be a sad reunion. Her stepdaughters have university degrees, and her son is working for one of Sharon's brothers, but she hopes he will go to university next year. Speaking of brothers, one of them, the one I have met, also passed away. She has had a tough few years.

On to something else—this is getting sadder by the minute. "What about your shoe sales business? Are you still doing that?" I ask.

"It was a good business for thirty years, but about three years ago I had to quit. It was too hard to compete with the Chinese and Indian factories. I now work for my brother, who has a media advertising company," she says, sounding a bit cheerier.

"I don't remember if you follow any religious faith," I say.

"I was raised Methodist, but I don't go to church. I feel I am spiritual and have a special personal relationship with God," she replies.

As we talk, she casually takes off her sweater and starts loosening the collar of her blouse. Hot flash! I would recognize that move anywhere. "What a segue!" I laugh and tell her that the next questions were about menopause. "I have had all the symptoms for the last five years, but the main one is getting fat and ugly on the outside, but not the inside," she says. I disagree with her assessment of herself, but we commiserate about hot flashes and night sweats. She doesn't take any medications.

"What about hobbies? What do you do in your free time?" I ask.

"I love movies, cooking, and eating. But I also go to the gym, and I love walking," she says.

I ask her how South Africa is different since apartheid has been abolished. She says, "South Africa is a lot different since apartheid—yes, most definitely—they don't call it the rainbow nation for nothing. We are all so blessed and privileged to live here amongst previously disadvantaged people who have embraced the new South Africa. That doesn't mean we don't have problems, politically and from a crime perspective, but try to tell me any other place in the world that doesn't. The younger generation are forgiving, and I work with an amazing bunch of people, black and white. Unlike the older generation, they are open-minded to the government, the good and the bad parts of many undelivered promises and corruption."

"So you still like living in Johannesburg?" I ask, surprised at her enthusiasm for her country. She has lived here all her life and she loves her city, but if she could persuade her son to go with her, she might consider moving to Australia, where one of her brothers has a home.

"I know how I describe you, but how would you describe yourself?" I ask.

Funnily enough, she says the same thing I thought. "Loud and bubbly, a girl who loves to entertain and go out with family and friends, and a person who loves her family and friends madly."

The wine is long gone and we are starving, so we are heading out for dinner soon. After hearing of all her losses and the change in jobs, I am not quite sure of her final answer. "Are you happy?" I ask.

"Yes, I am very blessed and grateful for a wonderful life, which I wouldn't change if I had to do it all over again, except maybe I would have made more time and effort to meet new men and a potential life partner after the death of my husband."

~

I flew from Johannesburg to Cape Town, and the contrast was staggering. It was hard to believe I was in the same country. According to several articles I have read, Cape Town is in the top fifty tourist destinations in the world. Unlike Johannesburg, where I was the only one on a tour, the double-decker tour bus I rode to see the sights of Cape Town was full. It is a beautiful city enveloped by flat-topped Table Mountain and the lovely coastline that makes up the southern tip of Africa. We drove through the city and then along miles of coastline, with beach after beach for sunning, swimming, and surfing.

As lovely as it was on the outside, the tourist brochure I picked up said it best. "Cape Town is a city of contrasts and tells the tale of two cities: one that boasts a thriving creative economy, premier tourist destination status and incredible natural beauty, juxtaposed with social problems and poverty that are directly related to our colourful past and troubled history." I was told the crime rate was not as bad as Johannesburg, but I was also warned not to wander alone at night. I don't wander alone at night in any big city, so that was no problem for me.

Like Sydney, Australia, Cape Town has several surfing beaches not far from the city centre. I took a bus out to Camps Bay Beach for a few hours of relaxation and then took in lunch at one of the trendy cafes across from the beach. Later, I visited the Victoria and Alfred Waterfront in the historic part of Cape Town's working harbour. Out in the harbour sits Robben Island, where Nelson Mandela spent eighteen of his twenty-seven years in prison. It is now a tourist attraction, something the former inmates would likely never have imagined.

I guiltily decided to take advantage of the city's modern offerings instead of soaking up the cultural and historical landmarks. I chose to feed my addictions instead. Yes, addictions, plural. I was not only addicted to massages and spas, but seemed to have fallen for fortune-telling as well. It was a good thing that in most countries I have visited these were relatively cheap activities. Luckily for me, I found everything at the V & A Waterfront. I was able to have a pedicure, a massage, and a tarot card reading, all within two hours.

The fortune-teller told me that not only would I find Mr. Right soon, but that he was going to be rich and empowering. (Sounded good to me.) She also told me I had to focus on myself more. (I think I have that covered with this trip.) And she said I need to let some stuff go from my past. (I thought I had, but maybe not completely.) This Mr. Right thing keeps coming up. I wonder where that corner is?

On my second day in Cape Town I joined up with a group of seven others to travel from there to Winhoek, Namibia, my fortieth country. My tour mates were a couple from Seattle, in my age category, a couple from London in their twenties, a girl from London who turned forty on the trip, and a girl from Australia in her thirties. We had a very young, white South African tour guide, who was also our driver. It was nice to have a small group so we were able to move around our tour van. The van was bigger than an ordinary van, but smaller than a bus, and we could walk around in it. This was good for game viewing, and we were also able to get on the roof if we wanted. The van wasn't air-conditioned, however, and we almost melted more than once.

From Cape Town we drove through a very dry region heading towards the Namibian border. The landscape of brown fields and rolling hills reminded me of the central part of southern British Columbia, where my sister lives. When we arrived at the western coast it was, surprisingly, quite desolate. We saw no homes for miles. We stopped at one restaurant that sat alone on a beach, but there was no one there. It wasn't until we arrived in the tiny town of Lamberts Bay that we found people and a place to eat.

Lamberts Bay is famous for Bird Island, where a nature reserve provides protection for the Cape gannets. The rocks were blanketed with thousands of these birds. We took some time to have lunch and stretch our legs on the breakwater, but the smell of the birds eventually drove us away.

Our overnight stop was at cabins in the middle of the sandstone mountains of Cedarberg. Our hostess was as rough and ready as you can imagine, but she fed us an incredible meal of pumpkin, lentils, feta, chicken, and lamb. The best part was the malva we had for dessert. Malva pudding is a sweet pudding served hot with custard and/or ice cream made with apricot jam, a South African speciality, and I knew this was going to become a favourite.

In the morning we explored the cave art in the surrounding mountains. The sign said they cannot be dated precisely, but are similar to art that has been identified as up to six thousand years old in other areas. These rock paintings depict the experiences of the San Bushmen who inhabited the area for twenty thousand years. We found many pictures of animals and people. My favourites were those of the curvy big-butted woman. (Maybe I have some African roots?)

So concluded my trip in South Africa, as the next day we would be crossing the border into Namibia. I knew I merely covered a very small part of a very big country, but I learned a bit more about the past struggles and how the future was unfolding. I only saw the surface and could barely begin to understand it all. I certainly hope that things begin to equalize as the future generations become more educated and tolerant.

Chapter 37
Namibia

"You came to Namibia during the rainy season, which means I have good news and bad news for you," said our tour leader, Darren. The good news was that everything was green, flowers were blooming, and rivers were flowing. The bad news was the rivers were flowing over, roads were closed, and we had to miss a few of the highlights that Namibia offers.

Namibia, formally South-West Africa, was under South African rule until 1990. It is the second least densely populated country in the world, second only to Mongolia. I was not surprised by that statistic, because we drove halfway around the country and saw very few people, including hardly any tourists. The population is just over two million, with approximately 87 percent black, 6 percent white, and 6 percent mixed race people.

We crossed the border from South Africa into Namibia and spent our first night near the Orange River, which runs along the border between South Africa and Namibia. We went canoeing in the morning and were disappointed to find the river wasn't actually orange, but was named after William of Orange. The canoe trip was a welcome respite from the hours spent melting away in the tour van. Our peaceful paddle took us through an area in the Richtersveld Mountains, the oldest desert mountains in the world. We experienced bright blue skies, brown mountain peaks, colourful birds, fresh air, and exercise. It was glorious.

After that fantastic morning we hesitated getting back in the van, but of course we did, and headed north. The roads started out fine, even though they were gravel. However, they got progressively worse as the days went by. One day we got our fresh air and exercise by filling in the muddy road with rocks we dug up from the side of the road, so we could get through the muddy holes. That wasn't glorious, but we made it through without sinking into the mud, so it was worth it. We were thankful for the seat belts because some of the potholes were so big they couldn't be avoided, and we would be sent flying into the air if we didn't have them on, which was something we had to learn from experience. The temperature ran in the mid-thirties Celsius for most of the journey, so we always arrived at our destinations hot, sweaty, and ready to get out of the van. T. S. Eliot had obviously never travelled in this heat, on these roads. The destination mattered more than the journey. Fortunately, most of the lodges we stayed in had swimming pools, hot showers, and were set in very unique remote locations, which helped us forget our long day's journey.

We stayed a few nights near Fish River Canyon, the second-largest canyon in the world after the Grand Canyon. We arrived in time for sunset and Darren had arranged a "Sundowner Party", with wine and cheese, as a surprise for us. We had time to hike around a portion of the canyon's rim and then sat on the edge, looking down into the vast expanse and watching the setting sun illuminate the canyon. It was breathtaking.

Our drive through this sparsely populated country presented us with a varied landscape, from sandstone cliffs, dolomite volcanic rocks, flat-topped mountains covered in green vegetation and conical-shaped peaks, to vast wide-open spaces with nothing in sight for miles. We spotted kudu, zebra, ostrich, gazelle, and springbok. The springbok were the most fun to watch as the young ones "pronk", which is when they spring suddenly into the air. We also enjoyed watching ostriches try to outrun the truck. It was a close race.

The most beautiful landscape we drove through was the eastern edge of the Namib Desert. This is where orange actually meant orange. The sand was the most amazing bronze-orange I have ever seen. The sand is full of iron and it rusts, creating that warm bronzy tone. We were going to go for a long drive through the desert and climb one of the tallest dunes (said to be up to three hundred metres high and among the tallest in the world), but this was where we hit our first overflowing river. The river, in fact, washed out the road, and fallen trees were floating past at a rate too fast to safely manoeuvre around. Thankfully, we were able to climb one of the first dunes before we got to the river, and from its peak had a great view over magnificent desert sands. Because of the rain there were green shrubs and flowers growing in the dunes, which does not happen often. Darren said he had never seen the variety of greens we saw on this trip.

After days in these remote locations, we arrived in Swakopmund, a city of about thirty thousand, on the Atlantic coast. Surrounded by the Namib Desert on three sides and the Atlantic Ocean to the west, this area usually does not get extreme heat. But while we were there the temperatures were in the thirties. Established by the Germans in the late 1800s, the town has now become the thrill-seeker capital of Namibia. Our canoe guide on the Orange River called it "Little Germany", and I understood why when we arrived to find many colonial buildings and meet many people of German descent.

In Swakopmund, sand boarding, skydiving, quad biking, fishing, seal and dolphin watching and, sand yachting were just some of the thrill-seeking options offered. My British tour mate, Emma, turned forty the day we arrived, so she, Julia (our Australian tour mate), and I decided to skydive to celebrate.

On the day of our dive we were picked up and driven to a wide-open desert area, just outside of town. The skydiving school, complete with stand-up bar, was a buzz of activity. Parachutes were packed, jump suits were fitted, waivers were signed, lessons on the "dive position" were taught, and then we were driven further out to the dive spot. A small plane sat out on the desert sands and six of us, plus the pilot, hopped in. In order to make room for everyone, the interior of the plane was devoid of seats. Julia and I, our tandem partners, and two videographers sat cuddled together on the floor. We had a few laughs while we flew up to ten thousand feet. The men were all very funny and, I'm sure, used their humour to keep us from being nervous. It worked because I really wasn't scared or nervous.

We got a great view of the desert, the city, and the coastline before our time came to jump. Securely strapped to the front of our tandem partner, we wiggled our way to the open door and stood perched there while the videographer jumped out in front of us. Then we jumped! That first step away from the plane was exhilarating. Having the air forced against my face made me breathless for a second, and then I caught my breath as we were free-falling downward. I don't know how he did it, but the cameraman positioned himself in front of us as we flew through the sky. He had me blow kisses to him, all for the video, of course. Then we pulled the chute, which caused my legs to swing like those of a rag doll, and then down we soared at a slower pace. To add to the thrill, my partner did a few trick moves with the parachute that sent us in circles and backwards. My stomach lurched and my squeals grew louder, but it was so much fun. I didn't want it to end, but you can't fight gravity. We sailed down and I marvelled at the feeling of flying as the ground came up to meet us. Amazingly, we landed on our feet.

As we headed back into town, Julia said, "Did you notice the duct tape holding the plane together?" Thank goodness I hadn't, and thank goodness we had a safe ride. Skydiving in Africa? Am I crazy? Mom must really have been looking after me up there.

The fun wasn't over, however. I was also convinced to go quad biking, despite the horror stories I had heard of people crashing and hurting themselves. I was drawn in by the desire to see more of the desert and the sand dunes we had seen from the sky. Julia and I joined Steve, the quad expert, and off we went, out to the dunes. Our bikes were speed controlled so we couldn't go too crazy, and he instructed us to stay in his tracks and all was safe. We followed him up and down the towering bronze-coloured dunes, but didn't try wheelies like he did. We drove further into the desert and then doubled back for a spectacular view of the Atlantic. It was great fun, and by the end I wished I'd gone faster and tried riskier moves, so then I understood how people get carried away and it could be dangerous.

We headed out the next morning to travel further north, but I had time for a massage. The woman who did my massage said she could have helped me find an interviewee, so I got her e-mail address and said if I didn't find a woman before I left the country, I would contact her. I asked if she might do the interview for me, and she said she would be happy to do that.

We had another long day of driving, but it was broken up by a stop in Spitzkoppe, where we found an amazing outcrop of huge granite boulders jutting out of the flat landscape. We flew out of the hot truck and frolicked like kids over the rocks. We had a great time climbing the rocks, finding bushman paintings and spotting brightly coloured lizards.

That night we stayed in the tiny town of Usakos. The hotel owners were very sweet and made an Amurula birthday cake for Emma. Amurula is a delicious, creamy South African liqueur. The hotel staff at every lodge we stayed in also provided us with entertainment, and one of the songs they sang for us was the "Amurula Song", complete with actions. It was very funny, and by the end of the tour we were all singing and dancing to the song.

From Usakos we were supposed to drive along the Skeleton Coast, named originally for the whale and seal bones which covered the shore when the whaling industry was still active and the skeletal shipwrecks that sit offshore jutting out of the ocean. A constant dense fog and rocks offshore wreaked havoc on ships in the area. There are apparently over a thousand ships littering the coast. That, however, was the other part of the tour we had to forfeit because of the rain. The roads were blocked and we had to head inland, rather than stay on the coast.

We stopped in a small town to visit a Himba market. The Himba is one of the Namibian tribes that is still very traditional. Sitting on the ground, clad only in tiny goat-skin miniskirts, metal ankle bracelets, and several necklaces, were four Himba women. The orange theme continued here, as these women were covered in a paste of ochre and butterfat from head to toe. Their multiple braids were caked in the paste and draped down their backs. They do this to protect themselves from the sun. The women were happy to have us take their pictures and excited when we showed them their images. They sold jewellery, and I bought a bracelet that turned out to be PVC piping engraved with a traditional design. A lovely blend of modern and traditional art!

The Himba are a nomadic, pastoral people who follow the best grazing land for their cattle and goats, and their homes, like those of the Maasai, are made of cattle dung.

Another tribe we saw, but did not interact with, was the Herero tribe. The Herero are cattle farmers who measure their wealth in cattle, and the importance of cattle is shown in the hats the Herero women wear. We saw several women in town in traditional attire. They wore long colourful dresses and huge hats shaped like cow horns.

For the next two nights we stayed in another remote location, this time in the Damaraland region. When we were told we would be staying in tents, I wasn't happy about it, but they were "luxury tents", and only the walls were canvas. They were set up with wood floors, indoor toilets, and real beds, so they weren't too bad. From there we went out in search of the desert elephants.

There are only about two hundred of these elephants left and they can be hard to find. We were lucky, though, and found a huge herd in a lush grazing area. Darren let us out of the vehicle, and gave us instructions to keep quiet. Then he showed us signals for getting down low or keeping still, and even suggested we might need to run. We stayed upwind from the elephants and nothing dramatic happened. We just enjoyed a few hours of watching these magnificent and massive creatures grazing and tracking their way across the desert. It would have been a good story, though, if we had needed to run for the truck.

Our next stop was Etosha National Park, where we were all anticipating great lion sightings. Darren admitted, after the fact, that he thought we were there at the wrong time of year and would not find any. We were blessed, however, and saw several. If not for another car stopped at one location we would never have known they were there. Crouched in the tall grass not far from a waterhole full of gazelles and zebras were two females. We sat for quite a while watching them poke their heads up and listening to the guttural growls, but the anticipated run for dinner never happened on our watch. I was somewhat sorry I didn't get to see a "kill", but I was relieved as well. I probably would have closed my eyes anyway. All the men on the tour practiced their lion growl for days after that.

In our two days of game drives we saw hundreds of giraffes, zebras, black-faced impala, springbok, oryx, hartebeest, steenbok, and many varieties of birds, including ugly Corrie bustards and beautifully coloured guinea fowl. We also came across another group of lions and lionesses. It was interesting to find out that the manes of the males are not as big as in Tanzania, as they adapt to the hotter weather by having less fur. Our game drives would start to get boring, and then all of a sudden we would turn a corner and the road would be blocked by a tower of giraffes or a zeal of zebras. The zebras would move away, but the giraffes would stand their ground and stare us down.

Even though we were inconvenienced by the rains at times, we weren't caught in a deluge until our trip to Waterberg Plateau Park. The plateau rises more than two hundred metres above the savannah. It has lush vegetation, which is a real contrast to the savannah it looms over. We were on the plateau searching for the elusive rhinos when rain poured into our open jeep, drenching us and causing us to be cold for the first time in two weeks. We were teased by muddy rhino tracks in several locations, but because the brush was so dense, we never found the rhinos. They were probably just behind a bush staring back at us. It really was not one of our better days, but I kept reminding myself that I was in Africa looking for rhinos, and that was a wondrous thing.

With game drives completed, our final day was spent in Windhoek, the capital of Namibia, a city of around three hundred thousand people. We all had mixed feelings about ending our trip and arriving into the chaos of a city. Despite the rough roads and long drives, we enjoyed all the spectacular landscapes and wilderness we had experienced the last two weeks. After a good-bye dinner, we went our own way. It was another great group to travel with and an incredible tour.

In the morning, before I was to fly out, I was preparing to go into town to find someone to interview, but the desk clerk told me not to walk the twenty minutes into town because it was a Sunday and the streets were too quiet. She didn't think I would be safe. That surprised me, because I hadn't heard there were any problems. I was out of Namibian currency so I couldn't take a cab, and therefore didn't go. I knew I had the lady from Swakopmund to help with an interviewee, so I read my book and headed to the airport in the afternoon.

A few days after I left Africa I had an e-mail from Julia, my Aussie tour mate. The same morning I decided not to go to town, she did go. She had not spoken to anyone and started to walk into town on her own. She was robbed at knifepoint. Fortunately, the thief just took her purse and ran, but what a horrible way to end a holiday. She was shook up, but otherwise fine, and hadn't been carrying her passport or anything of much value, so she was lucky. Thank goodness I was given that warning. Mom must have been very busy watching out for me in Namibia.

On the way to the airport my taxi driver asked me what I thought of Namibia. I told him I loved what I saw, but didn't really know too much about the lifestyle of the people. He told me that half the population lives below the poverty line and that HIV/AIDS affects 15 percent of the population. Those were shockingly horrible statistics. I left feeling quite sad.

That was the end of the African portion of my journey. It is a vast continent, with vast beauty, vast poverty, and vast struggles. I have been fortunate to travel there twice in my lifetime and would love to go back again. I hope the future holds more promise than the past.

Bianca was the woman I befriended in Swakopmund. She was happy to do the interview for me, and ended up thanking me because through the interview she became more acquainted with Alexia, who had been her nanny and housekeeper for years.

~

Alexia – 51

Bianca wrote this first: "Alexia is a Herero woman. The Herero are a very proud, even on occasion arrogant, people who don't normally mix easily with any other tribes. They have traditional dress, which Alexia put on especially for the photo, and yes, they love their photos to be taken. They do not wear the traditional dress on a day-to-day basis anymore, but when her mother was growing up it was standard. Nowadays they have become more westernized and maybe the dress just became too hot!"

Alexia is fifty-one years old, but says she feels forty-five. She has been married for four years and lived with her husband for five years prior to that. (Bianca commented: The Herero women, even if treated badly, seldom divorce. They may run away, but never divorce. This is because the husband pays two head of cattle and six thousand Namibian dollars upon marrying her, and if she divorces him she has to repay the money and give back six cattle.)

Although this is Alexia's first marriage she has eight children. Bianca asks her their ages and she says she doesn't really know, but from around thirty-three to ten, five sons and three daughters. Alexia went as far as grade seven and says none of her children have finished school.

Alexia's parents were never married to each other. Her mother did marry eventually, but she says she does not remember much about her and is not sure how old she was when she passed away. Her father left the family early and she thinks he was a soldier and went to fight somewhere. He did not have much contact with her family, but she does know that he has also passed away. She feels her life is far better than that of her parents, who lived in extreme poverty.

She is very happy with her job and feels she is making a good living. She says, "Here I get clothing, food, furniture, and am able to live well." (Bianca wrote: I do spoil her; I don't think it is the norm, but I believe that I give where it is due, and she is an amazing second mom in this home.)

She is Catholic, as is her husband, and says religion is very important to her. She attends church on a regular basis and her children attend as well.

She was from Windhoek originally, but has lived in Swakopmund for the last nine years. She has done some travelling around Namibia, but has not been out of the country. If she could move to another country she would love to move to Australia. (Bianca wrote: Two of my sons have immigrated to Australia and I have hinted I may go there as well. Alexia said I would have to take her with me. I don't think she really knows where Australia is, or how far it is, either.)

She has never thought about where she would be at this age, as she doesn't think she has the vision to plan or hope for anything. She just takes every day as it comes.

She has no menopausal symptoms yet, but is on high blood pressure medication.

She describes herself as a woman with a strong personality, who is hardworking, caring, and loving. A perfect description of a nanny, I would say.

Alexia wants me to know a few other things about the Herero. One thing is about marriage: the wedding is a huge affair. The night before the ceremony the man sleeps in his wedding garments. The bride, in her white dress, stays at her parents' home. Each parent presents the daughter with a cow or goat. (If the parents have passed away the whole community rallies together and collects money to buy the animals.) The cow gets milked at the ceremony and then a cow or goat is slaughtered for the feast. That night the bride goes to sleep in her wedding dress.

She says that the men are still very much the head of the household and women have few rights. Alexia assures Bianca that the Herero make use of condoms, much more than the other tribes. Alexia also wants me to know that of the hundreds of children begging in the streets, few, if any, are Herero, because the Herero would never allow themselves to stoop to that level. They would rather take in an extra child from a sister, brother, niece, etc., than have a child roaming the streets. Bianca checked on this and found no Herero begging anywhere. Her comment on that was "Now if only everyone had that idea."

Chapter 38
Dominican Republic, BVI, Antigua, Barbados, St. Lucia

Caribbean Cruise

"When I sat in the ICU, willing you to live six months ago, I never believed you would be healthy enough to join me," I said to my sister, Lynda, when I met up with her and our niece, Colette, in Miami after flying in from Africa. We were poised to start our five-country cruise in the Caribbean. Mom really must have been looking after us from above. To see Lynda healthier than she's ever looked was such a gift.

Our Miami hotel was on the beach, but not in the best neighbourhood, so we just ate at the hotel and caught up on the last few months. In the morning, we took the bus to South Beach to check out the trendy stores and wander through the Art Deco neighbourhood, where palm trees and beautiful purple bougainvillaea line the streets.

Then we bid dry land farewell and boarded our cruise ship. This cruise was with Norwegian Cruise Lines, a line I had travelled with in the past, and the ship was the very same ship Lynda and I had been on the year before, so we gave Colette the tour, did the obligatory fire drill, and unpacked before our first dinner.

We had a great cruise, keeping busy day and night on port days and sea days. We had three sea days, but I only managed to read five pages of my book. Lynda and I are the same when it comes to relaxing—we can't do it. Colette didn't have our problem and actually knew how to relax by the pool or on a beach. We attended the ship's art auction and seminars and walked the deck, and I played in a couple poker tournaments. I won seven hundred and fifty dollars in one tournament, which almost covered the cost of the cruise.

Our evenings were jam-packed with dinners and a variety of entertainment, including three music and dance shows, a hilarious comedian, a great hypnotist, a four-man a cappella group, game shows, talent shows, an improv show, and an improv workshop. Poor Colette, who is only twenty-five, enjoyed herself with us old gals, but unfortunately there were not many young people for her to hang out with. I did stay up with her one night to dance under the stars at a deck party, but on most nights we were in bed by ten.

~

Dominican Republic

"Do you want to hire a van with us?" I asked a nice-looking man in the long queue we were in to get off the ship at our first port, Samana, in the Dominican Republic. (He looked around forty-three.) We knew if we had enough people it would be much cheaper and more fun than paying for the tours offered by the cruise line. My new friend agreed to meet us on the dock, but unfortunately we never found him. (I guess I wasn't at the right "corner" yet.) We did, however, find a couple from Miami, who were originally from Nicaragua and Cuba. As Spanish is the official language in the Dominican Republic, they made perfect travel buddies.

When we arrived at the dock, several tour guides approached us with their sales pitch. After sorting through the bunch we agreed to go with Martin, who offered a tour of the area for twenty dollars. A similar tour with the cruise line was around sixty dollars, so we were happy with that. The Dominican Republic is the second-biggest Caribbean Island in size and population, next to Cuba. The population is close to ten million, and over 40 percent of those people live below the poverty line. The area around the dock was similar to most cruise ports, with many lovely tourist shops and restaurants, but not far from town we travelled on potholed dirt roads, avoiding roaming dogs, cats, chickens, and goats. We found ramshackle homes and businesses and shabbily clad locals, looking less than impressed with a group of tourists gawking at them. We also passed several baseball fields and learned that baseball is the number-one sport in the country. This surprised me, as I thought soccer was the sport of choice in most Latin American countries.

Samana is on a peninsula on the eastern side of the Dominican Republic and Martin took us to the point, where we found a nearly deserted beach and enjoyed a few hours of beachcombing and relaxing on the beautiful azure Caribbean Sea, while trying out the local beer, Presidente. Martin was also proud to show us a small waterfall nestled in the bush not far off the road, where we watched some local kids leap off the top and into the river below. They were quick to come up to collect tips for their great feats, which we were happy to pay. Once back in town we set out and found an interviewee and our new friends, Aris and Joanna, were happy to translate.

~

Juliana – 55

I spot a woman selling jewellery near the dock who looks to be the right age, and ask Joanna if she can explain my quest and see if she is willing to answer some questions. Juliana, the woman, is reluctant at first, but asks her husband to look after the table while she talks to us. After Joanna and Aris explain a little further, and I stand by smiling as nicely as possible, she says she is happy to answer my questions.

She is older than I thought, telling us she is fifty-five years old. She has been married eighteen years, but knew her husband for twenty-five years before she married him. He keeps looking over wondering what we are up to. After most of the tourists leave their table he joins us as well. The other vendors at the craft market are curious about what we are doing.

She tells us she had sixteen siblings when her mom passed away. Then her dad married a woman thirty-one years younger than he and had six more children. Juliana didn't follow their example and only had three children. One was a daughter she had before her marriage. As we start talking about children, she gets a little teary and tells us that her first daughter got married at the age of fourteen and moved to the States with her husband. She returned home last year, to tell her mother she had lupus, and died shortly after. I ask Aris to tell her I lost a child as well, and she and I hug. Everyone's eyes have tears in them now.

"On to your other children," I say brightly. "Yes, they are seventeen and eighteen years old and have finished high school, unlike me, who only went until I was ten years old. They will go on to university too," she says proudly. Juliana's father had no education, while her mother attended school until she was ten years old.

The mood picks up more when we ask about religion. She belongs to an evangelistic church and says it's very important to her. She attends mass five days a week, along with her husband and children. She goes as far as to say her hobbies are, "Spreading the word of the Lord, going to church, and sewing."

I tell Aris that Joanna can handle the next questions and ask her to see how far she can get with questions about menopause. Juliana doesn't seem to have a problem with this at all, and tells us that she has been going through menopause for seven years, still experiencing hot flashes, night sweats, and irritability. This of course scares Joanna, who is only in her thirties, and doesn't make me feel much better—seven years!

When we ask if she would move to another country, she says, "Yes, the U.S. But now that my daughter is gone it isn't as important."

Not surprisingly, when asked if she is happy, her answer is, "So-so." We hug good-bye and go back to the ship. I felt bad, because I think we left her sad and thinking about her daughter. I know that pain, and it takes a long time to lighten.

~

British Virgin Islands

"Can I get recycled on the Virgin Islands?" I joked, as I am sure many women have, sailing into Tortola, the biggest of the British Virgin Islands. Rolling green hills, steep roads, and beautiful houses and resorts lined the sparkling coast.

We joined up with our friends from Florida, disembarked, and found a boat trip to the next island of Virgin Gorda, which we had heard was the best place to go for a day trip. Of course, we thought we were so clever getting the cheapest boat, until we got within about one hundred metres of Devil's Bay and they told us we had to get out and swim. If that part of the trip was explained, none of us heard it. The fact that they wanted us to swim in was ridiculous, but the saying "you get what you pay for" certainly rang in our ears. I don't know what we were supposed to do with our cameras and towels. While we were complaining, it became apparent that the waves were too big for us to safely swim in anyway, so they agreed to take us to shore.

Once on the island we were happy we made the trip. We found a beautiful white sand beach and followed a path through giant boulders that we climbed over and under and around to Devil's Bay. For the rest of the afternoon we hung out on the beach, drank pina coladas, and enjoyed the sun. The pounding surf made swimming a challenge, but Lynda tried it anyway. I had a great laugh watching her get tossed around and land on the beach with a bathing suit full of sand. How lucky we were to be there, just six months after almost losing her.

Back on Tortola, I walked around town trying to find an interviewee. The problem was, I couldn't find a woman who was actually born in BVI. It seemed everyone in the shops was from one of the other Caribbean Islands. I was disappointed I couldn't find anyone, but we sure had a fun day.

~

Antigua

"I'll look after you girls," said Twami, our Antiguan guide. He had scooped us off the dock amongst all the other guides vying for the passengers' trade. He was smooth, and we knew we would have fun with him. We started out agreeing to a quick twenty-dollar tour and ended up paying thirty-five dollars for an extended tour through the rain forest. Most of the island was brown and drier than the last two islands, but the rain forest was a lovely contrast, with lush tropical tree-canopied roads.

The salesman in him never quit, telling us he could take us zip-lining, snorkelling, or scuba diving if we wanted. We would have loved to say yes, but there just weren't enough hours in the day or dollars in our pockets to do it all.

The homes we passed were neater and tidier than those we saw in the Dominican Republic, but we saw none as opulent as the ones on the coast of BVI. Twami took us to the top of Shirley Heights, where we had a fantastic view of Montserrat and Guadeloupe, as well as English Harbour. He also pointed out Eric Clapton's house, which blended so well into the countryside that you could barely see it.

We ended the day with more relaxing on the beach, drinking Wadaldi, the local beer, and swimming in the beautiful turquoise waters of the Caribbean. When Twami dropped us off at the ship he slipped me his phone number. "In case you ever return," he said with a wink. Considering he had told us about his third wife, to whom he was still married, and his several children all over the island that he was supporting, I didn't keep the number.

While up at Shirley Point Twami found a reluctant candidate for me to interview.

~

Cynthia – 56

Twami asks a few of the ladies selling jewellery at the little market at Shirley Point if they want to be interviewed. I see most shaking their heads, but one lady looks at me curiously and agrees to at least listen to the questions. First, however, she says, "I am a born-again Christian. Are you a believer?"

Hesitantly, I say, "I believe there is someone looking out for us."

She doesn't appear to like my answer, but says, "I will answer what I can."

I know this isn't going to go simply, but start off with the easy questions. She tells me she is fifty-six years old and has been married thirty-eight years. She has two sons, twenty-eight and twenty-nine, and one daughter, thirty-four. She doesn't remember if her parents had any education and says she only went to primary school. "But all my children have finished high school," she says proudly.

I ask how long she has been selling jewellery here and she says, "I make it and sell it and have been on this spot since I was a little girl." As we talk, the other vendor women are listening and giggling and talking with Twami in their local language of Antiguan Creole. Twami is laughing along, but he won't tell me what they are all finding so funny. Cynthia doesn't seem as amused as the rest.

She has always lived very near Shirley Point, but has travelled to a few of the other islands nearby. She says she would never want to move anywhere else.

I know I am going out on a limb here, but I bring up menopause. "That is way too personal," she says.

I quickly go on to the next question, "Do you think your life is better than your parents'?"

"I won't talk about that, either," she huffs.

I know asking about religion is safe, so I ask about that. She is happy to discuss her faith and how important it is to her. She attends church twice a week along with her husband, but her children are not involved in the church.

I know you are grumpy, I think to myself, but say, "Are you happy?"

"Yes, I am happy, because of my faith in God." She isn't the first one to answer in that way!

~

Barbados

"I live in Canada six months of the year and come home to Barbados for the other six," Marson, our taxi-driver-turned-tour-guide, told us. Of all the taxis it was great that we picked his, because he was informative, efficient, and fun. We only had a few hours to see as much as we could because we had booked a submarine trip for the afternoon, and he promised to give us the whirlwind tour.

Marson took us to see the highlights of the ritzy areas of town. We drove around the golf course where Tiger Woods got married. It was apparently five hundred dollars a round, so we weren't surprised to see only one golfer. We also drove by many gated communities and well-manicured properties, including homes leased by Bill Gates and Richard Branson.

Then we drove through an area where the middle class live. Small bungalows on stilts lined the incredibly clean streets. Marson told us they have garbage pick-up twice a day. Our tour included several sugarcane plantations and the top of a hill overlooking the rugged Atlantic coast. We enjoyed the countryside of beautiful orange, pink, yellow, and red flowering tropical trees. It was a lovely island, and a shame that we couldn't have seen more.

Our much-anticipated submarine trip was not as exciting as we had hoped. The submarine *Atlantis* took us down to 150 feet, but the water was murky. We went over a coral reef which was colourless and a shipwreck that had very few fish exploring its deck. At the very end of the trip a school of silver fish swam by, interspersed with a few blue-striped beauties. I had been really spoiled with the incredible snorkelling I did in Bali, so that dip into the deep blue sea just did not measure up.

After the submarine ride I was determined to find an interviewee. Colette, Lynda, and I set out to find someone at the shops near the cruise terminal, and Colette succeeded.

∼

Amena – 49

Colette approaches a woman at the flower kiosk in the mall of the cruise terminal. She explains what I am doing and the woman says she will answer what she can when she doesn't have customers. Colette comes to find me and we go back to talk with Amena. She tells me the kiosk is not her business, but she has worked here for nine years. Previously she worked for an airline, but likes her current job much better, because it is less corporate.

Colette is good at guessing ages, as Amena is forty-nine years old. She tells us she was married when she was thirty. "But," she says sadly, "I have been divorced for the last five years."

She has a daughter, twenty-two years old, and a son, thirteen years old. Her daughter is in university, studying law. She seems embarrassed to say she only finished primary school and her parents only attended school for a few years. But she is happy to say that her parents are both still alive at eighty-six and eighty-nine years old, and are still married and healthy for their age.

"Do you think your life is better than your parents'?" I ask.

"My life may be better than theirs because I have more possessions, but I think I have less values," she answers sadly.

Amena says her hobbies are gardening and watching cricket, which is the number-one sport in Barbados. She has only travelled to Puerto Rico and has always lived in Bridgetown, Barbados. She says she wouldn't mind living in another country for a while to get experience, but she doesn't think she would stay long and has no country in mind.

She is Pentecostal and attends church weekly. "Religion is very important to me. I need it to survive," she tells me. Her children attend with her.

"Are you happy?" I ask.

"Not completely. I want to be in a loving relationship and that is not happening," she says with a sad look.

~

St. Lucia

"I will take you inside an active volcano," one of the many tour guides in Castries Harbour on St. Lucia announced. We thought that sounded like fun and joined his tour. St. Lucia is a volcanic island and more mountainous than many of the other islands, making the drive around it windy and a little frightening along some of the cliffs.

We drove through a few lovely little towns, through tropical rainforests, and past banana plantations. Then, after stopping at a few of the beautiful beaches, we drove into a volcano, as promised. The sign said that Soufriere Volcano is the world's only drive-in volcano. The strong, putrid smell of sulphur permeated the air, and we were told it was strong enough to discolour silver jewellery. We did not test it.

We paid a small entrance fee to walk the boardwalk around the crater, and watched bubbling volcanic mud pots and blowing steam vents. When we eventually got used to the smell we were thrilled to be that close to an active volcano. It hadn't had a big eruption since the 1700s, so we weren't too worried about it happening on our watch.

After our volcanic excursion we had lunch at a beachside restaurant, enjoying the view of St. Lucia's most famous landmark, the Pitons. These twin cone-shaped peaks jut out of the sea to over 790 metres. We enjoyed fresh prawns in a delicious local Creole sauce. Unfortunately, I didn't have time to find an interviewee.

The last day of our trip was spent at sea and we enjoyed taking advantage of all there was to offer: poker, a future cruise seminar, an improv workshop, the casino, and a fantastic Cirque show.

I was so happy to have been able to travel with my sister and niece. After I waved good-bye in the Miami airport, I looked up to Mom to thank her for watching over us. And off I flew to Cancun, to join my final tour group and finish my last five countries.

If you look like your passport photo,

you're too ill to travel.

—Will Kommen

Chapter 39

Belize

"Welcome to Belize. You are going to love our country. I'm sure you came for the diving, but don't forget we have some great Mayan ruins as well," said the man behind the customs desk, sounding more like a tour guide than a border guard. Then, as he looked at my passport, he said, "I must tell you that you are much better-looking than your passport picture." His warm welcome, spoken in perfect English, reminded me that Belize is the only Latin American country where English is the official language, and gave us the first indication of how friendly the locals were. I had to admit, after forty-five countries, most with a language I didn't understand, hearing English was comforting. Belize, formerly known as British Honduras, has had independence from Britain since 1981.

I had flown out of Miami to Cancun, taken a bus to Playa del Carmen, about an hour from the airport, and met up with my new tour group: six other Canadians, three Brits, an Aussie, and a Swedish gal. They had spent a few days there, but I had booked myself so tight that I joined them on day three of the tour.

We began our journey the next day with a four-hour bus ride to the Belize border, followed by a three-and-a-half-hour drive into Belize City, where we stopped only long enough to catch a ferry to the island of Caye Caulker. According to our tour guide, Sara (a dual Canadian/American), we would not have enjoyed Belize City. She explained that the high crime rate there was not something she thought we needed to experience firsthand.

After our long day of travelling in exhausting heat, I was delighted when I finally laid eyes on the palm-treed island with its streets paved in sand. Golf carts and bikes were the only wheeled vehicles on Caye Caulker, and brightly coloured one and two-storey hotels and restaurants lined the waterfront. From the moment we stepped onto the dock and saw the "Slow Down" signs, I appreciated the motto of the island, where no one is in a hurry and the locals reprimand anyone seen running or rushing about.

The island is only about four miles long and four streets wide, so exploring it doesn't take long. In the 1960s there was a hurricane that wiped out a piece of the island at one end, making it two islands. At the "split" between the islands, there is a funky open-air bar built on the shore, where locals and tourists mingle to watch the sunset. We joined in the evening ritual. It was a great way to unwind and absorb the ambience of this peaceful island.

Despite the fact that the island depends on tourism, Caye Caulker still has a small village flavour, with a cultural mixture of Mayan, Creole, Garifuna, Mestizos, and even a small group of Mennonites. It was strange to see the Mennonites in their traditional clothing, complete with straw hats and bonnets, pulling their carts along the sandy streets. Apparently, most of the wooden furniture on the island has been built by the Mennonite carpenters.

Most of the businesses are locally owned and kept small scale. As we wandered the sandy streets we enjoyed the unique music of the Garifuna. They are descendants of Carib and Arawak Indians who intermarried with escaped Africans from two slave ships that sank in the seventeenth century.

Our second day on the island we hopped aboard a thirty-foot sailboat and sailed out to the world's second-largest barrier reef. The action started at our first stop, when our guides threw bait in the water, and within minutes several nurse sharks were circling the boat. It was exciting to be that close to these sleek beauties, but that was the water we were about to swim in and those fins were not a welcoming sight to me. Our guide told us they were harmless, but that didn't really ease my fears. However, a few minutes later I took a deep breath and joined the group as we all jumped into the crystal-clear water.

Before we swam away from the boat, our guide started playing with one of the several stingrays that had slipped in among us. I was able to get close enough to pet the velvety smooth creature and was thrilled, until I found out that these were the same kind of rays that killed Steve Irwin. I had just assumed they were safe, the way the guide was playing. He explained that because they came to that spot all the time these rays would never strike out, like the one that killed Steve. I don't think I would have tested that theory if I had known how dangerous they could be.

I surprised myself by continuing on after all that, as I don't like snorkelling when I can't touch bottom, but the water was very buoyant. I was able to relax and enjoy hundreds of colourful tropical fish and beautiful coral, and was startled for only a second at the eel that popped up from under a rock. By the third stop I was keeping up with the guide, swimming hundreds of metres away from the boat and wondering what I was ever afraid of.

While we had been exploring the ocean below, the first mate had been busy chopping chilies, onions, and tomatoes. These, along with fresh shrimp, were soaking in lime juice to create a delicious ceviche, which was served along with rum punch while sailing back to Caye Caulker. The fresh sea air was intoxicating, as was the punch, making me feel like a teenager as we danced on the deck the whole way back.

That evening we dined at Jolly Roger's, a roadside BBQ joint. We really had no choice but to eat there, as Roger is a huge man who crowds the road in front of his grill and will not take no for an answer. He and his grill, along with a few picnic tables, are all that make up his restaurant, but the seaside location and the tasty food make up for the lack of structure. Roger regaled us with stories of his island as he grilled up fresh shrimp and snapper, and still managed to scoop up every other tourist who wandered by. We ended the night playing a trivia game in the local sports bar. Our multinational group came in second. This was a great end to a perfect day, which has definitely been added to my "favourite days" list.

We spent the next morning relaxing in preparation for our first "chicken bus" ride in the afternoon. The nickname for the bus apparently comes from the overcrowded conditions on what are retired school buses. Known for their extremely hard seats and lack of air-conditioning, this was one of those "experiences in local customs" I could have forgone. Our bus lived up to its reputation for being a stifling box, and by the time we reached San Ignacio, near the Guatemalan border, I thought I might melt into the seat. Instead, I managed to just arrive soaked to the skin in sweat. Our ecolodge, right outside of San Ignacio, had tiny huts, with barely enough room for our luggage and no air-conditioning or fans. I was not pleased to see that the composting toilets and cold showers were placed a long way from the huts. I was not a happy tourist. I was not sure if I was just getting tired of travelling or if the heat finally did me in, but I couldn't stop wondering if I had pushed myself to my limit. I really questioned why I was doing all this.

I was not very excited when Sara suggested we walk down to a nearby river, as it was still extremely hot, but off we went and my mood switched instantly when we soaked our sweaty bodies in the refreshing river. Within minutes we were surrounded by the local kids, and ended up playing with them. It then took no time at all to remember: this was what I was doing this for.

The next day we were offered many great choices for outings: horseback riding in the Mountain Pine Ridge Forest, caving in what looked to be an amazing underground network, or going to see the Mayan ruins of Caracol. I would have really liked to have gone to the caves, but as I was the oldest on the trip I didn't want to hold up the younger ones who were looking forward to a wild adventure of swimming, climbing, and squeezing through the caves.

Those of us who didn't go caving headed to Caracol. The guide tried to keep us interested by hinting we might see monkeys, and even jaguars. As we drove for two hours on windy, rough roads through the pine forest, which was infested with pine beetles, we didn't see the promised animals, and the drive was not the prettiest until we reached the broad-leafed jungle and found the ancient world of the Mayans. Before we arrived at the site, we had to stop to be accompanied by the military, as we were very near the Guatemalan border. This escort was supposed to make us feel safe, but it scared me, knowing there was possible danger. Plus, we were heading into Guatemala the next day, so this was not very comforting.

I was surprised to learn that Caracol was only discovered in 1938 by loggers seeking mahogany trees, because it covers a huge area. We explored three plazas, the central acropolis, and the two ball courts, and also climbed the massive pyramid which loomed over the jungle. Apparently occupied from 600 BC to AD 1100, this city once had over thirty-five thousand buildings and five plazas. Carved monuments, called stelae, and Mayan inscriptions were everywhere. Wandering amidst the massive monuments, temples, and pyramids, we couldn't believe that these structures were built without the help of draft animals, metal tools, or pulleys.

Our guide explained the ball game played was a team sport, where getting a ball through a hoop, without the use of the hands, was the goal. It sounded like a combination of soccer and basketball. The final score led to a rather different result than our modern games, however; the losers were killed.

After exploring Caracol, our tour van stopped so we could explore a huge cave, and then hike down to Big Rock waterfall. What we thought was a great idea, turned out to be more trouble than it was worth. After we enjoyed a refreshing swim, showered under the waterfall and hiked back up, we found our driver trying to work out what to do about a dead battery. (He had left the lights on.)

We were hours from town, had no cell reception and no food, and it was getting late in the afternoon. There were two other cars in the parking lot and our guides tried to open the hoods to see if we could "borrow" their batteries, but they couldn't work out how to remove them. We had to wait for the owners to return two hours later. Thankfully, they were more than happy to help us out. I had already learned a lot about ancient history that day, but then learned a very handy modern-world trick. We removed our battery, put theirs in, started the van, unhooked their battery, put ours back in, and the car just kept running. I had no idea that would work.

We arrived back in time to swap stories with those who had gone caving. They spent hours exploring a long cave system, and it turned out to be quite a workout, but they loved it. I was jealous of their adventure, but happy I didn't try it myself. I may have been the fittest I had ever been, but wouldn't have been able to keep up with them.

As our time in Belize drew to a close I reflected on all that I enjoyed in this country: the laid-back lifestyle, the fusion of cultures, the beautiful beaches, the jungle, and the history of the Mayans.

While on Caye Caulker I had asked Charlie, the woman who ran the snorkelling tour company, if she knew a local around fifty years old that I could interview. Charlie was American and married to a local. When I returned from our snorkelling trip, she was eager to take me to meet the woman she picked. We hopped into a golf cart and drove the fifty metres to a little house on the beachfront. There, lounging in a hammock, was a lovely woman, whom Charlie introduced by saying, "This is my mother here on the island."

She then turned to the woman and said, "Ilna, this is Donna. She wanted to meet a local who was around fifty and I told her you were fifty-three. You have been my mentor here and I love you, so I wanted her to meet you." Then Charlie drove off.

~

Ilna – 77

Ilna laughs as Charlie leaves and I am a little confused as to why. She extracts herself from the hammock with an easy agility. Her perfect white teeth shine through her sly smile and she says, "I am seventy-seven," and then we both laugh. I thought she looked a little older than fifty-three, but would have never put her at seventy-seven years old.

I tell her of my quest and we decide we will do the interview regardless of her age. She has a pleasant essence about her and I like her immediately. She tells me she was born on Caye Caulker. Her grandfather was a fisherman, as was her father in his early years. Her father eventually became a shopkeeper on the island, which was not an easy task. Most of what he sold had to be picked up on the mainland. He would sail several hours to pick up the goods and then sail back, but if the weather turned bad, he would be stuck for days.

She tells me that in her younger years, there were only about four to five hundred people on the island. The roads were made with coconut husks, they had no electricity, cooked on fires, and had thatch-roofed houses. She remembers many carnivals and dancing groups going from house to house for various celebrations, and she says she is sorry to see most of their traditions dying.

Today, she says, there are about 1,500 people and the island has all the modern conveniences, including the Internet. Tourism has been growing for the last twenty years, which Ilna finds a blessing and a curse. Between her, a few of her eight siblings, and one of her daughters, they own several of the buildings along the beach where they live and have rental properties.

She was married for twenty years, but has been divorced for more than that. She has four daughters. Three live in the States and one lives on the island. Ilna has a university degree, as do all her daughters, with one currently in law school. Coming from such a small island, that is quite an extraordinary feat.

She was the school principal on Caye Caulker, until her girls needed to go to high school. As there was no high school on the island, they had to move to Belize City. When they attended university they all moved to Miami. Ilna was able to get work in schools everywhere they lived, but eventually moved back to the island to retire.

She is Catholic, but doesn't always attend mass on Sundays. Her daughters have not kept up their religion.

She has travelled around Central America, Europe, and the States, but she loves her place on the beach, swinging in her hammock, having her family and friends close, and "slowing down", as the island motto dictates. She says she would travel again, but would not want to live anywhere else.

I don't really have to ask, because it is obvious, but when I ask if she is happy, that sly smile comes out again and she says, "Yes, I am extremely happy and contented."

Twenty years from now you will be more disappointed by the things that you didn't do than by the ones you did. So throw off the bowlines. Sail away from a safe harbor. Catch the trade winds in your sails. Explore. Dream. Discover.

—Mark Twain

Chapter 40

Guatemala

"Do you truly believe the world will end on December 21, 2012?" I asked the Mayan shaman, who was working out the symbols and numbers for my horoscope. I looked deep into his eyes, to see if there was a flicker of doubt, but found none.

"Yes, I truly believe that life as we know it will be over by then. It has already started. The tsunami in Asia and the disastrous earthquake in China are the beginning of the end."

The Mayan calendar ends on December 21, 2012, when the sun will align with the centre of the Milky Way for the first time in twenty-six thousand years. I am told not all Mayans believe the world will end, but they do believe there will be a positive physical or spiritual transformation at that time. I want to believe in the latter scenario.

I had been in Guatemala for about a week when Jose, the Mayan shaman, came to the hotel to do my horoscope. I was expecting his wife, who was in her early fifties, to come for my session, and was disappointed when he showed up. He was a lovely fellow, but of course I wanted to have my horoscope done and sneak in an interview. The arrangements for the session had gone through three other people before the actual appointment was made, so it was not surprising it didn't happen the way I had hoped. I also expected to find a Mayan shaman dressed in traditional clothes and looking somewhat mystical. Jose, however, was dressed in khaki pants and a polo shirt, with no obvious "aura" surrounding him.

We had a lengthy discussion about the Mayan calendar, 2012, and how he thought we should live our lives until then. "Live life to the fullest, don't waste time with negative things, and enjoy everything," he told me. I assured him I was trying to do just that, but did not tell him what I had been doing for the last year. I wanted to hear his predictions first.

He said, "You are magical and a shaman. You should be sharing your experiences in writing. You are good at helping others with problems by pointing out the positive." (No mention of Mr. Right or that elusive corner.) He tried to explain the chart of symbols and numbers he had done but lost me within minutes. Somehow, I wasn't sure that I would make a good shaman, as he predicted, but since he didn't know about my journey, I did find it interesting that he thought I should write. It was an interesting way to spend a few hours.

The day of the horoscope concluded the first two weeks of my Central America tour, and only the Aussie girl and I were carrying on from that group. We met up with a new group to complete our tour. Our new tour leader was Annalu, from Costa Rica. My "favourite list" continued to grow, as I loved Guatemala. I was initially nervous to enter a country with a reputation for being dangerous, but although we were met at the border by guards with rifles, we found the whole process extremely easy. (It didn't hurt to have our tour guide to walk us through the process.) We had no troubles, nor did I feel uncomfortable or unsafe at any time.

The new group was all women (except the tour guide's boyfriend), so my last chance to find Mr. Right on a tour was over. They were all nice, but there was a little tension among some of the girls whose personalities just did not blend well. I just tried to stay out of it. My first roomie was a great gal who is Vietnamese/Canadian/Australian. She holds all three passports. She arrived without her luggage and was panicked about what to do. We were leaving the next day and the plane that might have her luggage on it wouldn't arrive for three days. I convinced her to use her insurance money, buy some clothes, use my small pack, and hope they would deliver her luggage to our next country. This reminded me how lucky I had been. After thirty-seven plane trips, I hadn't ever lost my luggage.

From the Belize/Guatemala border, our three-hour drive to Flores was made comfortable because of the van Sara managed to find money in the budget to rent. The tour guides can work out the transportation in their budget as they see fit. After no one had enjoyed our first "chicken bus" experience, she seemed to keep finding money to upgrade our transportation.

Although Guatemala's lush countryside was similar to Belize, the difference in culture and economy was obvious within minutes of the border. The villages and homes were more ramshackle and there were more traditionally dressed people everywhere. I was told and have read that 40–80 percent of Guatemala's fourteen million people are Mayan. I can't find a consensus of the exact percentage. Many of the Mayan women have kept to their cultural identity by wearing colourful, handwoven, intricately embroidered dresses, skirts, and blouses. Apparently, the different patterns on the clothing can help distinguish which of the twenty-three tribes they come from. They also have different hats or head coverings from tribe to tribe. Some looked like turbans, some like scarves, while others looked like they have just piled a small blanket on their head, but all were as colourful as could be.

Our first stop was Flores, a tiny island on Lake Peten Itza, which is the second-largest lake in Guatemala (thirty-two kilometres long). The island is attached to the mainland by a causeway.

Despite the afternoon heat rising to over forty degrees Celsius, I wandered the island's narrow cobblestone streets. I admired the brightly coloured houses, climbed up to a historical Spanish church, and sat in the plaza watching the locals. The island was officially founded by the Spanish in 1700. I was there during Semana Santa (Easter week) when, from Palm Sunday to Easter Sunday, there are processions through the streets, depicting scenes from the Passion of Jesus Christ. A large group of traditionally dressed women and men in modern clothes were busy throughout the afternoon decorating a float for the evening's parade.

The main reason we stopped in Flores was because of its proximity to Tikal, which is a very impressive Mayan ruin site dating from 400 BC to AD 800. We were up before dawn so we could arrive when the gates opened at six a.m. We went early to try to avoid both the scorching heat and the crowds. Our guide was a bird expert and was giddy with excitement every time he saw a bird. I'm not even sure he cared about the ruins. At one point he came to a full stop, smiled widely, and had us all squat down. We were all excited, thinking he had seen a jaguar or at least a monkey, and were disappointed when he pointed out a wild turkey. The ocellated turkey looks more like a peacock than a turkey, but none of us felt the same thrill he seemed to derive from the sighting.

The jungle surrounding Tikal was spectacular, with its exotic bird calls, cicada chirps, and screeching howler monkeys. We saw two animals I have never seen before: a mapache, which looks like an elongated raccoon, and a cotuza, which looks like a huge rat. Wandering along the dirt paths between the huge cedars, ceibas, ficus, creeping figs, and vines leading to the ruins would have been enjoyable even without the ruins. Of course, it is a UNESCO World Heritage Site.

The ruins, however, were also as magnificent as promoted. The archaeological area covers sixteen square kilometres, where more than three thousand structures have been found. We spent hours hiking, climbing, and exploring the pyramids, temples, acropolis, plazas, and statues. We learned more about the stair-step design of the pyramids that were built in the main plazas and were the heart of the Mayan cities. Each pyramid had a temple on the top. Our guide told us about, and showed us, statues of the rulers of the city and the local gods. He suggested that the Mayans who built the statues may have used hallucinogenic drugs, as the faces and bodies of many of the gods were very frightening. I think he was right. There were some strange figures there!

We climbed to the top of three of the pyramids, one over sixty-five metres high. I found it amazing that they allowed us to climb the ancient buildings and that most of them had no railings, uneven steps, and no safety precautions. Selfishly, I was happy that I had the opportunity to do this, but I know in the future they will probably stop people from climbing. The view from the top, looking over the jungle below, was spectacular.

As we hiked, we passed many structures that were only partly uncovered, making me think again that it would be a great job to unbury the past.

By midday it was too hot to climb or hike, so sadly, we left. I would have loved to spend many more hours exploring, but not in that heat. I felt sorry for all those we passed who were just starting their tour; I couldn't have hiked another minute. We were all very happy about the pool down the road.

The group decided we would put in extra money to get another private bus to take us to Rio Dulce, our next destination. In retrospect, it is too bad we had such a bad experience on the first chicken bus, because it would have been great to hang out around locals more, but we all really enjoyed the comfort of air-conditioning too much to try again. Guatemala is a mountainous country, and as we drove along, I had to wonder if some of the smaller hills might have had Mayan structures underneath. Maybe I need to become an archaeologist in my next life.

Rio Dulce is a very busy, crowded town located where Lake Izabal meets the Rio Dulce, a river that leads to the Caribbean. It is also a port stop for boaters who travel the river to Livingston at the Caribbean end. We stayed at an ecolodge on the other side of the river from town. The lodge was in a beautiful setting on the river, surrounded by jungle on three sides, with small bungalows connected by elevated boardwalks over a marsh. The only downfall was that the washrooms were about one hundred metres away from the bungalows, and navigating along the boardwalk in the dark was not my idea of fun. I am not sure if it was the heat, menopause, or the anxiety of my trip coming to a close, but I wasn't sleeping well and had to use the washroom several times every night. (I did manage without falling off.) I realized that "roughing it" does not appeal to me nearly as much as it used to. It's also sad that I rate all accommodations by where the washrooms are.

The jungle behind the lodge offered a hiking trail, and forgetting how hot it was, I agreed to go for a hike. Sometimes I just don't think. We had only gone a short way when I was completely soaked in sweat. I was proud of myself for not turning back, however, and I continued to the top of a hill overlooking the lake, river, and Castillo de San Filipe, an old fort that sits on the riverbank. Being above the canopy of the jungle, looking down at the gigantic ferns, was breathtaking. We crossed several suspension bridges swinging over the jungle floor, which I have no problem with, but one of my fellow hikers was frightened, so we didn't stay too long. I was happy for the pool back at the hotel, but it turned out to be almost as hot as a bath. Instead, I lined up for the one of two showers shared by at least twelve bungalows. I had to keep reminding myself to go back to the "glass-half-full" philosophy.

As was always the case, the next day brought me back to that philosophy easily. We took a boat trip to Livingston, about forty kilometres down the river. We passed fishermen, rustic homes, and several modern vacation homes. We stopped at a women's cooperative where Mayan handicrafts were being made and sold, and at one spot on the river we were greeted by small children in dugout canoes, who presented us with bright red tropical flowers. They then tried to sell us turtles, crabs, fish, and handicrafts. They were so young, maybe three to seven years old, and I was worried about them out on the river in their wobbly canoes, but I guessed that it was a daily routine and they seemed to know what they were doing. They then led us to their home, which was a rickety wooden hut on stilts, directly over the river. They were definitely used to the water and could likely all swim better than I could. We were invited into their home, where their parents sold woven baskets, local shells, and carved wooden trinkets. We all bought a little something, as we couldn't resist helping the kids who were so cute.

Closer to our destination, the river became very narrow and tall canyon walls of white limestone loomed on either side. Trees and vines clung to the water's edge and we spotted flocks of white herons, egrets, and several eagles perched within the branches. When we arrived at the marina in Livingston we docked alongside fishing boats that had several pelicans perched casually on the decks, not at all bothered by people passing by. They are very gangly scavengers with huge beaks. I wouldn't want to get in their way—they looked quite frightening.

Livingston sits at the mouth of the river on the Bay of Honduras and is only accessible by boat. It is a small town famous for its Garifuna community. It is promoted as "More Caribbean than Guatemalan." I saw about five men wearing colourful knit reggae hats that covered their abundant hair and heard a group of musicians playing a funky beat, but I didn't get a "Caribbean" vibe. The ocean wasn't turquoise blue, the beach was filthy, and I saw more Guatemalan people than Garifuna. The town is also famous for its cuisine, and although we only had one meal there, I can agree that that promotion is accurate. I tried *tapado*, which is a fish soup cooked with coconut milk and coriander. It was a feast for the eyes and the stomach. A huge bowl arrived at the table with a whole fish protruding out of the broth, and it was full of prawns and crab.

It was definitely one of those times that the journey is more important than the destination. I really enjoyed the scenic boat trip, meeting the local kids in the canoes, and visiting the women's cooperative; Livingston itself didn't do it for me.

Our drive the next day was delayed by a flat tire. We all had to wonder if it was a coincidence that it happened only about a kilometre past a tire shop. (There was a nail in the tire.) Fortunately, our driver got us to the side of the road without incident, changed to the spare, drove back to the shop, and we were back on the road within an hour. We drove along windy mountainous roads, through Guatemala City and into Antigua. I was extremely happy we did not stop in Guatemala City, as it was huge, dirty, busy, and not very inviting.

The city of Antigua definitely goes down on my "favourite city" list. It is in the central highlands of Guatemala, surrounded by three volcanoes. It has cobblestone streets lined with colourful colonial buildings, many beautiful churches, and fascinating ruins.

We were in Antigua for only one night the first time, but in that one night I truly fell in love with the town. It has so much charm, and being Semana Santa made it that much more special. I threw my bags in the room, headed out to take in the town, and within minutes was swept up in a procession parading through the streets. Everywhere were crowds of spectators and stunning floats. Hundreds of young children dressed in purple robes paraded the streets, some swinging incense, while others were burdened under a huge float carrying the statue of Jesus swaying precariously on top. It took at least fifty boys to carry each float, and the strain showed as sweat poured off their faces. The band that followed didn't really fit the scene; the men wore black suits and baseball caps. The atmosphere in town was one of celebration and it was fun to be a part of it.

We drove to Panajachel the next day, stopping in Chichicastengo for market day. (I love that name.) Chichi, as it is nicknamed, is famous for its traditional K'iche' Maya market, and it was as good as its reputation, which we were thankful for, because the road leading to it was long and winding and not in the best condition. We passed many farms, with steep sloping fields, and wondered how they manage to grow crops and irrigate at such an incline. Watermelon must be easy to grow, because there were many stands along the roadside with the melons beautifully displayed in various formations, each stand appearing to try to outdo the other.

Chichi is another cobblestone town with narrow alleys and lovely old buildings, including the four-hundred-year-old church of Iglesia de Santo Thomas. On market day we found the town full of colourful stalls, filling the square in front of the church and overflowing into the alleyways. I climbed the eighteen stairs (representing the eighteen months of the Mayan calendar) to the entrance of the church to have an overview of the market. In front of the church I found an effigy of Maximon sitting in the doorway. Maximon, I learned, is a "folk saint" worshipped by some Mayans. He wears a black cowboy hat, a suit jacket, a big colourful tie, and black pants, has a large mustache, and always has a lit cigar in his mouth. The effigy was being protected by two guards of the brotherhood, and is moved every year to a different location, only being brought out during Semana Santa. Worshippers offer him money, liquor, and cigars in exchange for good health, good crops, and various other favours. He seems an odd choice for a saint, and I am sure there is more to the story that I didn't hear.

The market sold everything from embroidered clothing and bags to pottery, masks, plants, candles, pigs, chickens, and tools. Small kiosks for food were dotted throughout as well. Even though I was tired of shopping, I enjoyed wandering amongst the stalls, sitting with the kids on the streets, and talking to any vendors who could speak some English. I bought a couple embroidered bags and believed the first woman who told me she stitched them herself, until I saw the exact same bag at a stall around the corner.

I eventually wandered out of the market area and found the most unique cemetery I have ever laid eyes on. All the monuments were painted bright colours, and from a distance it looked like a miniature city. I was continually surprised by the striking colours of Guatemala. I loved it there!

We finally arrived in Panajachel on Lake Atitlan in the late afternoon. The lake is surrounded by three volcanoes and is beautiful, which is more than I can say about the town. I am really becoming a tourist snob, but the town is devoid of charm and completely overtaken by tourists and tourist-oriented stalls. I imagine those who love shopping would like it, but it was disappointing to me.

The next day, however, we went out on the lake to a restaurant and rest area that was absolutely divine. Casa del Mundo was a welcome respite from the crowds in Panajachel, and we spent hours lounging on its deck and swimming in the cold, clear lake. But I couldn't sit still for long, of course, and when an offer came to take a boat to Santiago, another village across the lake, I couldn't resist.

When we first arrived I was a little worried that it was just another tourist trap, but the line of stalls that filled the main street leading into town had beautiful and unique handicrafts and artwork. And once in town we were stunned by the street art being created for Semana Santa. The streets were carpeted with detailed designs made from dyed sawdust and flowers. The locals were busy decorating street after street. The surprising part was that those time-consuming pieces of art were created to line the procession route and would be destroyed when the procession paraded on top of them. I was told they redo them every day, sometimes more than once a day!

We hired a young boy, Diego, to take us to see Santiago's version of Maximon. Cigar smoke poured out of the small room where two of the Mayan Catholic brotherhood sat protecting their deity. He was draped in scarves, wore flowery purple pants and a big black cowboy hat. We joined the line of locals who were bringing offerings and asking their favours, this being the only week they could visit him. After some of the gang bought some embroidered pieces, we took a pleasant boat ride back to Panajachel. It was another fantastic day.

We travelled back to Antigua for Easter Sunday, and to me, this is something everyone should do at least once in their lives. Every street in the city had the colourful flower and sawdust carpets, created over and over, as procession after procession paraded through town. During the day I watched one family making their design, using carrots, mangos, pineapples, tomatoes, and cabbages. I spoke to one of the daughters, who told me her family had been doing this for years, creating two a day, for three days. It must cost them a fortune. They had barely completed it, when the procession came to walk over it. The procession was followed by locals, who scrambled to pick up what wasn't ruined. Hours of work destroyed in seconds, and the family stood proud and happy to see it happen. This tradition of the carpets dates back to the sixteenth century and was meant to ease walking on the uneven cobblestone streets. This particular carpet certainly wouldn't have served that purpose, but it was unique.

The evening processions were magical. As the smoke and aroma from the incense filled the air, causing a mysterious aura, hundreds of black-robed men and women paraded through town. The women carry floats slightly smaller than the men's, with the Virgin Mary adorned on the platform.

I was happy I included Guatemala in my fifty countries and loved almost every minute in this beautiful country. I had always known that Guatemala had a tumultuous past, but was surprised to learn that its civil war lasted thirty-six years. I was told by our tour guide that in that time over two hundred thousand people were killed or disappeared. A peace accord was only signed in 1996.

While in Antigua, a woman at my hotel arranged an interview for me with her mother, Maria.

~

Maria – 58

The daughter has given me directions to her mother's house and I am where I think I should be, but there are no numbers on the doors. All the homes are attached and have huge, windowless wooden doors, each painted a different colour. I knock on two wrong doors before I find the correct one. Maria calls through the closed door. She's speaking Spanish, but I assume she is asking who it is. "I am Donna, your daughter told me you would be expecting me," I say in English, hoping she understands me. I only assume she speaks English, because her daughter does. The huge door opens slightly, and after she sees me she opens it wider.

Maria is surrounded by little girls, and she says in perfect English, "These are my granddaughters." I enter the house to find the reason for the huge doors. They also serve as garage doors, and there inside the house is the family car. There is no wall separating it from the dining room. As we carry on into the house I see the only windows are at the back, where doors open on to a courtyard shared by all the other homes in the building. Her furniture is mostly lovely antiques, and they are squeezed into the tiny rooms that make up her home.

I explain my quest, and as the girls run around playing, we start the interview. Maria's daughter told me her mom was fifty-one. I am not sure if that was so I would interview her mom, or she really didn't know, but I am quite sure she is older than that. So my first question is, "How old are you?" She replies, "I am fifty-eight years old."

"How old were you when you got married?" I ask. This question opens a conversation I don't see coming. She tells me she has been married for thirty-seven years to a man whom she can't find a kind word to describe. She says he doesn't like her family, drinks too much, doesn't give her money, never does anything with her, and she would divorce him if she wasn't Catholic. I have to assume he doesn't understand English, as he is sitting in the next room!

She becomes even more bitter when I ask about her parents. She explains that her parents were never married, and she lived with her mother until she was seven. Then she moved in with her father and stepmother, who she says was very strict. She was not allowed out of the house, except to go to school, until she was eighteen. It seems she didn't like her stepmother any more than her husband.

It seems I keep bringing up sad stories lately. I hope talking about her own family will brighten the mood. It does work, and she is delighted to tell me about her three daughters. Maria has a university degree and is an English teacher. Her daughters have high school educations, all work as secretaries, and have provided Maria with seven grandchildren, five of whom are running around this room.

As her husband is a doctor, I am quite sure she won't have trouble talking about menopause. She tells me she had a hysterectomy twenty years ago, but still has hot flashes and night sweats. She chooses not to take any medications, as she believes HRT causes breast cancer.

From the religious statues in the house I am sure she is religious. She tells me she is Catholic, as are most Guatemalans, and that she is a "guard" for Jesus. "What is that?" I ask. "I go to the church two or three times a week, clean the sanctuary, bring flowers and sweep up." This brings up another problem she has with her husband, as he doesn't attend church with her. She says her daughters attended occasionally.

This is obviously an upper-middle-class home, and I ask how her life was affected during the civil war. Her answer has me shocked and confused. "We didn't have a civil war," she says. I don't know how to respond. She continues, "It is much more dangerous now than any other time in my life. I spend most of my weekends in Guatemala City with my mother and it is violent and unsafe to walk the streets."

My mind is reeling; I am momentarily speechless while thinking of the horror stories of the civil war I had been told earlier in the week. I don't have nearly enough knowledge about the situation to debate this with her, so I just ask if she would move to any other country if she could. "No, I could never move away from my family," she says with conviction.

I am sure I know the answer to the question, "Are you happy?" She answers quickly, "Not really. I am always frustrated with my husband."

I leave thinking how sad it is to find this woman, who is obviously much better off than the majority of Guatemalans, but is unhappy and not nearly as warm as many other less fortunate people I have met.

Chapter 41
Honduras

"It is going to be hard to beat the last week," I said to my tour mates on the way to the Guatemala/Honduras border, and they all agreed. The border crossing was easy. We didn't even have to get out of the van. Our tour guide took our passports, and twenty minutes later we drove into my forty-eighth country!

Our first stop was in Copan Ruinas, a sleepy little town only fifteen minutes from the border. Although the town had quaint buildings, a central plaza, cobblestone streets, an old church, and a market, it didn't have the charm of Antigua. The heat may have had something to do with my first impressions, though, as it was extremely hot, dry, and dusty.

Not surprisingly, the town of Copan Ruinas is near the Mayan ruins of Copan. The site is not as big as Tikal, but there are more sculptures, carved stellae, and well-preserved hieroglyphics than the other Mayan sites. Giant carved figures and contorted faces decorate the plazas and pyramids. One of the highlights of Copan is the Hieroglyphic Stairway, a giant monument with sixty-three steps and thousands of glyphs, which tell the history of the royal house of Copan. This is the longest known text of the Mayan civilization. The lush jungle and the colourful guacamayas parrots swooping overhead enhanced this great archaeological outing.

We headed to La Ceiba on the Caribbean coast the next day. The group dynamics had gone from bad to worse as the days passed, so it was a long day of driving in a van full of tension. I was very happy to see the dock in La Ceiba, where we caught a boat over to the island of Utila.

Utila, one of the Bay Islands, is about twenty-nine kilometres away from the mainland and is only thirteen kilometres long and five kilometres wide. It is a laid-back island, reminiscent of Caye Calker in Belize. It is another island with no vehicles, other than golf carts, quads, and bikes. There were about six thousand people living on the island.

A few of us went kayaking through the middle of the island, from one side to the other. We went unguided through a maze of channels, so were pleased we got lost only once. I felt like we were in the middle of a *National Geographic* adventure. Mangroves covered the channel, creating a tunnel, and the only noise was the sound of our paddles and birds chirping.

About an hour into the trip, we saw a lone shabby-looking character, sitting in an old wooden boat on the side of the channel. None of us said anything until we passed him, but we were all extremely scared. I had all sorts of scenarios running through my head. We were miles from anything or anyone, and saw no reason for him to be there, so we feared he was a drug dealer or smuggler of some kind. He may have been both, but he didn't bother us, and we just paddled past as fast as we could.

After two hours of paddling we came out to a secluded white sand beach, with gorgeous turquoise water lapping its shores. We could see waves hitting the reef offshore and couldn't believe our luck to have this magical beach to ourselves. The water was warm and wonderful. We spent a few hours relaxing, swimming, and regaining our strength to paddle all the way back. I was exhausted by the time we returned, but I loved it.

The next day we hired a boat to take us snorkelling. The reef was part of the same reef we snorkelled through in Belize. We had three stops on tiny islands, and were able to snorkel from the beach. I spent hours floating above breathtaking coral and schools of brightly coloured fish.

We stopped for lunch on an island that was a mere strip of land, just wide enough for a road down the middle, with houses on either side built on stilts over the water. I was surprised to see the children didn't have fins instead of legs. The road and the inside of their homes was the only solid ground.

The bus trip to our next stop in Tegucigalpa was hot, sticky, and uncomfortable. "Tegus", as it is known to the locals, is the capital of Honduras, and it was definitely not my favourite city. When we hit the outskirts we came to a standstill in the traffic. It took us over an hour to inch our way into the city, and during that time we had a front-row seat to view the slums. Thousands of shacks and huts sprawled across the hillsides into town. We were warned it was not a safe city to explore on our own, and we heeded the warning. Instead, we ordered pizza and watched TV in our rooms.

Honduras did not warm me the way Guatemala did. I found the people aloof, the culture invisible, and the weather too hot. However, I might have been too tired to appreciate it. After all, I had been on the road a long time and not every country could be on my "favourite" list.

The owner of the hotel in Utila agreed to be my interviewee.

~

Dean – 57

I have finally pinned Dean down to spend some time with me to do the interview. She has been too busy running the hotel, looking after her grandson, taking in laundry, and training her new puppy. She is a little reluctant to be interviewed, but finally agrees.

As the hotel is on the ocean, we sit at the picnic table on the lawn and enjoy the cool ocean breeze as we talk. I already know she is fifty-seven, and she and her merchant marine husband have owned the hotel for sixteen years. "How long have you been married?" I ask.

She laughs when she says, "We have been married for thirty-seven years, but I have known him since I was twelve years old. We were both born here on the island, as were my parents." I ask about her parents and she says her mom died at sixty-two, but her father is healthy and happy at eighty-three years old. He was a teacher, and has moved to the mainland. She says her life has been easier than her parents', but doesn't elaborate.

"Tell me about your children," I say.

"I have three children, and two of them are attending university at a Seventh Day Adventist university in the States. I am actually flying out tomorrow to attend one of their graduations," she says excitedly. She explains that many of the Utila islanders are Seventh Day Adventist. It is a big part of their lives.

I can't believe after all these countries I keep forgetting to switch up the questions so I don't jump from religion to menopause, but here I go again. "I guess you are finished with menopause?" I say, expecting at her age that she is done.

Again, she laughs and says, "No, I still get hot flashes and night sweats. They started ten years ago and haven't stopped."

"Yikes! Please don't let me have them for ten years!" I whine. She says she does not take anything for the symptoms, but knows many women who take HRT.

"Would you move to another country if you could?" I ask.

"No, I love my island. I wouldn't want to live anywhere else," she says.

And finally, I ask a question I am sure I know the answer to. "Are you happy?"

Her jolly laugh fills the air and she says, "Yes, very happy."

Chapter 42

Nicaragua

"Nicaragua is the last country I ever expected to visit," I told my tour guide as we got to the Honduras/Nicaraguan border. "The name alone conjures up images of conflict and guerrilla warfare. I was only going there because it was included in the tour, and I assumed that if the tour company went there, it must be safe," She alleviated my worries by explaining, "Nicaragua is considered the safest country in Central America and the third-safest place in the Americas, next to Canada and Chile. The major conflicts between the Contras and the Sandinistas ended in the early '90s, tourism is on the rise, and crime against tourists is minimal."

The border crossing between Honduras and Nicaragua went as easily as the last few, and we were on the road to the city of Granada in a very short time. I was thankful for our tour guide, her knowledge of the paperwork needed, and how stress free these crossings had been.

Our first stop was Granada. It was a quieter version of Antigua in Guatemala, with Spanish Colonial architecture, narrow cobblestone streets, and beautiful churches. We arrived in time to wander around town and take in the local market in the central plaza, the heart of every colonial town, explore a few of the churches, and enjoy dinner at an outdoor restaurant on the main drag. From our table we watched all the evening activities. Break-dancers, who could contort their bodies into unfathomable positions, young boys manoeuvring giant handmade puppets playing out a traditional story, and wandering minstrels kept us entertained for several hours.

There were plenty of street kids trying to sell little trinkets, and to some they were a bother, but to me they were fun. The fact that these young kids, who probably don't go to school, live in poverty we couldn't imagine and perhaps have no parents, can speak English, work out exchange rates, make change, put on the pout, and persuade tourists to buy stuff we don't need, is amazing. Like most street kids worldwide, I found them smart, cunning, and a joy to talk to. (I also now own many trinkets I don't need!)

Our driver got to work trying to find someone for me to interview. He told me the first night, though, that he was having trouble finding a woman who hadn't had a hysterectomy. I said, "Why are you even asking women that?" He said, "I heard you asked about menopause and I didn't think a woman who had a hysterectomy would go through menopause." He had already discounted his wife, sister, and his boss's wife. I was surprised so many of them had had hysterectomies, but was also surprised that he was giving it so much thought. I told him that it didn't really matter about the hysterectomies, but he was on a mission to find me the best interviewee, and I was grateful for the help.

The rest of the week in Nicaragua was okay, but the battle between some of my tour mates continued, making some days a little tense. By trying to keep out of it, I ended up being the "go-to girl" for both sides of the battle. The girl who caused most of the stress asked me if I would share a room with her the rest of the journey. Lucky me! In one conversation she managed to cut down Americans, Swiss, and people who did not attend church weekly. All this in front of Americans, Swiss, and people who did not attend church weekly. I chose to keep my mouth shut, save the rest of the group from her, and agree to share a room with her until the end of the trip. I am not a saint (I don't even attend church weekly), but this seemed the easiest way to solve the problem.

Nicaragua is famous for its lakes and volcanoes, and Granada is a perfect place to see both. The town is on the shore of Lake Nicaragua (also called Lake Cocibolca, just to confuse people), the biggest lake in Central America. A short distance from Granada is the Masaya Volcano, the most active volcano in the region. As recently as 2003, the Masaya Volcano shot a plume over four kilometres into the air. A sign in the parking lot at the volcano read that you must park facing down the hill, in case you need to make a hasty exit. I thought this was a joke, until we were told that several cars were destroyed in the 2003 eruption. It was frightening, but fascinating, staring down into the crater and seeing and smelling the smoke billowing out. We survived unscathed.

The Mombacho Volcano, also near Granada, erupted thousands of years ago and spewed huge rocks into Cocibolca Lake. As a result, 365 islets, now called Las Isletas (Little Islands), were formed in the lake in front of Granada. The islands vary in size and usage. There is one big enough for over one thousand people, but many with only enough land for a few fisherfolk in their ramshackle homes. Several others accommodated a hotel or luxurious house, which seemed extremely out of place. Nicaragua is the second-poorest country in the Americas, next to Haiti, yet some of the homes were beyond luxurious. Thinking about the street kids and then viewing these homes illustrated that the gap between rich and poor in the country is extremely wide.

We had an exhausting but enjoyable day kayaking throughout the islands. Purple water hyacinths blanketed the shoreline, pink water lilies popped up everywhere, and beautiful flowering scrubs and mango trees grew on many of the islands. We also spotted egrets, cormorants, ospreys, magpie jays, and kingfishers.

We took a break from paddling to visit the ruins of Castillo San Pablo, a Spanish fortress, built in 1784. We climbed to the top of the fortress to find a breathtaking view of the lake, the volcano, and the impressive golden-yellow Cathedral of Granada that looms over the city.

Back in the kayaks, we made our way to "Monkey Island". It was fun watching several different species of monkeys playing in the branches, swinging from one tree to the next and leaning into the boat looking for food. I was disappointed, however, to learn that the monkeys were not indigenous to the island, but have been put there for the tourists.

I really enjoyed Granada and was sad that I would have to leave. Our next stop was the island of Ometepe, in the middle of Lake Nicaragua/Cocibolca. The island was formed by two volcanoes rising from the lake. The two volcanoes, Concepcion and Maderas, are joined by an isthmus to form one island in the shape of an hourglass. The island is about thirty kilometres long, with around forty-two thousand people making their living from livestock, agriculture (coffee, cocoa, plantains), and tourism. I am not sure I would like to live at the base of two volcanoes. Concepcion is considered an active volcano, and in 2005 they had an earthquake measuring 6.2 on the Richter scale, which is said to have been caused by increasing pressure within it. Maderas is considered dormant.

The ferry ride to Ometepe took an hour and the views of the volcanoes were stunning. Our hotel was on the lake, in full view of the Maderas Volcano. The point of staying in Ometepe was to climb one or both volcanoes. Out of our group the only takers were our guide and her boyfriend. Either hike was over eight hours long, and wasn't something I was up for.

I chose to go on a solo walk along the lakefront. It was a cloudy day and I had the beach to myself for most of the walk, but every once in a while someone would run by with a machete. The first time I was quite frightened, but eventually I worked out that they were on their way to work and not out to chop off a tourist's head. I was joined by several pigs, sniffing and snorting their way through the debris on the beach. That was an odd sight; I don't think I had ever shared a beach with a pig. It wasn't the most inviting beach, but I would probably have had a completely different opinion on a sunny day.

Some of us went horseback riding in the afternoon, which is often dodgy in these countries, and this "ranch" lived up to that reputation. The saddles, stirrups, and horses were not the greatest, but off we went anyway. A few of the horses didn't get along, and after one kicked up at another, one of the girls got off her horse, took the bike of the guy who was riding beside us, and went back to the hotel. He jumped on her horse and we carried on. Not far in we encountered a short-lived but heavy rainstorm and all ended up drenched, but still we carried on.

We rode through an area where living conditions were very poor. Most homes were dilapidated shacks without plumbing, and we saw many people bathing, washing dishes, and doing laundry in the little water left in the streams. Mangy dogs, pigs, and cows wandered aimlessly along the dirt roads. We passed many plantain, avocado, and mango plantations and ended up at a natural spring, "The Eye of the Water", where they have built a large swimming pool. It was a nice break to get off the horses, but we didn't have our bathing suits, so instead we just soaked our feet for a while. We galloped the horses along the beach back to the hotel, which was the highlight for me, and I was glad we had carried on.

On our last evening in Nicaragua, our tour guide gave us a brief rundown of the tragic history of the last forty years. In 1972, there was a devastating earthquake that killed over twenty thousand people and left more than two hundred fifty thousand homeless. The president at the time apparently used the relief money for many things, but very little of it for relief. The Sandinistas overthrew that government in 1979 and ran the country until 1990, but all that time there was constant fighting against the CIA-backed Contras. The U.S. placed a full trade embargo on the country at the same time. (It sounds like giving with one hand and taking back with the other.) Then, in 1998, Hurricane Mitch caused major mudslides, burying villages, killing over 3,500 people, and damaging 70 percent of the roads.

The war has been over since 1990, when the Sandinistas were defeated. But they returned to power in 2006, with Daniel Ortega as president again. I talked to several people who thought he was the best thing for the country, and then others who thought the opposite. So, although we found it as safe as we had been told, it is a country that needs a lot of rebuilding and is still in crisis.

Our driver did manage to find a fifty-three-year-old woman who hadn't had a hysterectomy. I spent a few hours with her when we were in Granada.

~

Estebana – 53

Finding Estebana's home is easy, because it is about five doors down from our hotel. The building is similar to Maria's home in Guatemala, with the large wooden doors and a courtyard in the back. Estebana opens the door and welcomes me into her living room, which is the first room inside the front door. It is quite dark, as the only windows are at the back of the house looking out into the courtyard.

I am a little surprised that she has agreed to the interview because she seems very shy. I try to break the ice by telling her about my trip and that this is my forty-ninth country. She seems to be warming a bit, so I start. "Are you married?" I ask.

"No, I have never been married," she says. Then, she tells me she has two children, a daughter thirty-three and a son thirty-two years old. She doesn't tell me anything about their father, but she does tell me she lives here alone. Both her children have partners and children, but neither is married. She says her parents were married but divorced after a few years.

"My daughter is in third-year law and my son is a civil engineer," she says with great pride.

"Are you working?" I ask.

"I was a secretary until a few years ago, but I don't work now," she says quietly, and offers no explanation as to how she supports herself now.

As far as religion goes, she says she is Catholic and it is very important to her. "What about your children? Do they go to church?" I ask.

"I raised them in the church and it disappoints me that they are not involved in the church now," she says sadly.

Estebana is putting on a brave face, but I don't think she is enjoying this. The driver must have told her about the menopause questions, though, so I will carry on. "Do you have any menopausal symptoms?"

She tells me that she has had all the symptoms for ten years! "They were so bad for a while that I didn't want to speak with anyone and was unhappy for years," she says.

"Did you take any medications?" I ask. She says she didn't, but knows many women who take HRT. I think this probably explains why she seems so shy, and I realize she has gone way out of her comfort zone to be speaking to me.

"Do you feel your life is better than your parents'?" I ask. She says her life is much better than her parents', but says for many years during the "crisis" (the Contra War), life was horrible. Her description was almost identical to that of the women in Hungary and Poland who described their lives during Communism. She explains that there was not enough food; they would have to get up very early to search out items they needed, line up for hours, and then often get to the front of the line to find the shelves empty.

"How long was it like that?" I ask.

"At least five years. And I had many friends killed or go missing. It was a horrific time," she says. I am speechless. I don't know what to say. How do I go on from here?

I take a moment to compose myself and finally say, "It seems life is better now, but would you move to another country if you could?" She says she would, but has no country in mind.

I think we are both happy this is coming to an end, and I ask the final question, "Are you happy?"

Surprisingly, she says, "Yes." I thank her for speaking with me, and as I leave I see her smile for the first time.

It is good to have an end to journey toward, but it is the journey that matters, in the end.

—Ursula K. Leguin

Chapter 43

Costa Rica

"She's alive!" I shrieked after I read the e-mail from my friend Ann. Until then, I was convinced that she had died. I hadn't heard from her in over a year, and the last time I spoke to her she had told me she was having a biopsy taken and was waiting for the results. When I didn't hear back, I thought the worst. Her e-mail read, "Can I join you in your last country?" First I laughed, then I cried, and then I was mad at her for not e-mailing sooner.

I received that e-mail about five days into my Costa Rican tour, and the day before I was off to spend a week in Orotina, at the home of another friend. After the shock of her resurrection wore off, I e-mailed Ann to give her heck and then tell her I would love it if she could come down, but it would have to be soon, as I only had a week left. A week left! No wonder I was not sleeping, my stomach was in knots, and I was weepy.

The last week of the tour was great (despite the girls' squabbles), and Costa Rica joined my list of "favourite countries". Again, I was amazed how quickly the landscape and surroundings change simply by crossing a border. As we left Nicaragua and entered Costa Rica, the forest became a richer green and the living conditions improved immensely. We travelled through green rolling hills dotted with farms surrounded by stone fences. It was reminiscent of Scotland, especially when the misty rain began.

We continued climbing, entering the mystical cloud forest on a rutted dirt road, until we reached Monte Verde. Through the clouds, which I am told are a constant fixture, we caught glimpses of the vine-covered trees and the deep green foliage of the jungle. Annalu told us that 25 percent of Costa Rica is set aside for national parks and protected areas. I had a permanent grin on my face; it was breathtaking.

We arrived in the small town of Monte Verde, nestled in between the Monte Verde Cloud Forest Reserve and the Santa Elena Cloud Forest Reserve, eager to explore the area. The cool, misty mountain air was refreshing after weeks of exhausting heat. The main street was lined with an adrenaline junkie's dream shops, selling adventure trips for zip-lining, canopying, hiking, mountain biking, canyoning, horseback riding, and rafting. And, for those who prefer a quieter pace, the area is a nature lover's paradise, with tours of the unique diversity of flora and fauna. The town was full of young backpackers and adventure seekers.

The stronger economy, of course, came with higher prices. Our dinner the first night was delicious, but expensive compared to the last few countries. The 15 percent tax and the 10 percent tip, that were added automatically, made the bill even higher, and harder to work out for our group of still bickering women. But with higher prices came good service, good food, clean surroundings, a proper toilet with toilet paper, and hot water, and that I was definitely ready for.

The next day everyone was up early to get in all the activities we had lined up for the day, but the sleepless nights had caught up to me and I didn't feel well. I missed the early morning jungle hike and the zip-lining, much to my dismay. I rallied for the afternoon hike to Monte Verde's Hanging Bridges and was glad I did. The views from the bridges, which are suspended high over the jungle floor, were breathtaking. Our guide, who was extremely knowledgeable about the area and passionate about the conservation of the ecosystem, led us through virgin forests, pointing out all the plants, including several varieties of orchids, and we climbed through the centre of a strangling fig tree. We were also excited to see a silver fox, a coati (a raccoon-like creature), and many creepy crawlers.

Back at the hotel that evening, the group held a "fifty" party for me. The appetizers were displayed in the shape of a five and a zero, and they gave me a certificate to commemorate my journey. It was very sweet. I just wish I had felt better.

I would have loved to have spent some more time in that area, especially when I woke up the next day feeling better and raring to go. But the disadvantage to tours is the tight schedule, so off we went to LaFortuna. A two-hour drive back down the mountain, through the pastoral landscape, and then a short ferry ride on Lake Arenal brought us to La Fortuna de San Carlos.

Looming over the town is the Arenal Volcano, considered the most active volcano in Costa Rica. The people of these last few countries like to live dangerously, it seems. In 1968, the previously quiet volcano erupted, burying three small villages and killing over seventy people. Since then there have been ash columns, rumblings, and glowing lava flows daily. In May 1998, eruptions damaged two square kilometres of area around the volcano.

And yet we went on an evening hike not far from the volcano. We enjoyed more of the dense, lush jungle, listening to and watching the monkeys. Then we sat on the banks of a nearby river, ate pizza, and watched the "volcano show." As darkness fell, we could see rolling red lava spilling down the side of the volcano. No one seemed worried, and I suppose there are scientists following the activity, but it scared me! However, it was a spectacular phenomenon to watch.

With volcanoes come hot springs, so we spent the remainder of the evening at a hot springs park, complete with ten pools of varying temperatures, waterfalls, water slides, and swim-up bars. It was a great way to relax, and again I realized how very lucky I am.

Early the next morning, two of us went on another great adventure, which took us on a two-hour drive past many farms of sugarcane, pineapple, oranges, and guavas. Our destination was the Cano Negro Wildlife Refuge, where the forests, grasslands, and marshes of the area provide shelter for various endangered species, such as cougars, jaguars, tapirs, ocelots, and several species of monkey.

The tour began with a three-hour floating safari on the Rio Frio through a tropical rainforest. When we reached the canal on the river that leads to Lake Cano Negro, however, the water was so low that we could go no further. As I am sure they were aware of that before we got on the boat, it was a little disappointing, but the boat trip itself was so fascinating, we were not terribly upset.

Our guide on the Rio Frio was another very experienced naturalist, who pointed out many different birds, including storks, herons, hawks, cuckoos, swallows, trogons, and kingfishers. We watched monkeys swinging from trees, sloths hanging out, caimans sunning themselves, turtles snapping, and bats sleeping in the trees. We even spent part of the journey back in Nicaragua, as the river continues on into that country. I really enjoyed the day.

The last full day of the tour was one of the best. I felt completely healthy again and we went on the wildest white-water rafting trip I had ever been on. Our guides were all young and experienced, which was a good thing for me when I flew headfirst into the river. Fortunately, I didn't have time to be scared. As soon as I came to the surface they grabbed me under my arms and pulled me back in the raft. The group had a good laugh at my expense; they said it didn't look like we had hit any rough water, but all of a sudden I was in the air and then in the river. I had no idea how it happened, but was glad those boys were so fast.

We screamed through several rapids, where we had to lean in, drop to the floor, or paddle like crazy, and then we meandered down the calmer stretches enjoying the scenery. The guides kept us entertained in the quieter moments, one by manoeuvring his small kayak, doing trick turns, twists, jumps, and dunks. Another showed off his agility by sitting at the front of my raft, grabbing a branch from an overhanging tree, lifting himself out of the boat and, after we floated under him, dropping himself in the back of the raft. It was *pura vida* day!

Pura vida is an expression heard everywhere in Costa Rica. It literally means "pure life", but it used to mean "full of life", "purified life", "this is living", "going great", or "cool!" It is used as a greeting, a farewell, to express satisfaction, and in many other ways. Even if they are speaking English, which many do, they will throw in *pura vida* when they can.

All good adventures must end, so from the river we were picked up and driven to the capital city of San Jose. Reaching the city and hitting gridlock was a rude reality check that not all of Costa Rica is green. We inched our way through the city until we finally reached our hotel. Nothing I saw from the windows of the van prompted me to venture far from the hotel.

Our last dinner together was a great meal at a trendy spot not far from the hotel. There were a few of the girls I was sad to say good-bye to, including our guide, Annalu. But as a group this was a bad one, and as we headed to bed, I was not unhappy to be going my own way.

My next stop, for the last week of my journey, was the home of my friend Ann Marie, who lived in a town called Orotina. She gave me careful instructions on how to catch the bus from San Jose to her town. The journey took about an hour and a half and cost a dollar and a half. The bus travelled through rolling hills that were not nearly as green as up north. I learned later that this year had been one of the driest ever.

Ann Marie used to work in an office beside mine in Victoria. We had known each other for years, but had not been close friends. So it was very nice of her to invite me to stay with her, and even nicer when she said Ann was welcome as well. I phoned Ann, my long-lost friend, as soon as I arrived on Tuesday, and we picked her up at the airport in San Jose on Wednesday. Not many friends could e-mail one day, talk on the phone the next, and be on a plane the day after. What a great way to wrap up my journey. I could barely contain my joy when I saw her coming into the waiting area. I really believed she had died. In her defence, she said she had e-mailed me during the year. I believed her, yet I didn't remember ever receiving them. Of course, I was just happy to hear that the biopsy had turned up negative and she hadn't been sick at all.

She and I met over thirty years earlier at a job I held for only three months. She was my mentor for that short time, and after I left we would run into each other from time to time. Forward twenty years and she came into a dental office I was working in and we reconnected. We sat on the board of the Help Fill a Dream Foundation together for several years and travelled to South America together. Hiking to Machu Pichu was probably the pivotal moment of our friendship. Sharing a pup tent at 3,600 metres, during a gruelling four-day hike, can really cause two people to bond.

Ann and I both settled in comfortably to Ann Marie's beautiful home overlooking the Cordillera Mountain Range. Over the last few years, Ann Marie and her husband, who is a Tico (Costa Rican), had built the house, a pool, and a guest *cabina* and decided to try out life in Costa Rica, running a bed and breakfast. They did an incredible job of creating a tranquil spot to relax and enjoy the warmth and beauty of the country.

Our week was spent with equal parts of relaxing and exploring. Ann Marie was the perfect hostess, not only to us, but also to two of her friends from Toronto. We spent several days relaxing and reading by the pool, and although it was enjoyable, it was still a very hard thing for me to do. If I couldn't relax after a year of moving every day, I don't think I will ever work it out!

Of course, my favourite days were when we were exploring the area. Ann Marie and her friend Ginny, an American woman who has lived in Orotina for the last ten years, took us to three nearby beaches: Jaco, Hermosa, and Herradura. We girls had a great time driving along the dramatic coastline, walking the black sand beaches, lunching at a seaside cafe, window-shopping at the luxurious shops at the yacht club, and shopping in Jaco at the tourist shops that filled the streets of the little beach town.

Another day we went zip-lining at nearby Tura-Ba Ri Tropical Park, where we had great fun zipping over five hundred acres of tropical rainforest and gardens. It was a big day for Ann, who is afraid of heights. She was scared to death, but signed her life away with the rest of us, and off we soared above the beautiful scenery. Between lines we hiked through amazing foliage and crossed three hanging bridges, which were also a challenge for Ann, but she made it! It was yet another exhilarating day to add to so many I was lucky enough to have throughout the year.

Ann and I also spent two days in Manuel Antonio National Park. Manuel Antonio is the smallest of Costa Rica's twenty-five national parks, but has the widest variety of mammals and birds. We stayed in a beautiful hotel set in eleven acres of rainforest, with private nature trails and access to two pristine white sand beaches on the Pacific Ocean.

My last great adventure was a guided walk through the park. Our guide had lived in it before it was a national park. His grandfather farmed the area and his father was one of the first wardens. He was very passionate about his park, and had a skill for finding tiny insects, hidden animals and birds we would have never seen without him. We were able to get very close to sloths, including two babies, lizards, bats, iguanas, and white-face monkeys. The interesting trivia I picked up from him was that trees only have rings in countries that have distinct seasons, so the trees in Costa Rica do not have rings. I wonder how they know how old they are?

The other interesting thing I learned during the week was that Costa Rica was the first country in the world to constitutionally abolish its army in 1948. It is still one of only perhaps twenty countries that do not have a military. It seems to have done them no harm, and compared to their neighbours in the north, they have had no need for one. Costa Rica is on my 'favourite list" and I will be back one day, as there was much more to see and do.

While staying in Orotina, Ann Marie lined up an interview for me with Rebecca, her aesthetician.

~

Rebecca – 48

Ann Marie, Ann, and I sit at the back of Rebecca's popular shop waiting for her to be free to visit with us. She comes back looking a little rushed, but sits down and with a wide smile says, "Si, I'm ready." Her English is better than my Spanish, but Ann Marie will translate when needed. It feels more like a hen party, with Ann sitting in on the interview as well.

Rebecca tells us she is forty-eight years old and has been married thirty-two years. "That means you were married at sixteen!" I exclaim.

"Yes, and I only knew my husband for two months before we married. My mother was sick about my decision to marry so young, but I did it anyway," she chuckles.

Her expression changes to a sadder one when she admits her mother was probably right. She is obviously feeling comfortable with all of us and admits that six years into the marriage, and a year after the birth of their first child, her husband had a child with another woman. She went on to tell us that not only did she stay with her husband, but after eight months she adopted the boy and raised him as her own, and went on to have a third child with her husband. Ann Marie is surprised to be translating this, as she did not know this story, and is surprised that Rebecca is revealing it to us. We are all touched by her kindness to her husband and the boy, and all of us are a little teary-eyed.

"How far did everyone get in school?" I ask. Rebecca says she went as far as grade six, as did both her parents. Her daughter, the oldest child, is a speech pathologist; the middle boy didn't finish high school; and the youngest finished grade thirteen and now works with his father as a woodworker and carver. She also points out that her father still works. He sells shoes out of the front of Rebecca's shop.

"What about religion?" I ask. She tells us that she found her faith as a Christian twenty-five years ago and attends church every day. Her husband does not attend, nor do her sons, but she says her daughter attends occasionally. And for the first time, there is actually a connection between religion and menopause, because she says, "I prayed to God to help me when my hot flashes started, and they went away." She hasn't taken any medications, but knows many women who do.

"Would you ever move out of Costa Rica?" I ask. She says she has travelled a bit around Costa Rica and went to Panama when she got married, but that is as far as her travels have taken her. She loves her country and would not want to live anywhere else.

"Do you have any hobbies?" I ask. She explains that not only does she have her shop, but she also has a sewing business, so she doesn't have time for hobbies.

I ask, "How would you describe yourself?"

We are all touched when tears well up in her eyes and she says, "I am a very hard worker, like my father." Again, we are brought nearly to tears, feeling like her answer says so many things, in very few words.

She is a lovely woman, who opened herself up to us, as we all got to know her, her pain, and her happiness. Her final answer, when I ask if she is happy, is, "Si." And even after everything she told us, I believe her.

~

I loved Costa Rica, staying with Ann Marie, and getting to spend time with my long-lost friend Ann. We had a fantastic time together as we celebrated the accomplishment of my goal to visit fifty countries in fifty weeks.

I flew home excited to see my family and friends, sleep in my own bed, and rest! But I worried about putting on real shoes, and getting on with "real" life.

Once the travel bug bites there is no known antidote,
and I know that I shall be happily infected until
the end of my life.

Michael Palin

Epilogue

I am definitely infected by the travel bug and don't ever want to find the antidote. The year was more than I ever imagined. I don't remember who sent me the Facebook map that led to the dream, but I am thankful to them. Other than not getting an interviewee in every country, the year couldn't have gone better. My "stupid mistake list" was much shorter than my "favourite list", so I couldn't have wished for more.

I met many amazing people who shared their lives and life stories with me. My hope that I would find women to answer my questions was fulfilled, and most of them agreed shortly after meeting me. I was humbled by many of the women who answered yes when asked if they were happy, knowing how little they had and how hard they struggle to help themselves and their families. Almost every woman was hardworking, ambitious, and lovely. I believe we women of "fiftyish" are a generation of "Superwomen"!

My year was filled with lessons of other cultures, religions, lifestyles, and history. I hope I can keep up the compassion, tolerance, and patience I developed along the way.

I didn't find that elusive corner where "Mr. Right" was waiting for me, but I wouldn't have had time for him anyway. However, all those fortune-tellers can't be wrong, so I will continue to look carefully around every corner.

I will never stop exploring the world, but even after fifty countries I still believe that we in Canada—and especially we in Victoria—are the luckiest people in the world. Our quality of life and our environment are absolutely the best there is!

The year was truly **A DREAM COME TRUE!**

About the Author:

Donna Marie Lynch

Donna Marie Lynch was born in Victoria on Vancouver Island in British Columbia, Canada. As much as she loves living on the island, she has a passion for travel, having visited forty-three countries around the world before she started this journey. Now she has been to seventy-six countries.

In 1993, after her precious daughter Carly died at ten-months-old, she battled her grief by researching and publishing *I'm Bored*, an information guide for teenagers. Now, after her mother passed away, she has written *50ish*.

Donna was a travel agent for a short time, a casino dealer in the Yukon, and has worked as a receptionist and office manager in dental offices throughout Victoria, but her passion for travel has her continually taking extended time off to travel.

The dream that started this journey might have been just a dream for some, but she was determined to make it a reality—and she succeeded, without ever doubting it could be done!

34111260R00198

Made in the USA
Charleston, SC
01 October 2014